THE WHEEL
OF FORTUNE

By the same authors
THE BOOK OF LOVE NUMBERS
FORTUNE-TELLING BY DICE
FORTUNE-TELLING BY RUNES
THE NUMEROLOGY WORKBOOK

THE WHEEL
OF FORTUNE

How to Control Your Future

David and Julia Line

THE AQUARIAN PRESS

First published 1988

British Library Cataloguing in Publication Data

Line, David, 1946-
The wheel of fortune: how to control
your future.
1. Fortune-telling by numbers
I. Title   II. Line, Julia
133.3'354   BF1891.N8

ISBN 0-85030-618-3

*The Aquarian Press is part of the Thorsons Publishing Group,
Wellingborough, Northamptonshire, NN8 2RQ, England*

Printed in Great Britain by
Woolnough Bookbinding Limited, Irthlingborough, Northamptonshire

1 3 5 7 9 10 8 6 4 2

CONTENTS

To F.M.L. . . .

INTRODUCTION

Start at the beginning, go through the middle until you reach the end. It sounds obvious, but that's exactly how to treat *The Wheel of Fortune*. By following your own path through the book, we hope that you will build up an accurate picture of your own personality and prospects — or those of others — and turn future trends to your own advantage.

The book uses the ancient disciplines of astrology and numerology to construct the pictures, starting with the broad spectrum of your birth sign and then compounding the picture as more numerological detail is added.

But do remember that, as the number of permutations increases, space limitations prevent a proportional increase in detail, so be prepared to intertwine your own intuitive conclusions with the information on these pages.

Now turn to the first chapter, determine your birth sign and discover how astrology can make the first turn of your Wheel of Fortune . . .

CHAPTER ONE

Your Birth Sign: The Starting Point

You are probably well-acquainted with your birth sign already but just so that you can double-check a table is given below showing the sun's ecliptic path through each of the twelve signs of the zodiac commencing at the vernal equinox, on 21 March, when it enters the sign of Aries.

> 21 March – 20 April ♈ Aries – The Ram
> 21 April – 21 May ♉ Taurus – The Bull
> 22 May – 21 June ♊ Gemini – The Twins
> 22 June – 23 July ♋ Cancer – The Crab
> 24 July – 23 August ♌ Leo – The Lion
> 24 August – 23 September ♍ Virgo – The Virgin
> 24 September – 23 October ♎ Libra – The Scales
> 24 October – 22 November ♏ Scorpio – The Scorpion
> 23 November – 21 December ♐ Sagittarius – The Archer
> 22 December – 20 January ♑ Capricorn – The Goat
> 21 January – 19 February ♒ Aquarius – The Watercarrier
> 20 February – 20 March ♓ Pisces – The Fishes

The twelve birth signs have positive and negative characteristics which, to a greater or lesser degree, bear upon those they rule. Their strong, yet subtle, influence can be seen at work in all of us. You've only to watch a fastidious Virgo washing her lettuce for the umpteenth time to make sure it's clean and germ-free, or a secretive Scorpio exerting his strong will upon someone to realize just how true this is. However, the influence of your birth sign doesn't stop here. It not only plays a major role in determining your character but it can also steer you, albeit gently, towards a particular career, and could make certain parts of your body more susceptible to problems than others, and it might even explain why you feel a stronger affinity towards some colours, precious stones, trees, flowers more than others.

This chapter contains an analysis of each of the zodiac signs, so turn to your sign and perhaps you will get to know yourself a little better . . .

ARIES ♈

Symbol: The Ram
Dates: 21 March – 20 April
Ruling Planet: Mars ♂
Colour: Red
Gem Stones: Diamond, Ruby, Bloodstone, Opal, Chrysolite

There's nothing wishy-washy about an Aries, man, woman or child. They all know what they want and they're quite capable of going out and getting it, because one thing they certainly don't lack is initiative. They are self-assertive, enterprising and adventurous. Just because something hasn't been done before, won't stop an Aries from boldly going ahead. They are pioneers; courageous, fearless and prepared to push themselves forward with every opportunity that comes their way.

They are the first of the zodiac signs and their attitude is 'me first' every time. They also need to see quick results from their labours. No Aries likes to sit around watching the grass grow, they want everything done yesterday if at all possible and at times, when matters seem to hang fire, they become restless and fidgety. They are bright, lively, impulsive and exceptionally quick-thinking which helps them to keep one jump ahead of any competition they may encounter. They do, however, need to feel free to come and go as they please, finding it difficult to conform to restrictions and regulations. What's more they are frank, sometimes to the point of rudeness, so one golden rule to remember is never ask for the opinion of an Aries unless you're prepared to hear the truth.

Unfortunately, as with all the other signs, our go-getting Aries does have a negative side to his character which needs to be kept in check. Often in his rush to get everything done in ten minutes flat, he will find that he's been in too much of a hurry to pay any attention to details and this can cause him problems.

He is also inclined to be over-optimistic and, needless to say, he finds any technical hitches irritating, especially when they're caused by his own thoughtlessness. And it's at such times that he will tend to take his bad temper out on the nearest person.

If there is one quality that an Aries does need to develop, it is tact. It's all very well giving an honest appraisal but there really is no call for the brusque, offhand way he handles people at times. He needs to learn to suffer fools just a little more gladly. Very occasionally they can go completely over the top letting their aggression run riot, when they seem not only argumentative and insensitive but also down-right rude into the bargain. Less bark, bite and a few lessons in diplomacy would certainly improve the Aries character at times.

In their personal lives all Aries are extremely physical characters with strong sexual drives. They are passionate, demonstrative and inclined to come straight to the point. If you're looking for tact and refinement in a lover then an Aries probably won't fit the bill but if you're looking for quantity and a basic, earthy (if occasionally) selfish approach, then an Aries should do nicely. But please don't ever sigh wistfully for eloquent words, flattery, fuss and attention because you won't get them from one of our Rams.

When it comes to choosing a suitable career there are several points which an Aries needs to bear in mind. He or she needs constant challenge, competition to pit wits against plus the opportunity to use his or her initiative to the full, but above all else there must be heights that he or she can swiftly rise to. An added bonus would be physical activity of some kind as these characters need to work off their surplus energy.

On the health front, Aries is traditionally associated with the head and brain, which seems very apt for such head-strong individuals. Aries types seem to be susceptible to severe headaches, migraines, inflammations of various sorts and, due to their impulsive streak, many are accident prone — the head being particularly at risk.

KEYWORDS
Positive: pioneering, courageous, enterprising, impulsive
Negative: impatient, unreflective, aggressive, insensitive

TAURUS ♉

Symbol: The Bull
Dates: 21 April – 21 May
Ruling Planet: Venus ♀
Colour: Red/Orange
Gemstones: Emerald, Amethyst, Moss agate, Sapphire, Turquoise

'The salt of the earth' accurately describes Taureans and no one could ask for a better friend. Naturally cautious they may be, slaves to routine they can become, but if you're looking for someone practical, steadfast and reliable with both feet planted very firmly on the ground, then it has to be a Taurus every time.

They are productive and industrious, methodical and deliberate, enduring, patient and constructive – but why? Because although mentally unshakeable, they need to feel materially secure and it is only by putting their positive characteristics to constructive use that they manage to achieve the safety and security they so desperately crave. The need to possess is very strong and they tend to conserve anything and everything in case it comes in handy one day.

Friendships are also important to Taureans and many will remain in regular contact with old school pals well into middle age. Comfortable, preferably luxurious, homes are yet another of their little foibles and that's where they are at their very best. They have an eye for beauty, good colour sense and an enormous appetite for good food and wine – you could hardly expect a bull to survive on the odd handful or two of hay and unfortunately many pay the price for their over-indulgence.

Even from a negative point of view there's not a great deal drastically wrong with Taureans. Some tend to be unoriginal but that's because they often find a comfortable rut to get stuck in. Others are stubborn and rather self-centred while to a few, criticism or contradiction act like the proverbial red rag. Over-possessiveness is by far their worst bullish trait. Next time you are with a Taurean just try counting the number of times they pointedly remark 'that's mine' during the course of a conversation.

In their private lives it's marriage or nothing for a Taurus as it's in this particular area that their possessiveness can show up in its worst light, with the odd touch of irrational jealousy thrown in at times too for good measure. But if these negative characteristics can be kept under control, they make loving, responsive partners. They are affectionate, sensual, sensitive and well aware of their sexual charms which they instinctively know when to turn on to the best advantage.

Most Taureans simply have jobs, whilst it is other people who have careers. All they ask for is a good steady position with a guaranteed index-linked pension upon retirement and they're happy.

They don't want to take risks and jockey for position with their competitors although they are not afraid of hard work and responsibility rests easily on their shoulders. They are trustworthy, patient, persevering individuals with a sound sense of material value and an innate dislike of waste.

Many become builders, farmers and bankers, some find the Civil Service attractive, while others become accountants, surveyors and economists. The talented few are drawn quite naturally into the arts.

Physically Taurus is linked with the throat, neck, thyroid gland, sexual glands and the ears. Throat infections can cause recurrent problems from early childhood onwards with overweight and goitre lurking in later life. Earaches can also be bothersome especially in high winds and the females of the species could possibly experience some discomfort with their wombs once past childbearing age.

KEYWORDS
Positive: practical, industrious, reliable, balanced
Negative: stubborn, dull, possessive, self-indulgent

GEMINI ♊

Symbol: The Twins
Dates: 22 May – 21 June
Ruling Planet: Mercury ☿
Colour: Orange
Gemstones: Moonstone, Agate, Tourmaline, Lapis lazuli

Plenty of staying power and stamina are what's required if you want to try and keep up with a Gemini. You may possibly manage to keep abreast of him or her for a short while but there's no way you'll ever get to be one step ahead because that's their forte. Gemini's are born restless and spend their entire lives 'on the go' constantly seeking variety and change purely for it's own sake. They are fidgets and infuriatingly good at everything they do. To make matters worse they pick things up with tremendous ease because they are so incredibly versatile and adaptable. Like the planet that rules them, they are mercurial and just as hard as quicksilver to pin down.

Life could never be described as dull with a Gemini around. They are witty and humorous, engaging conversationalists (not only in their own language but probably in two or three others as well). They are as inquisitive as cats, wiley as foxes and as nervously excitable as a whole string of racehorses. They usually have fine minds, above average IQs but unfortunately it is their innate inconsistency that lets them down every time. They are never on the same wavelength for more than five minutes and always in two minds about everything.

Gemini's are just about bearable, if a little exhausting, in a positive frame of mind but when their darker, negative qualities come to the surface you had better watch out as anything could happen and probably will. Then their funny stories tend to degenerate into third-rate gossip. Beware of any favours they try to do because there is bound to be a catch and although they may smile sweetly to your face who knows what is going on behind your back? They seem to be even more inconsistent than usual, rush around at even greater speed still getting nowhere fast and seem unable to take anything seriously even when it is really important. In fact, to be in the vicinity of a negative Gemini is a most unnerving experience.

To be personally involved with one of these twins certainly will not be plain sailing and the entire venture could quite easily end up on the rocks unless someone cool, calm and collected takes the helm at a very early stage.

It is difficult to say whether Gemini's have feelings like everyone else or whether they simply have difficulty in expressing them, because to the casual observer they certainly seem to take love and marriage very lightheartedly, appear coolly affectionate towards their partners, in public anyway, and at private parties are always ready for a spot of audacious flirtation. Unfortunately due to their inconsistent natures many are also likely to keep a second string to their bow as a matter of course so that they do not feel they are missing out on anything.

Gemini's make superb middle-men. They love to wheel and deal, to travel, make new contacts, experience change but they also need to exercise those razor-sharp minds of theirs or they soon become bored. They also shy away from any hard, dirty work so anything too physically arduous or taxing would be out of the question. The transport industry, printing, publishing or the media should appeal to them as well as any vacancies for agents, representatives, brokers and merchants. A market stall would seem an appropriate outlet for some of their talents but perhaps being a mind-reader with a travelling circus would suit them best of all.

Not surprisingly it is the nervous system that lets Gemini's down health-wise as well as the respiratory tract, the hands, arms, hips and sciatic nerves. There is a whole range of problems that can catch up with these restless twins at some time or another which includes nervous exhaustion, rheumatism, pulmonary disorders, asthma, pleurisy, bronchitis and pneumonia.

KEYWORDS
Positive: versatile, intelligent, restless, communicative
Negative: inconsistent, over-active, cunning, exciteable

CANCER ♋

Symbol: The Crab
Dates: 22 June – 23 July
Ruling Planet: The Moon ☽
Colour: Yellow/Orange
Gemstones: Ruby, Carnelian, Crystal, Chrysophase, Moonstone

Crabs are strange creatures, outwardly tough and crusty, with huge claws and thick shells yet soft, sensitive and easily wounded once their protective armour-plating has been penetrated. Cancerians tend to employ much the same self-preservation tactics as their symbol the crab. On the surface they appear confident, strong and very sure of themselves but beneath that thick veneer which they build up layer by layer over the years lies a shy, vulnerable romantic.

People born under this sign need to feel secure and set great store by their homes and families towards whom they are tremendously loyal and caring. They are clannish and patriotic, intuitive and receptive, with retentive memories and shrewd brains. They are also great collectors and will fill their homes with souvenirs and keepsakes often to the irritation of their partners.

Cancer is a water sign ruled by the Moon which not only affects the ebb and flow of the tides but can, it is believed, also affect the emotions. Cancerians are certainly subject to swings of mood and will often allow their emotions to colour their judgement. At times they appear outgoing and positive while on other occasions they become withdrawn and prefer their own company. They are imaginative, often artistically talented and many will develop some form of ESP because they are particularly open to psychic influences.

Unfortunately negative Cancerians can be extremely 'crabby' people. They are easily flattered and often have brittle, eggshell-thin egos. Say the wrong thing at the wrong time and they will either dissolve into tears, retreat into silence or snap back in a most unpleasant manner. They wallow in self-pity, let their precious homes and possessions become untidy and harbour grudges over the most trivial details.

Cancerians are homelovers at heart. They have strong paternal feelings and make fine parents always ready to come to the aid of their offspring when they are in trouble, and always ready to give advice and encouragement when it's needed. They are shy, sentimental and incorrigible romantics, they are also incurably jealous and need constant reassurance of their partner's fidelity of mind as well as body. They are tender, demonstrative lovers, protective partners but at times they can be a little too clinging and possessive within a relationship.

Cancerians seek more than financial rewards from their careers – they need job satisfaction as well. They like to feel they are fulfilling a need and doing something really worthwhile and, what is more, the atmosphere has to be just right. Too much stress and pressure will only send our sensitive crabs scuttling for cover. These people have great depth of feelings so anything from the nursing profession where they would be caring for others, to raising tender seedlings in a nursery or market garden would be appropriate. They need time to do a job properly not tight budgets and deadlines to work to. Being born under a water sign means that the sea holds a special appeal for them and even in the role of brewer, publican, caterer or hotelier they would still be peripherally involved. Many are also to be found in such areas as interior design and property sales and development which stems from their strong domestic feelings. A few find archaeology a fascinating area to work in perhaps because they are such innate collectors who like to save and preserve everything for posterity.

Physically the weak points in the Cancerian armour are the stomach, alimentary system, skin, knees, breasts and female reproductive system. Crabs of both sexes could be prone to digestive or gastric disturbances while the ladies should add breast disorders and possible womb problems to their list of things to watch out for.

KEYWORDS
Positive: sensitive, intuitive, romantic, loyal, home-loving
Negative: lacking in confidence, moody, clinging, vulnerable

LEO ♌

Symbol: The Lion
Dates: 24 July – 23 August
Ruling Planet: The Sun ☉
Colour: Yellow
Gemstones: Tiger's eye, Onyx, Sardonyx, Amber, Citrine

Leo's are fascinating and infuriating; attractive and annoying; compelling and irritating all at one and the same time. Whether you love them or loathe them, it makes no difference, as you certainly will not be able to ignore them because they simply will not let you.

They are born leaders, always impatient to take command and that is just what they are going to do come hell or high water. They never do anything by halves but always in that dramatic, larger than life style of theirs. Even a trip to the library can become a Hollywood production for a Leo and they will never miss an opportunity to tell you how clever, intelligent and important they are. They are outspoken, forthright and very, very sure of themselves.

Leo's work hard and they play even harder. They tend to look at everything in broad, overall terms – minor, petty details are beneath their dignity – and then they look around for someone to delegate everything to so that they can go off and enjoy themselves with their admiring followers, preferably on a sun-soaked beach or at some exclusive nightspot.

They are arrogant, conceited and pompous but their generosity and warm hearts can bring sunshine into the darkest corner and is strong enough to melt even the frostiest face. They know just how far they can push you before they turn on the charm because it's all part of the act, and all Leo's are born Thespians, in which they play the starring role of 'The Great I Am'. However, they do have one small flaw in their stage make-up – they cannot resist flattery and whether it is sincere or not you can have them eating out of your hand for as long as you are prepared to tell them how wonderful they are.

To list all the Leonine faults would take forever but basically they can be self-opinionated, intolerant, conceited, bombastic, snobbish, patronizing and eminently forgivable when all is said and done.

Leo's rarely settle down to one particular partner early in life as they need time to sample everything that is on offer. They also need to find a partner worthy of their affections and this could take quite a while because, in their opinion, few deserve this great honour. And what if they made a mistake? That would never do. However, once the perfect mate is found they are sincere, generous and whole-hearted in their feelings, will do anything they can to make life a bed of roses and it goes without saying that they are wonderful lovers, if a little lazy and selfish at times. And in return for the precious gift of their love they expect nothing more than total devotion – what else?

In their working lives, Leo's need to rise to power as meteorically as possible and stay there. They are hard task-masters, expecting nothing less than 100 per cent effort at all times, but they are also fair-minded and generously reward those who serve them well. With Leo careers it is not so much the area of operation that is important to them but the position and title they have within it, and they should aim for managerial posts such as chief executive, director, chairman, organizer and so on, although anything connected with the leisure industry, films or exotic travel would be right up their street.

The heart, circulatory system and the back are all Leo trouble spots as well as the ankles (Leo's never have weak knees). Most of their problems such as cardiac and spinal afflictions can be avoided provided they take reasonable care of themselves, avoid excess and do not try to burn the candle at both ends for longer than is really necessary.

KEYWORDS
Positive: generous, dynamic, born leader, pleasure-loving
Negative: conceited, bossy, intolerant, easily flattered

VIRGO ♍

Symbol: The Virgin
Dates: 24 August – 23 September
Ruling Planet: Mercury ☿
Colour: Yellow/Green
Gemstones: Carnelian, Peridot, Sapphire, Jade, Jasper

Virgoans are cool, calm and collected. In all their undertakings they are precise, methodical and correct right down to the last little detail. They prefer to work with hard facts and a logical approach, feelings and emotions are never allowed to cloud the picture even for a second.

They are highly intelligent individuals; always ready to learn and improve themselves, easy to educate and scholastic in their approach. They fit in readily and willingly to a strict routine because it provides them with an abundant supply of rules and regulations to observe and adhere to and Virgo's do like to go by the book whenever there is one available.

They are practical and conscientious; shrewd and discerning; highly critical and extremely choosy. They are also very reserved which can occasionally make them appear cold and stand-offish. They never act impulsively and always analyse a situation with great care, paying particular attention to any small print, before actually committing themselves.

Virgoans are also very health conscious, sometimes to a ridiculous degree, and they do demand a high standard of cleanliness and hygiene in their homes if not actually a completely sterile and germ-free environment.

Occasionally the organized, highly efficient, practical Virgoan character can get out of hand and it is at such times that their virtues take on the appearance of vices. Then their rigid self-control is allowed to completely override any emotions they may be feeling and dismiss them as weaknesses; they become so obsessed with order and perfection that they start to fuss and interfere with everything and their mania for personal cleanliness defies description.

Relationships are often difficult for people born under this sign especially ones of an intimate nature. They are pure, modest and rather virginal at the best of times and sexual encounters tend to upset their normal poise and decency. They prefer to be worshipped from afar rather than at close quarters. Emotionally they find it difficult to let themselves go and to express their feelings. For this reason their lovemaking tends to be rather mechanical and as with most other things in their lives, done to a set pattern and fitted in as part of their unchangeable routine. Virgoans undoubtedly make excellent breadwinners/housekeepers but rather unexciting playmates.

Careers are of special importance to Virgoans because they provide the perfect outlet for many of their talents and abilities. They love to systemize and analyse; to sift and assimilate; to inspect and also, in certain circumstances, to serve. They are also practical, adaptable and virtually unflappable. Book-keeping, statistical, clerical and secretarial work should appeal to them as would computer programming or a job involving high technology. Nursing could also prove suitable particularly in an educational or advisory capacity.

Virgoans are rather inclined to imagine they have all sorts of weird and wonderful things wrong with them, but most astrologers are prepared to narrow the field of possible Virgoan trouble spots down to the abdominal region, spleen, intestines, and central nervous system. Typical complaints for people of this sign are ulcers and nervous disorders, intestinal upsets and appendicitis.

KEYWORDS
Positive: practical, methodical, reserved, fastidious
Negative: over-modest, emotionally repressed, critical, fussy

LIBRA ♎

Symbol: The Scales
Dates: 24 September – 23 October
Ruling Planet: Venus ♀
Colour: Green
Gemstones: Opal, Chrysolite, Tourmaline, Lapis lazuli

The balanced scales, Libra's symbol, represent not what Librans are but they they are constantly striving for and occasionally manage to achieve – equilibrium. It is an elusive quality which they find difficult to hold on to for long periods and there are several reasons for this. Kind, easy to get along with and utterly charming they may be, but because they are also easily influenced by the demands of those around them they rarely manage to stay on course for long. Just when they have finally decided never to get side-tracked again along comes someone with a good idea or a persuasive argument and they lose balance and change direction once more. Their judgement of others is usually infallible but when they have to use it for themselves that is when they become indecisive and try to sit on the fence.

They are diplomatic, co-operative and intelligent with good colour sense, an innate appreciation of art and an eye for beauty. Ideally they would like to live in a perfect world where problems and difficulties never arise. But they don't and because they dislike unpleasantness they will often bend over backwards and go to practically any lengths for a little peace and quiet. A Libran is always prepared to compromise if that is what a difficult situation seems to require of him. He usually looks to the future with cheerful optimism and this is probably his greatest single asset which serves to sustain him when the balance of his life has been temporarily shifted out of line.

Librans have few bad points and those they do possess tend to harm their owners far more than anyone else. Sometimes they are too soft and easy-going for their own good. They can be changeable, lacking in confidence, untidy and frivolous. Even if you add all their faults together, they would hardly amount to anything serious or even mildly disturbing.

In private, Librans very often allow their partners to walk rough-shod all over them and they have no one to blame but themselves. They like things on an even keel and in order to achieve this within a relationship they often find that their views and opinions tend to take second place for most of the time. Head-on confrontations and heated arguments are not Libra's style at all. They are kind, caring and tender, sentimental, soft-hearted and romantic. They need to be in tune with their partner both mentally and physically for their relationship to work well and even at times when the going gets a bit tough they are still prepared to give their all in the hope of better days (and nights) to come once the rift between them has been mended.

The world of big business where fierce competition, tight deadlines and quick turnovers is the name of the game is not for a Libra. They work best in a quiet, peaceful atmosphere where stress and pressures are minimal and where people and their feelings are still the most important consideration. Social and welfare work attracts them and anything connected with the arts would also suit the Libran temperament. The diplomatic service, marriage guidance, counselling and advisory services, cosmetics, textile design, antiques, hairdressing and beauty treatment would also be worth their consideration when selecting a suitable career.

The kidneys, lumbar region, and the skin are all parts of the body astrologically associated with Libra and some could experience problems in these areas particularly in the form of kidney complaints such as stones, and lumbago.

KEYWORDS
Positive: cheerful, easy-going, beauty-loving, helpful, intelligent
Negative: indecisive, changeable, too easily influenced, untidy

SCORPIO ♏

Symbol: The Scorpion
Dates: 24 October – 22 November
Ruling Planet: Pluto ♇ and Mars ♂
Colour: Blue/Green
Gemstones: Turquoise, Beryl, Aquamarine, Malachite

The Scorpio character is perhaps the most difficult of the twelve to describe because Scorpio's are very private individuals. They are rather like icebergs with two-thirds of their person hidden from view below the surface. They are strong, silent and enigmatic. Their self-control is rigid and icy, their feelings run deep but are rarely displayed in public and their hawk-like, penetrating eyes have an uncomfortable way of boring deep into your very soul.

They are perceptive and analytical; strong-willed and courageous; subtle and imaginative. Scorpio's undoubtedly have charisma and people are drawn to them like moths to a flame. They are attractive, mysterious and fascinating. They have hidden depths which they prefer to plumb alone. Their convictions are passionate, their actions purposeful, their thoughts intense and their motives always closely-guarded secrets.

Scorpions in the wild only use their stings when they feel physically threatened and people born under this sign also have stings in their tails which they will not hesitate to use if circumstances dictate. When looking at the darker side of their nature they can be stubborn and vindictive; resentful and destructive; brooding and wilful. And just as a cat will play with an injured bird, some are capable of great cruelty.

Strong sexual impulses run through Scorpio veins. They are hot-blooded, passionate, demonstrative and completely overpowering. They want to possess their partners, body and soul, and to become the be-all and end-all of their existence. They are also insanely jealous and because they are very secretive themselves they tend to think everyone else has something to hide which makes them highly suspicious of their other half's comings and goings, often for no good reason. But should a good reason ever materialize then their methods of questioning can make the Spanish Inquisition look like *Children's Hour* by comparison.

Scorpio's work better on their own than within a large organization or a partnership. They are extremely self-contained, very sure of themselves and prepared to take full responsibility for their actions. Praise means little to them as they are already well aware of their own worth and they can take or leave encouragement. They should be able to find something which appeals to them from the following list of career possibilities – surgeon, lawyer, investigator, soldier of fortune, researcher, psychologist, scientist, analyst, undertaker, faith-healer.

The genitals, bladder, rectum, throat and nasal bones are traditionally associated with this sign and the most common troubles that Scorpio's fall prey to are nasal catarrh, polypi, adenoids, rupture, renal stones and genital problems.

KEYWORDS
Positive: passionate, mysterious, magnetic, deep, strong-willed
Negative: secretive, vindictive, jealous, stubborn, cruel.

SAGITTARIUS ♐

Symbol: The Archer
Dates: 23 November – 21 December
Ruling Planet: Jupiter ♃
Colour: Blue
Gemstones: Jacinth, Topaz, Moonstone, Turquoise

If there is one thing Sagittarians must have, it is room to breathe. Not because they are moody and prefer their own company but because they are adventurous, active and sporty. They love wide-open spaces, vast rolling landscapes and new horizons to explore. They are frank, open and sincere, physically and mentally active and so full of life that they need to let off steam through sheer, physical exertion. They are like new-born foals, still wobbly on their legs but already impatient to experience at first-hand everything the world has to offer. They are happy, carefree and optimistic; versatile, open-minded and receptive. Give an Archer his freedom and a few opportunities and if he does not actually change the world he will certainly leave his mark on it somewhere along the way.

Unfortunately all that latent energy and *joie de vivre* can make Sagittarians rather careless and extravagant. They need to pay more attention to detail and a little less to speed. Sometimes, too, they forget that other people have feelings to be considered and tend to be tactless and outspoken at the wrong moment. They are also inclined to be boastful and prone to exaggeration.

It is a rare person indeed who can get a restless Sagittarius to agree to tie the knot and put down roots. And it is an even rarer one who can get them to stay in one place for any length of time. In private their feelings are sincere and their approach conventional and down to earth. They are demonstrative, passionate and extremely physical. They are faithful, loyal and honest but should they ever feel, even for a second, that they have been trapped then they will move heaven and earth to regain their freedom.

Sagittarians would work well in a sporting or an intellectual environment provided there is plenty of room to manoeuvre and that their job was not too routine or boring. They need to stretch themselves to the full, to have scope to develop further and a breath of fresh air occasionally would be much appreciated. The Law, Civil Service, university research or a translators/interpreters position would be suitable as would any of the following – promoter, politician, sportsman/coach and anything to do with animals or travel.

People born under this sign are, as a rule, a pretty healthy crowd but the areas most at risk for them are the hips, thighs, and sciatic nerves. Rheumatism, sciatica and hip disease head their list of possible problems which may be brought on by over-exertion and an excessive zeal for physical exercises and heavy training.

KEYWORDS
Positive: freedom-loving, adventurous, intellectual, active
Negative: restless, outspoken, tactless, careless

CAPRICORN ♑

Symbol: The Goat
Dates: 22 December – 20 January
Ruling Planet: Saturn ♄
Colour: Indigo
Gemstones: Garnet, Ruby, Malachite, Jet

'Softly, softly, catchee monkey', should be the Capricorn motto because if there is one thing people ruled by this sign possess it is infinite patience. They are also modestly ambitious and lay their plans with the utmost care and precision.

They never do anything rash or impulsive preferring to plod steadily, deliberately and cautiously on until they reach their goal.

They are prudent, methodical and disciplined; level-headed, frugal and conscientious. No matter how difficult life becomes or how frustrating it sometimes seems Capricorns will never give up once they have set their sights on something in particular. They stay cool in a crisis, are able to concentrate in even the most disruptive conditions and always pay particular care and attention to even the smallest details which many another person would simply fail to notice. They are tremendously hard-working, serious, self-contained units.

When viewed from a different angle, Capricorns can appear rather mean and selfish because they seldom take even the odd minute off every now and again simply to relax. They drive themselves far too hard for the majority of the time, worry over the slightest little problem and tend to take a pessimistic view of life, always expecting the worst to happen and then feeling quite cheated when it doesn't. They tend to be too conventional, too cautious and too single-minded. All work and no play could make Capricorn boys and girls rather dull unless they actively do something about it.

It is not easy to gauge a Capricorn's feelings even on an intimate one-to-one basis because they are so conservative about everything – even their emotions. They certainly won't run to long flowery speeches and meaningful glances when a few short words will convey their message.

Marriage is one thing they think long and hard about, carefully weighing the pros and cons and never, ever being in a hurry to reach a decision. They also seem to marry well and often choose a partner who has good connections, a private income and occasionally both. They are not particularly affectionate, demonstrative or ardent lovers but they make up for their lack of passion in many other ways taking their family commitments and responsibilities very seriously indeed. Once a Capricorn has said 'I will' you can be sure that he/she means it.

Capricorns make excellent managers and administrators. They are resourceful, trustworthy, thrify and reliable. They never let their feelings cloud their judgement and they seem to positively thrive under a huge workload. Engineering, science, statistics, systems-analysis, finance and politics all offer them considerable scope as do the construction industry, teaching, estate management and local government.

The skin, bones and joints in particular, the knees and the digestion are all Capricorn weak spots and many of the associated problems such as skin rashes, spots, eczema, nervous dyspepsia and flatulence can be directly traced back to either over-anxiety or a tendency to bottle things up.

KEYWORDS
Positive: disciplined, conscientious, patient, responsible, hard-working
Negative: over-cautious, penny-pinching, narrow-minded, unfeeling, anxious

AQUARIUS ≈

Symbol: The Watercarrier
Dates: 21 January – 19 February
Ruling Planets: Uranus ♅ and Saturn ♄
Colour: Violet
Gemstones: Garnet, Jade, Chalcedony, Ruby

'This is the dawning of the Age of Aquarius' or so twentieth century songwriters and astrologers are always telling us and Aquarians are certainly people who like to move with the times. They are highly intelligent with colourful imaginations, reliable intuitions and inventive minds. There is nothing dull or run of the mill about people born under this sign. Their ideas are original; their methods revolutionary and unorthodox and their actions unpredictable. They are friendly and broad-minded with very definite leanings toward the intellectual side of life. They find anything new and unusual extremely attractive, especially if it is of an artistic or scientific nature.

Aquarians are born humanitarians. They care a great deal not only about the state of the living world around them but also the plight of the people in it. They have high ideals to live up to, progressive thoughts to turn into deeds and reformative ideas to put into action. As luck would have it, they also possess a boundless supply of energy to make this possible and an Aquarian with a cause to champion can be an awesome sight.

Unfortunately not everyone seems able to appreciate, or even comprehend, what these enthusiastic individuals are trying to achieve and their motives are often misunderstood or simply ignored. They can at times appear fanatical, cranky and eccentric, rebellious, unconventional and odd. In their crusade to put the world to rights they frequently give the impression of being rude and tactless because they always come straight to the point, perverse and obstinate when they refuse to accept plain facts and down-right offensive should anyone dare to ridicule their actions.

Marriage and close personal relationships can be disaster areas where Aquarians are concerned because they tend to view life on a much larger scale than everyone else. It is the masses they want to please and getting tied down to one particular partner only serves to cramp their style. They can be too dispassionate and independent for their own good and although they never intend to hurt anyone, especially those they are fond of, they frequently end up doing so. With these people it is the old, old story of the cobbler's children being the worst shod – Aquarian charity seldom begins at home. Friendship is fine if only it could remain like that but once duties, responsibilities and expectations start to creep into the picture that's when the rot sets in.

There are many career avenues open for Aquarian minds to explore simply because they are interested in so many different aspects of life – the more new-fangled and modern the better. Science, medical research, electronics, engineering, computers and aeronautics would all be worth consideration as would publishing, photography, journalism and the media. In fact anything technical should appeal. And it goes without saying that politics, animal and human rights organizations or conservation work fits the bill perfectly.

On the health front the lower legs, and the circulation are all traditionally vulnerable Aquarian zones and they could be particularly susceptible to circulatory problems, varicose veins, blood disorders, pulled tendons and spained ankles.

KEYWORDS
Positive: intelligent, progressive, reformative, humanitarian, original
Negative: eccentric, unpredictable, unconventional, rebellious

PISCES)(

Symbol: The Fish
Dates: 20 February – 20 March
Ruling Planets: Neptune Ψ and Jupiter ♃
Colour: Red/Violet
Gemstones: Amethyst, Bloodstone, Aquamarine, Pearl

Pisceans are quiet, unassuming people who lack the drive and aggression that is so often required to play a starring role on life's stage, preferring instead to take a back seat as far away as possible from any pressures and responsibilities. They are naive, guileless, very unworldly and totally lacking in ambition. They do not seem to have the first idea about how to handle money and find it exceptionally difficult to organize themselves and get some semblance of a routine into their easy-going lives.

They are sympathetic, compassionate and make first-class listeners although when it comes to giving sound advice that is an entirely different matter. Emotionally they are hyper-sensitive; they cannot bear to see anyone suffering or in pain and are easily moved to tears.

However, they do have one strong point, and it is something all true Pisceans possess – a fertile creative imagination. They are receptive, impressionable and intuitive, subtle, fluid and philosophical and, at times, positively inspired. They tend to convey their ideas best through poetry, music and art and the contributions that they make in this area can be thought-provoking and often bordering on brilliance. They are also highly susceptible to psychic influences and many will be found to possess powers of ESP possibly in the form of clairvoyance or clairaudience.

Pisceans are never particularly positive about life at the best of times but on an off day they should be left to get on with it by themselves until the mood passes because nothing you can say or do to try and help them will have any beneficial effect whatsoever. They are temperamental, touchy and ungrateful. They get their affairs into a grand and glorious muddle and then they either look for someone else to blame for their predicament or try to drown their sorrows in the nearest pub. They are impractical, indecisive and frequently incomprehensible.

In private Pisceans are potential disaster areas. Upon first acquaintance they appear shy, thoughtful and in need of love and understanding. Their vulnerability is appealing and brings out the protective instinct in other, stronger individuals and that is just what they want – someone to look after them because they are basically insecure. They are tender and romantic; gentle and submissive; spinners of dreams but beware, they are also clinging, suspicious and moody. Rather like waifs and strays, they can make very good pets if you are prepared to devote all your time and energy to their every need but if you are looking for an equal partner with whom to shoulder the responsibilities of a home and family life you will be very lucky indeed to find these qualities in a Piscean.

When it comes to seeking employment people of this sign seldom set their sights very high and are quite content to muddle along provided they are not given too much responsibility and the pressures are few. Pisces is a water sign so the sea and anything connected with it is immediately attractive while the arts could provide an outlet for their creative talents. Some find the priesthood beckons while others go in for caring work involving either people or animals. And many fine mediums can be found in the Piscean ranks.

The feet and gastro-abdominal system are astrologically linked with Pisces, and Pisceans certainly do have trouble standing on their own two feet. They can also experience other pedestrian problems such as bunions, corns, excessive sweating, fallen arches and ingrowing nails as well as stress-related stomach disorders and a weakness for cigarettes, alcohol and certain drugs because of their escapist tendencies and depressive moods.

KEYWORDS
Positive: imaginative, sensitive, receptive, artistic, gentle
Negative: indecisive, impractical, gullible, over-emotional

CHAPTER TWO

The Number

You should by now have a picture of your astrological symbol and what it means in your mind. Let us now move on to the first stage in building the numerological component. To do this we take the most immovable facet of your life, your date of birth, and reduce it to a single figure.

Write out your birth date in full and, using the example shown here, add the numbers together until a single figure remains.

13 November 1961 (13.11.1961) becomes:
$$(1 + 3) + (1 + 1) + (1 + 9 + 6 + 1) = 23$$
then $(2 + 3) = 5$

So the date of birth number for someone born on the 13 November 1961 is 5.

Before we show how your birth sign and date of birth combine to give a more detailed picture of your personality, first check out the broader image in this chapter. The page number for your date of birth number is:

Number	Page
ONE	25
TWO	27
THREE	28
FOUR	29
FIVE	30
SIX	32
SEVEN	33
EIGHT	34
NINE	36

ONE: THE LEADER

Symbol: The Stag
Ruling Planet: The Sun ☉
Colours: Yellow, Bronze, Golden brown, Orange and Gold
Gemstones: Citrine, Topaz, Amber

One is the number of adventure and ambition and people born under this vibration are capable of great achievement. They love to explore new possibilities, both physical and mental, and are prepared to work twenty-four hours a day in the pursuit of their aims and not give up even when an obstacle standing in their way looks insurmountable.

They are tenacious, single-minded and tremendously independent; energetic, decisive and determined to the point of obstinacy about any task they undertake. Their actions speak far louder than any words and the results they achieve speak for themselves.

Those with a birth date number of a One will always get things done, usually in a novel way, and all by himself if necessary. These people do not seem to need help of any kind. They are inventive, creative, and original as well as being workaholics with a capital 'W'. Nevertheless because of their dynamic personalities and undoubted talent for leadership others are attracted to them like bees to honey. They are powerful, pioneering and very popular.

However, when viewed in a less favourable light their drive and energy could well be mistaken for overt aggression; their commands and orders for bossiness and tyranny, and some of their more progressive ideas for eccentricity. And a One with time on his or her hands (which is usually rare), can be like a bear with a sore head. They will either snap and growl at everyone and everything until the mood passes or lounge idly about refusing to lift a finger.

In their private lives One's are loyal and sincere. They take their commitments and responsibilities very seriously and tend to be over-generous where presents and treats for their partner are concerned. What is more they simply hate friction and argument of any kind, not that they cannot hold their own but because they find them unproductive and a waste of time. A One will opt for a speedy compromise. Jealousy is not a problem they have to cope with, but should an indiscretion ever come to their notice they can be utterly ruthless and totally without pity in the way that they deal with the guilty party.

In an intimate setting they are charming and affectionate but always in full control of themselves. They are demonstrative and caring; know all the right moves and how to make them but they never, ever lose their heads even in the heat of the moment. Their rigid control rules their heart every time.

As far as a career is concerned Ones like to take command preferring to work alone or as the leader of a small, well disciplined team. They need plenty of scope to use their creative talents to the full and plenty of fresh ground to break in order to satisfy that pioneering spirit of theirs perhaps as designers, inventors and engineers or even, should the opportunity arise, as trouble-shooters and explorers.

One is ruled by the Sun and traditionally associated with the heart and circulation, so irregular blood pressure, palpitations and heart disease are all problems people of this vibration should watch out for. Bright sunlight can also cause them eye problems and they should take special care when travelling abroad in hot climates.

KEYWORDS

Positive: pioneering, creative, independent, original
Negative: obstinate, intolerant, tyrannical

TWO: THE SENSITIVE

Symbol: The Butterfly
Ruling Planet: The Moon ☽
Colours: Green, Cream, White
Gemstones: Jade, Pearl, Cat's eyes, Moonstone

Two follows one in numerical order, and second place is just what a Two likes to take – the limelight is the last place they want to be seen in. They are shy, retiring and very self-conscious, preferring to follow rather than to lead, to encourage and support but never instigate.

People born under this vibration are gentle and imaginative; deeply intuitive and artistic; emotional and easily hurt. They need to feel secure, both physically and financially, and can be so careful with money that they often deprive themselves of comforts when there really is no need. Two's are all avid collectors of one variety or another. Some will collect knowledge and information while others assemble a vast assortment of souvenirs which they cannot bear to part with.

Twos are neither boisterous nor forceful. They never do anything in a grand manner because this would only focus attention onto them and they positively thrive in quiet, orderly surroundings well away from the main stream of life. They are gentle, submissive and very receptive. In fact, many are found to possess powers of ESP usually in the form of clairvoyance. They are co-operative, understanding and make very good listeners which could account for their popularity and their wide circle of friends.

The main problem that any Two has to contend with is constant swings of mood. Their number is ruled by the Moon which affects the rhythms of so many things on this earth such as the tides and the female cycle, so it is small wonder that her subjects are emotional Yo-Yo's. They experience tremendous extremes of feeling and seldom achieve equilibrium for any length of time. Twos can either be found on a fragile, temporary high or, more often than not, wallowing about in the depths of despair imagining that the whole world is against them.

Twos need someone to lean on and in personal relationships they often team up with a strong partner who can provide them with reassurance, encouragement and above all the security they so desperately crave. They are romantic, sentimental and affectionate; kind, loving and loyal. They make devoted, if over-protective, parents and will always be the first to bear an olive branch when a row or disagreement has occurred. Unfortunately it is usually the Two who has caused the rift in the first place. They are possessive and clinging; over-emotional and as changeable as the wind. They need constant demonstrations of their partner's affection and tend to imagine problems where none exists.

They also suffer from extreme jealousy and the other unpleasant symptoms such as suspicion that go with it. Twos are certainly not easy people to live with and need to be handled with kid gloves to avoid damaging their wafer-thin egos.

Anonymity is what a Two seeks in his working life and once he has secured a position he is usually quite content to remain there until he reaches retirement age. He is not one to dream of a seat on the Board of a high-powered executive office, he just wants peace and quiet with few worries, cares or responsibilities resting on his shoulders. These people make excellent clerks, store-keepers, secretaries, teachers, researchers and back-room boys and girls. They seek nine to five hours, job security and, of course, a good pension scheme.

Health-wise, Two has long been associated with the digestive, lymphatic and nervous systems, synovial fluids, stomach, breasts and ovaries. Their main problem is usually depression as well as digestive and stomach upsets of various kinds which tend to stem from anxiety.

KEYWORDS
Positive: emotional, receptive, understanding, shy, romantic
Negative: jealous, suspicious, moody, possessive, insecure

THREE: THE VERSATILE

Symbol: The Otter
Ruling Planet: Jupiter ♃
Colours: Mauve, Violet, Pale purple, Lilac
Gemstone: Amethyst, Garnet

Anything you can do a Three can usually do better and with very little apparent effort. They can be absolutely infuriating and tremendous fun all at the same time because they have such brilliant, quick-silver minds – as anyone who has engaged a Three in a battle of wits will testify. They are satirical, witty, discerning and, in conversation, generally at least one mental jump ahead. They are incorrigible show-offs, have the luck of the devil and somehow always manage to land on their feet.

When talent was being handed out Threes must have been at the head of the queue as there seems to be very little they cannot accomplish when they have a mind to. They are versatile, expansive and very ambitious. Their ideas are original; their methods are shrewd and clever and their energy boundless. People ruled by this vibration work hard and play hard. What is more they rarely miss an opportunity for self-advancement because they always have their wits about them and their eyes and ears wide open.

However, like everyone else, they do have their faults. They cannot bear to be upstaged by anyone and although they love giving orders and bossing people around, when the boot happens to be on the other foot and someone attempts to tell them what to do, it is time for the firework display to begin. And woe betide anyone who tries to take advantage of a Three's warm nature. They are well known for speaking their minds and certainly will not leave the culprit in any doubt as to how they feel about the transgression.

A great many Threes seem to steer clear of serious emotional commitments for as long as possible, and they are difficult characters to tie down, but once they do decide to settle they usually choose a partner for their brains first and beauty second, because they need mental as well as physical stimulation if the relationship is to last.

Threes are exciting and impulsive lovers just so long as you never try to complete with them for first place. They are generous, warm and loyal, entertaining, good company, sociable and full of amusing stores and good ideas. In fact life can never be dull or boring when there's an unpredictable Three around. They are neither jealous nor possessive but once they have decided, for one reason or another, that a relationship has gone past it's 'sell-by date' they are quite capable of ending it without futher ado and will walk away without even a backwards glance. A Three will never give anyone or anything a second chance once their interest has waned.

Journalist, writer, artist, musician, entertainer are all career possibilities for people of this number as they like to be in the public eye. There is certainly nothing shy or mediocre about any of them. However they are so multi-talented that they ought to do well in any field of endeavour that they find attractive provided there are not too many rules and regulations to restrict them and provided of course, that they are in charge.

The liver and the disposition of bodily fats are traditionally associated with this number. Problems in these key areas could arise for some Threes while others may find they are most susceptible to neuritis, sciatica, skin troubles or stress related disorders probably caused through overwork.

KEYWORDS
Positive: versatile, brilliant, talented, sociable, energetic
Negative: outspoken, frivolous, insubordinate, wasteful

FOUR: THE BUILDER

Symbol: The Bee
Ruling Planet: Uranus ♅
Colours: Half-tones, Electric Blues/Greys
Gemstones: Sapphires of any shade

Fours are life's builders. They are practical, down to earth individuals who construct their lives carefully, systematically and with great precision. In fact an orderly existence is second nature to anyone ruled by this number. They seem to have a place for everything and, naturally, everything is always in its place.

Fours are veritable pillars of society. They are solid and respectable; utterly trustworthy, efficient and totally reliable – their word is their bond. What is more they are so calm and stable that they rarely lose their heads and are virtually impossible to upset. And in a situation when everyone else seems to be in uproar and chaos it is usually a Four who will step in and get matters back on an even keel because they adopt a steady approach, have a flair for organization and an enormous capacity for hard work. These people actually thrive on it.

However, when a Four is having an off day, which fortunately is not too often, then it is a different ball game. Efficiency temporarily goes out of the window and carelessness creeps in. Tenacity crosses the borderline into stubbornness; an overdose of order and discipline makes them appear dull and pernickety and their usual cheerful optimism becomes eclipsed by a dark cloud of gloom and despondency.

In their private lives, Fours are extremely conventional and tend to follow the time honoured tradition of courtship, engagement and marriage, in that order. They are also great homelovers at heart and will take a great deal of time and effort to get the right accommodation for their family's needs although they will never live beyond their means to achieve their desires.

They make kind, considerate husbands and wives, are devoted to their partners and will go to great lengths to make them happy. They are always ready to give advice and support when asked and always prepared to lend a hand when someone is in difficulty. While they are not actually jealous, domineering people they do like to be kept informed of their partner's movements as a matter of common courtesy and become highly suspicious if there are any free periods in their loved one's timetable which they cannot account for.

Even in their love-making Fours tend to follow a strict pattern and routine; this intimate area of their life needs to be organized and kept under control just like everything else. While they may be not unpredictable, exciting and inventive they are certainly not selfish and their main objective is to ensure that their partner's needs are fulfilled.

In their working lives Fours are an asset to any employer because system and order is the name of their game and they are first division players. They are also honest, industrious and reliable. They should be able to find a niche almost anywhere that requires a superb organizer and administrator but the areas which attract them most are farming, engineering, dispensing, accountancy and the building trade.

Traditionally depression and bouts of melancholy are the main health problems associated with this number together with anaemia, neck and head pains, spasms and cramps. Occasionally some will also develop mysterious ailments or symptoms which are particularly difficult to diagnose, but this tends to be the exception rather than the general rule with Fours.

KEYWORDS
Positive: steady, practical, organized, stable, respectable
Negative: gloomy, careless, suspicious, dull

FIVE: THE ADVENTURER

Symbol: The Swallow
Ruling Planet: Mercury ☿
Colours: Light shades of any colour particularly Grey
Gemstones: Diamonds and any pale, sparkling stones

Five is the number of adventure and people born under this vibration know how to live life to the full. They need to experience anything and everything that appeals to them and are constantly searching for something new to try or somewhere different to go. Not only do they enjoy travelling on the physical plane, to the far ends of the earth if possible, they also love to explore new ideas and concepts.

They are talented, clever and original; resourceful, industrious and alert; with fertile, creative imaginations, quick wits and boundless energy. They are restless, fidgety, impatient individuals, constantly on the go. They positively thrive on excitement which they are quite capable of manufacturing for themselves, stretching themselves to the limits and burning the candle at both ends.

Life is one long gamble to a Five. They often chance their luck by taking the most alarming risks always in the hope and expectation of getting rich quick – and occasionally fortune does smile on them. But even when things go wrong you can never keep a Five down for long. They will soon come bouncing back full of new schemes and ideas which they feel this time simply cannot fail to succeed. Deep down they are all secretly afraid of failure and this is what continues to motivate them when less resilient mortals would be inclined to admit defeat.

Fives tend to have a great many minor character deficiencies rather than one or two major ones. To name but a few they are conceited; sarcastic and critical; often hurt people's feelings unintentionally with some thoughtless remark or deed; are far too quick-tempered and impatient with others and much too hasty and impulsive for their own good at times. Their fidgety behaviour can be intensely irritating and their rapid thought processes almost impossible to keep pace with. What they need is to drop their lifestyle down a gear or two, but that is rather like asking a leopard to change his spots.

To numerologists this is also the number of pure and simple sexuality and the private life of a Five can be interesting to say the least. A strong sexual drive is part and parcel of a Five's make-up. As with all other areas of their lives, they need to experience, experiment and explore every possibility before finally committing themselves.

They are earthy, sensual and demonstrative play-mates; unpredictable, imaginative and almost insatiable. Anytime, anyplace, anywhere is fine as far as a Five is concerned. They are generous to a fault, attentive, sympathetic, loyal and here's the rub – not averse to the occasional extra-marital relationship too. People ruled by this sign can be very jealous and unforgiving when their suspicions are aroused.

A suitable career for a Five always poses something of a problem because of their restless natures. Quite often they will set out in one direction only to change horses in mid-race and go off at an entirely different angle. They need constant challenge, stimulation and, preferably, little or no routine or their attention will soon wander. Anything connected with travel, foreign languages, communications or the media should appeal as would literary and public relations work. The Stock Exchange, Lloyds and the Commodity Market are also distinct possibilities because whether they use their own money or that of a client the element of risk is still involved.

Health problems traditionally linked with the number Five are fairly predictable given the nature of the beast. Insomnia, nervous and mental disorders and an over-active thyroid head the list with respiratory problems, anxiety and breakdowns coming a close second. Perception and sensory organs can be put under stress because Fives live so much on their nerves and complete physical exhaustion is also possible in some cases.

KEYWORDS
Positive: adventurous, resilient, restless, resourceful, sensual, speculative
Negative: conceited, quick-tempered, easily-bored, lustful

SIX: THE PEACEMAKER

Symbol: The Dove
Ruling Planet: Venus ♀
Colours: All shades of Blue except the metallic hues
Gemstones: Turquoise, Emerald

Ruled by Venus, the planet of love and beauty, represented by a dove symbol of tranquillity and calm, it is hardly surprising that Sixes desire nothing more from life than a little peace and quiet. People ruled by this number are homely, domesticated and utterly devoted to their families. They are honest, reliable and well-balanced. They like life to run as smoothly as possible and will go to great lengths to keep stress and unpleasantness at bay in all areas of their lives – especially in the home.

Home is where a Six's heart lies and that is where you will see them at their best. Furniture and furnishings are chosen with care and imagination and somewhere in amongst all the pictures, paintings, pottery ornaments and overflowing book-shelves you are sure to find one or two examples of their own handiwork.

They are intelligent and imaginative; artistically inclined and very creative. They have a flair for design and a way with colours that is second to none. Many are also gifted in other areas of the arts such as music, poetry and writing. But whatever their forte it has to be expressed for them to feel truly fulfilled.

While the home and family always come first, Sixes are also extremely sociable, gregarious individuals with a great many friends and acquaintances who they like to entertain informally, but well. They are born hosts and hostesses who seem to known instinctively how to make others feel comfortable and just how to put people at their ease.

Sixes have few real faults; however their innate desire for perfection occasionally gets out of hand and they fuss and worry over trivial little details. And their desire to help others cope with their problems is sometimes mistaken for interference or nosiness. What is more, it is virtually impossible to do anything in return for a Six – they know how to give and they are very generous but when it comes to receiving that is another matter entirely. They simply do not know how.

Sixes lean to the ideal in matters of the heart and the age of chivalry will never die while there is still a Six around to champion its cause. They are romantic, tender and affectionate; loyal, faithful and loving; fair, reliable and sometimes too considerate for their own good as they can easily be taken advantage of. They always put their partners needs first and will go to almost any lengths to avoid possible rows, arguments and confrontations.

On a purely physical level, Sixes do not score quite so highly. The language of love flows tenderly from their lips, their eyes are deep pools of expression but their bodies certainly take some coaxing. They prefer to worship from afar and passion is something they find difficult, but not impossible, to get to grips with. It just takes them a little longer to get the opening speeches over and done with.

Careers for a Six fall into two distinct categories. On the one hand they could follow their natural inclination to help others and there are a great many ways in which they can be of service either as doctors, nurses, vets and welfare workers or in the fields of marriage guidance, counselling or the Ministry. On the other hand they are undoubtedly talented individuals and many become fine artists, craftsmen, interior designers, musicians, poets and sculptors. But the atmosphere in which they work needs to be harmonious and preferably not too stressful and competitive for them to give their best. Sixes do not work well to strict deadlines and tight profit margins.

The areas of the body traditionally associated with the number Six and most likely to give rise to problems are the lumbar region, circulation, throat and kidneys. Circulatory disorders are perhaps the most common ailment and some women who come under this vibration have a tendency to suffer discomfort of one kind or another with their breasts.

KEYWORDS
Positive: creative, artistic, homely, paternal, considerate, romantic
Negative: fussy, trivial, interfering, anxious, stubborn

SEVEN: THE MYSTERIOUS

Symbol: The Owl
Ruling Planet: Neptune ♆
Colours: All shades of Green, Yellow and Gold
Gemstones: Any milky white stones, Moonstone, Cat's eyes, Moss agate

Sevens are magical, mystical and very mysterious. They are solitary beings and the web of secrecy which they wear around them like a cloak only seems to make them appear even more fascinating and attractive.

They tend to keep themselves to themselves and the few friends they do have are chosen with great care and extreme caution. People ruled by the number Seven actually do need to spend long periods of time completely alone with only their thoughts to keep them company because this is vital to their spiritual and mental well-being.

They believe that their mission in life is to gain wisdom and understanding and that their goal is to find the answers to some of life's, as yet, unanswered questions. A quest which they take very seriously indeed. They meditate, study, research and seem to spend most of their waking hours in a little world all of their own peopled entirely by dreams and fantasies of their own creation.

Many will be found to hold highly unorthodox beliefs while a few will even create new religions of their own which will suit their needs. And the vast majority will at some time in their lives become irresistibly attracted to mysticism and the occult in the hope of answering some of the riddles in the esoteric teachings of past cultures and civilizations. They are imaginative, intuitive individuals who often possess well-developed powers of ESP usually in the form of clairvoyance and psychometry.

Sevens like to experience life first hand and preferably in its raw, natural state. They care little for money or physical comfort and when travelling, which they frequently do, it is usually light and always off the well-beaten tourist tracks. They want a taste of reality not cheap imitations and pretence.

Like everyone else Sevens do have their faults and weaknesses. They need to keep at least one foot on the ground some of the time if they do not want to lose complete touch with the physical world around them. And they also need to make a greater effort to get along with others. Sometimes they are difficult to understand because of the wavelength they operate on and at other times they give the impression of being sarcastic and aloof because they do not suffer fools gladly. And they can be incredibly lazy especially when there are household chores that need attention.

Still waters inevitably run deep and it is only within the close confines of a relationship that Sevens can really let off steam and afford to drop their guard for a minute.

They are passionate, demonstrative lovers who, even after many years of married life, never seem to lose that initial sparkle and excitement. There is something charismatic about them all. They are understanding, good-natured and sincere with tremendous reserves of feelings which they have their own unique way of expressing. They are not particularly possessive or jealous, they dislike arguments of any kind, preferring to discuss grievances calmly and in a sane and civilized fashion. They seem almost too good to be true and they are but do not ever expect a relationship with a Seven to be a union of body and soul because that is not how it works. Their soul is locked away behind a door marked *Private* and that is how it will always be although you may on occasion be allowed a quick peep through the keyhole – but no more than that.

As far as a Seven is concerned work can represent one of two things – a pleasure if they are in the right job, and that is not very often, or a tedious means to an end if they are not. They are difficult to place because they rebel against routine, simply cannot work to order and do not make very co-operative subordinates. All Sevens eventually come to terms with the fact that money has to come from somewhere in order to survive and pay the bills and those who cannot find jobs which provide satisfaction simply work twice as hard in their spare time doing their own thing.

But the lucky few will become researchers, librarians, archaeologists, philosophers, astrologers, teachers or even perpetual students.

In numerology the Thalmus, spinal canal and the mental and nervous processes are all traditionally linked with this number. Most Sevens tend to be stronger mentally than they are physically although depression and moodiness is something they constantly need to guard against. They also seem to have particularly delicate, sensitive skins and over exposure to the sun's rays or strong chemicals could cause them problems.

KEYWORDS
Positive: solitary, secretive, intellectual, philosophical, imaginative
Negative: impractical, unrealistic, moody, aloof, physically lazy

EIGHT: THE MATERIALIST

Symbol: The Ant
Ruling Planet: Saturn ♄
Colours: Dark grey, Dark blue, Purple and Black
Gemstones: Dull rubies, Amethysts, Black diamonds and Dark sapphires

Success is the name of the game that all Eights instinctively know how to play – they simply make up the rules as they go along. They are tough, materialistic and adaptable and all tarred with the same brush. They have a tremendous capacity for hard work, boundless energy, no scruples whatsoever and an overwhelming desire for power and social status. Their application is relentless, their effort concentrated and their goals and targets clearly defined. They are fired with ambition, driven on by determination and capable of anything.

Eights are tough, strong individuals who see and do everything on a grand scale, and they are nobody's fools. They acquire wisdom the hard way through first-hand experience in the school of life, certainly not from text books in a synthetic environment. These are self-made men and women and whatever their final achievements may be, you can be sure they have sweated blood and shed tears in the process.

Unfortunately Eight is a difficult vibration to live under. In numerology it is the number of great reversals, as its shape suggests, and those who come under its rule will almost certainly know the bitter taste of failure as well as the sweet smell of success at some time in their lives. Fate has a nasty way of coming along and knocking an Eight off his perch just when he least expects it. And when she does you can be sure it will be spectacular because these people never do anything by halves. They also have a ruthless streak which they will not hesitate to display when charm, flattery and all else fails. They will resort to any trick, however low and underhand and stop at nothing to get what they want.

A relationship with an Eight is an emotional minefield with neither party knowing where the bombs are planted or what disguise the enemy will be wearing. But more often than not rampant, unreasoning jealousy will be the foe and it certainly will not be very well camouflaged.

This undesirable character trait is an incurable problem from which all Eights suffer and one which can wreck a relationship if it gets out of control. In public they seem so confident and self-assured but in private they need constant reassurance and a non-stop show of affection to keep their fragile egos bolstered up to full strength.

They are not easy people to live with at the best of times because not only do they have difficulty in expressing their emotions, they also tend to go to extremes. One moment they can be kind, gentle and understanding and the next minute off-hand, detached and unapproachable. And it is anyone's guess what their mood will be. They need to choose a partner who has infinite patience and a hide like that of a rhinoceros for there to be any chance of their relationship working at all. Even then it will still be a gamble.

While the personal life of an Eight may be precarious, their career progression should hopefully run as straight as a die, right to the very top. Success is of paramount importance and tenacity is their middle name. They crave nothing more than power and recognition and will sell their souls if necessary in order to achieve it.

Commerce and industry are both fields in which Eights excel. They have first-class business brains and many become executives, financiers, brokers, bankers, lawyers, supervisors and organizers. Others find the world of politics and local government attractive, because its affairs are usually conducted in the public eye and that is where an Eight desperately wants to be. He not only needs to succeed – he also needs to be seen to have done so.

The skeletal system, skin, teeth, gall bladder and spleen are all traditionally associated with the number Eight and liver troubles, headaches, rheumatism and intestinal problems are a few of the most common ailments which people ruled by it are prone to.

KEYWORDS
Positive: tough, materialistic, strong, ambitious, tenacious
Negative: mercenary, ruthless, obstinate, jealous, unscrupulous

NINE: THE VISIONARY

Symbol: The Badger
Ruling Planet: Mars ♂
Colours: Pink, Rose, Crimson, Red, Purple
Gemstones: Rubies, Garnets, Bloodstones

Nine is the number of mental and spiritual supremacy and those ruled by it have a genuine concern for their fellow man. They feel they must somehow strive to restore quality and meaning to life and to right some of the wrongs in society today. And not just within their own immediate environment but on an all-embracing, global scale. They care about the plight of the third world, they want to liberate all those living under political tyranny and they are prepared to speak out against pollution and the decimation of our planet – nuclear disarmament being one of the greatest dreams. They are do-gooders who pursue their goals with grit, drive and determination.

Nines are both inspired and inspiring. They are quick-thinking and even quicker acting. They are courageous, selfless and born fighters which is hardly surprising with Mars as their ruling planet. They have great imaginations, artistic flair and enterprising natures. They are ambitious but unless they can be at the helm they soon lose interest in a venture.

They tend to hold very high opinions of themselves and their own worth and many consider that playing a subordinate role is beneath their dignity. They strongly resent criticism, even when it is constructive and well-meant, although when it comes to their own way of speech, which is usually plain and very much to the point, that is rather a different matter. This does not always win them friends or influence people; in fact, quite often it achieves the reverse. On occasion they are also very impatient and much too impulsive for their own good. They go from Stop to Go without heeding the amber light which wisely counsels caution.

Nine is also the mystical number and many of its subjects are gifted with powers of telepathy and clairaudience. Some may also experience prophetic dreams or unpredictable flashes of insight into the future.

In their private lives Nines are warm and considerate. They are passionate, imaginative lovers and life is certainly never dull when they are around. They are loyal, trusting, honest and only jealous when given good cause to be. They dislike rows and arguments within a relationship and seem to have the knack of not only disagreeing without anger but also of reaching a compromise with a certain degree of humour. But woe betide any outsider who dares to interfere in the running of their personal affairs – then the fur will fly.

Nines crave love and a physical show of affection almost as much as they do world peace, and for this reason many make fools of themselves if they fall into the hands of an unscrupulous partner who is prepared to use physical attraction as a means of manipulation.

Everyone else has careers but Nines are different because they have vocations and callings. They seem to know instinctively, and usually from an early age, what they want to do or be although their pathway to success is rarely smooth. Above all they need to feel that through their work they can somehow help others less fortunate than themselves to achieve a better quality and understanding of life. Many become teachers, lecturers and doctors, others enter the world of politics and diplomacy while the more artistically talented often turn to music, writing or painting.

The muscular and uro-genital system, sex glands, kidneys and red corpuscles are all traditionally associated with the number Nine. Those ruled by this vibration seem to be particularly susceptible to contagious disease and they are also very accident prone because of their impetuous nature. They should always remember to look at least once and then count to ten before they even think about leaping anywhere.

KEYWORDS
Positive: humanitarian, ambitious, determined, visionary, idealistic
Negative: impulsive, impatient, conceited, resent criticism

CHAPTER THREE

The First Combination

You have now determined your birth sign, date of birth number and seen the general influences these two fundamentals bring to bear. Let us now find out how they combine. In the following pages you will find your particular combination such as Leo/Three or Pisces/Five.

Here the main attributes of the signs and numbers are combined and, in some cases, characteristics are reinforced while in others, oppositions may negate or cancel some specific traits. It is at this point you must start bringing your own intuition into play to adjust the meanings to suit your own circumstances. Obviously, not every possible detail can be incorporated so the results must be treated in broad terms.

Now turn to your personal sign/number combination.

ARIES-ONE

Planetary combination: Mars/Sun

Whenever One attributes are added to an already dynamic Aries nature, this usually proves to be a strong, powerful combination of sign and number.

Aries-Ones are ambitious, enterprising and self-propelled. They thrive on competition, rise to a challenge and will drive themselves on to the point of physical collapse in order to reach their goal. They are robust, born leaders and always ready for the fray. They love to live dangerously, and are prepared to take risks and cut corners if it means they can steal a march on everyone else. They are positive, decisive, if a little too impulsive at times, and desire nothing more than to be extremely successful, king of the castle and centre of attention all at once.

They are capable of great effort and indeed achievement, but what they find it almost impossible to do is relax. They are hyper-active and always geared up and ready for the next move.

Quarrels and arguments punctuate their lives like commas and full stops and occasionally they can become violent when their feelings are running particularly high. They are bossy, head-strong and stubborn; power-mad, hot-blooded, intolerant and insensitive.

KEYWORDS
Positive: ambitious, forceful, adventurous, pioneering
Negative: impulsive, thoughtless, quarrelsome, over-active

ARIES-TWO

Planetary combination: Mars/Moon

The number Two tends to soften the aggressive, go-getting Aries character which means that those ruled by this combination are honest and hard-working if a little too tense and over-emotional on occasion. They are independent and energetic; whole-hearted and sincere. They appear to have tremendous sense of purpose in life and the enthusiasm which they generate is almost infectious.

They are competent, determined individuals who know their limitations and rarely take on any commitments which are beyond their capabilities. There is nothing pretentious or boastful about any of them but this does not mean that they will let others walk all over them. They will soon shout if they feel unjustly treated or unfairly criticized.

Aries-Twos don't like to feel indebted to anyone and prefer to do everything for themselves. They carry this stubborn independence of theirs to extremes and will resolutely shun all offers of assistance even at times when they could really do with all the help they can get.

What is more, they are not particularly tolerant souls and find it very hard to make allowances for other people's shortcomings. Often they permit emotion to colour their thoughts, making some of their actions appear impulsive and ill-timed; certainly not based on sound judgement. They are also highly strung, excitable individuals who will flare up angrily when pushed too far.

But whether viewed in isolation or *en masse* their greatest fear is of restriction. To them life would be intolerable if it had to be lived within close confines or under a rigidly imposed routine.

KEYWORDS
Positive: independent, honest, purposeful, capable
Negative: intolerant, impulsive, stubborn, highly-strung

ARIES-THREE

Planetary combination: Mars/Jupiter

Aries-Threes have really got their acts together. They are capable, positive, enterprising and, more often than not, successful. Their attitude is very free and easy and they tend to take things much as they come. But even when the going gets tough their natural bouyancy and cheerful optimism somehow always see them through. They are irrepressible.

People ruled by this combination of sign and number are energetic and usually very good humoured individuals. They lead busy, action-packed lives and it makes no difference whether they are nine or ninety, they simply cannot resist an opportunity to show off and demonstrate to others just how clever they are. They are bold and courageous; clever and resourceful. They have the luck of the Devil and the innate ability to lead and inspire others.

However, their daring and ambition can sometimes get them into hot water especially when they act in haste or without due care and consideration. They are also incurable fidgets who become restless and impatient at the slightest little hitch or hold-up.

Their greatest bugbear comes in the form of rules, regulations and red tape; they simply cannot cope with personal infringements and restrictions of any variety. Consequently they are rather inclined to rebel and often find themselves at loggerheads with people in authority.

KEYWORDS
Positive: bold, ambitious, energetic, optimistic
Negative: rebellious, hasty, reckless, fidgety

ARIES-FOUR

Planetary combination: Mars/Uranus

When the number Four is added to a restless, impulsive Aries it tends to act rather like a brake. While it will not stop them completely it will certainly slow the pace down a little and make them less likely to make silly mistakes.

People ruled by this combination are capable of great, if rather unusual achievements; will almost certainly attain their goals and ambitions although they cannot expect success to be handed to them on a plate. They will have to struggle all the way using every last ounce of courage and determination they possess in order to earn it.

Aries-Fours are active, independent and fuelled entirely by nervous energy. They are workaholics who do not even know the meaning of the word 'relax' let alone how to do it. They are never satisfied unless they have got plenty to think about and something positive to get their teeth into. All work and no play certainly does not make them dull boys and girls — that is what keeps them happy.

On the deficit side of their character, stubbornness and obstinacy are their main faults although they are not particularly tolerant of other people's little foibles either. Their temper is best described as hot, hasty and hair-triggered.

KEYWORDS
Positive: active, ambitious, enduring, hard-working
Negative: over-active, stubborn, intolerant, quick-tempered

ARIES-FIVE

Planetary combination: Mars/Mercury

Aries-Fives are dexterous, determined and decisive. They pick things up quickly and with ease; and when it comes to passing on ideas and information to others their speech is persuasive and their arguments sound. They make fine orators, and their ability to debate has to be seen to be believed.

Their brains work well and at high speed, their wit is ready and razor sharp and their humour is usually at the expense of someone else. These people could sell rice to the Chinese if they had a mind to.

Aries are passionate individuals with strong sexual drives and feelings so an extra helping of Five earthiness and sensuality is tantamount to a hormonal overdose. Frequent cold showers and hard physical labour are recommended if the beast within those ruled by this sexy combination is to be kept under any sort of control.

Aries-Fives have their fare share of character flaws, the worst of which is finding fault with others. They are critical, tactless and far too outspoken. They are also quarrelsome and sarcastic. However they can usually run mental rings around most of their opponents so their arguments seldom end up coming to actual blows.

KEYWORDS
Positive: witty, clever, decisive, persuasive
Negative: lustful, promiscuous, tactless, critical

ARIES-SIX

Planetary combination: Mars/Venus

The number Six brings peaceful, creative qualities to the Aries character and Aries-Sixes are artistic, imaginative and capable of expressing themselves both verbally and visually. Their work is usually highly original and their output tends to be prolific. They like to improvise and experiment with new methods and techniques but tend to become discouraged and lose interest if their efforts go unrecognized. Quick results and profits are what they are after, not posthumous honours and awards.

They are lively, enthusiastic men and women who are both attractive to and attracted by the opposite sex. They are passionate, impulsive and easily aroused. They usually experience many loves during their lives and tend to put off settling down with one special partner for as long as they possibly can.

When viewed in an unfavourable light they appear coarse and a little vulgar because their approach tends to lack finesse and their intentions are rather too obvious. Their private lives tend to go in fits and starts although their personal magnetism usually ensures that they are never completely at a loss for company. Their attitude is one of 'love them and leave them' and unfortunately when the right person comes along they can find it is very hard to mend their ways.

KEYWORDS
Positive: imaginative, creative, original, lively, attractive
Negative: easily-discouraged, sensual, insatiable, impulsive

ARIES-SEVEN

Planetary combination: Mars/Neptune

An Aries-Seven alliance produces a most unlikely amalgam of talents and temperament and one in which the good points of both components do not always rise up to the surface.

People born under this difficult vibration are imaginative, artistic, creative and, at times, positively inspired. They are always full of brilliant ideas which unfortunately are usually impractical, not financially feasible, or both. What they need is a strong hand to guide them as they lack the necessary drive and determination to convert their schemes into realities. In fact they are totally unrealistic and spend most of their lives wishing for the moon.

Aries-Sevens are dreamers who live in a world of fantasy and irrational fears. They seldom put their time or energy to constructive use because mentally and emotionally they are immature. They are sensation seekers, romantics, pretenders; moody, weak and dissatisfied. And their escapist tendencies could get them into a whole heap of trouble particularly where drugs and alcohol are concerned.

KEYWORDS
Positive: artistic, creative, imaginative, inspired
Negative: weak, emotional, immature, unrealistic

ARIES-EIGHT

Planetary combination: Mars/Saturn

Aries-Eights are pioneers. They are disciplined, determined and can be dangerous if you happen to be sharing the same target. They are born survivors who take set-backs and hardship in their stride. These people will get to the top come hell or high water because they are tough, self-reliant and relentless.

There is nothing at all spiritual or refined about an Aries-Eight. They are mercenary, money-grabbing and materialistic. Mammon is their God and it is to him they have sold their souls.

A combination like this is bound to have its bad points. Love and tenderness are two vital ingredients which seem to have been omitted from the recipe while greed, selfishness and unscrupulous behaviour seem to have been added by the spoonful.

Those born under this vibration will undoubtedly achieve their goals but success is all the sweeter when it is shared and they need to work much harder at their personal life if they do not want to add solitude and loneliness to their list of accomplishments.

KEYWORDS
Positive: ambition, self-controlled, determined, strong
Negative: avaricious, unemotional, ruthless, greedy

ARIES-NINE

Planetary combination: Mars/Mars

The sign of Aries and the number Nine are both ruled by Mars and a double helping of this fiery planet certainly make Aries-Nines a force to be reckoned with. They are active, energetic and practical; dynamic, decisive and domineering. They like to work with, and usually for the ultimate benefit of, others; however they must lead the team or they soon get bored and lose interest. They are efficient, well-organized and very businesslike. They are tremendously ambitious and set themselves a series of personal targets to aim at and goals to achieve.

Provided all that Mars energy is used in a constructive way and that they do not encounter too many obstacles and problems everyday life should run smoothly for Aries-Nines. However if they come up against too many petty rules, regulations and restrictions it could be a different story. They are impatient, reckless and head-strong. They are rather inclined to act on impulse, will fight for what they believe in and are certainly not afraid to speak their minds. Once they get excited then anything can happen and to hell with the consequences as far as they are concerned.

Those born under this vibration also have strong sexual drives and a great deal of their time and energy is channelled in that direction. Their private lives are colourful to say the least and not always trouble-free.

KEYWORDS
Positive: active, ambitious, efficient, goal-conscious, sensual
Negative: hasty, impulsive, aggressive, blunt

TAURUS-ONE

Planetary combination: Venus/Sun

This combination of sign and number produces individuals who want to be safe and successful. They have strong personalities, masses of self-confidence and an almost irrepressible inclination to show off whenever possible. They are attractive and popular with a whole retinue of loyal friends and admirers around them. They are warm-hearted, physically demonstrative and fun to be with.

However, on a rather more serious note, they do have a very materialistic outlook on life and like to surround themselves with status symbols so that everyone else can see how well they are doing. Their sense of values is strong and their craving for security sometimes reaches manic proportions.

Change is something they all resist strongly although they are obstinate about it rather than actually immovable. They also tend to over-indulge themselves where little luxuries are concerned and when it comes to turning on the charm in order to get something they want, Taurus-Ones are experts in this field.

KEYWORDS
Positive: confident, popular, materialistic, ambitious
Negative: over-indulgent, insecure, obstinate, crafty

TAURUS-TWO

Planetary combination: Venus/Moon

Emotional security is of paramount importance to a Taurus-Two. Love and affection are what they are looking for and anything else that comes their way is merely an added bonus. They are gentle, kind and loving; tender, romantic and sensitive. They are also cultured, refined and artistically gifted.

People ruled by this combination have excellent taste and tend to fill their homes with beautiful objects and rich, colourful furnishings. They are easy to get along with, good listeners and amusing conversationalists. They make caring parents, loyal friends and devoted, if rather possessive, partners.

Of course everyone has their failings and Taurus-Twos can be very moody. They will sulk for hours over some imagined slight and a harsh, unkind remark can make them retreat into silence for days on end. They are easily hurt, rather shy and retiring in the company of strangers and incurably jealous.

KEYWORDS
Positive: tender, affectionate, artistic, cultured
Negative: jealous, moody, emotionally insecure, easily-hurt

TAURUS-THREE

Planetary combination: Venus/Jupiter

Taurus-Threes are in love with life and all the pleasures that it can bring them. Socially they are always in great demand because they are charming, entertaining, flamboyant and extremely generous.

They are artistic and creative; versatile and outspoken; outrageously extravagant and theatrical in their mannerisms. In fact they spend money like water and then seem genuinely surprised when their bank account becomes overdrawn. They are like characters from a glamorous Hollywood production with homes like filmsets to match — comfortable, luxurious and well over the top.

Unfortunately the high life, over-indulgence and lack of exercise can cause them health problems in later life. Promiscuity and infidelity will eventually wreck all but the strongest marriages and there is, as yet, no elixir of life which will restore lost youth. Taurus-Threes tend to live now but they will inevitably have to pay later just like everyone else and their bill will almost certainly be high unless they mend their ways.

KEYWORDS
Positive: generous, entertaining, versatile, pleasure-loving
Negative: over-indulgent, lazy, vain, extravagant, wasteful

TAURUS-FOUR

Planetary combination: Venus/Uranus

Taureans are practical, reliable and industrious; Fours are solid efficient and hard-working; and Taurean-Fours are the by-product of both. They are the most productive, honest, well-organized, totally dependable people you will ever meet.

They are patient, methodical and deliberate. They will not hurry in case they make a mistake, they do not panic when a crisis looms and they never seem perturbed when progress is slow.

Security is important to these individuals and most of them will have a little nest egg tucked away somewhere for a rainy day. They tend to have fixed views and opinions about most things and seldom, if ever, do anything impulsive or out of the ordinary. They take responsibility seriously, never shirk their duties and make conscientious parents. In fact they are so cautious and conservative that it is hard to fathom what real pleasure or enjoyment they get out of life.

They are stubborn, predictable and very dull and boring at times. They are slaves to routine, dislike change in any shape, colour or form and once they have settled into their safe, cosy ruts that is really the end of the story, because nothing short of a major catastrophe will budge them ever again.

KEYWORDS
Positive: honest, hard-working, efficient, reliable, conservative
Negative: dull, boring, methodical, joyless, predictable

TAURUS-FIVE

Planetary combination: Venus/Mercury

The Taurus-Five combination is somewhat of a contradiction in terms, which makes it all the more difficult to analyse or define. People ruled by this vibration are logical and thorough because they are secretly afraid of failure. But once they have completed a project they like to go onto something completely different for a change.

The number Five provides the spirit of adventure which Taurus on its own sadly lacks. It also adds a dash of spice in the form of humour, nervous energy and natural buoyancy. It lightens the Taurean spirit considerably without pushing the subject to the point of recklessness or gay abandon. In fact it adds sparkle.

Sexually this is a lusty combination. Taureans are affectionate, sensual and possessive. Five is the number of sexuality. Put them together and the result is not quite a sex maniac but certainly an individual with strong animal drives, desires and preferences. Unfortunately Taurus-Fives are also jealous, suspicious and fickle. They lead complicated personal lives which usually feature difficult marriages or many short-lived relationships.

KEYWORDS
Positive: logical, thorough, diverse, cheerful
Negative: sensual, possessive, promiscuous, jealous

TAURUS-SIX

Planetary combination: Venus/Venus

Venus the planet of love and harmony rules this combination bestowing an appreciation of art and beauty; an eye for colour and form; a love of comfort and luxury and a desire for peace and domestic stability upon her subjects.

Taurus-Sixes are even-tempered, good-natured and considerate. They are sociable, friendly and diplomatic; homeloving, affectionate and loyal. They make model parents and faithful partners who are always ready to put the needs of their loved ones before their own.

Many Taurus-Sixes are artistically gifted while others are talented musicians, writers and poets. They are intelligent, creative and well-informed; charming, attractive and sincere.

They do not really have any major flaws in their character — just a few minor blemishes which are hardly noticeable. They like their homes to be just so and fuss too much on that score. Sometimes they are rather extravagant and will buy items they do not really need and because they will do practically anything for a quiet life they tend to be put upon with predictable regularity.

KEYWORDS
Positive: kind, considerate, talented, intelligent, peace-loving
Negative: fussy, extravagant, easily put-upon

TAURUS-SEVEN

Planetary combination: Venus/Neptune

Taureans are programmed at birth to be patient and methodical; industrious and reliable; not to do anything which will rock the boat or which is in any way progressive and unorthodox — in fact to do, but not to ask the reason why.

However, when Seven characteristics are also fed into the same computer that is when the print-out goes haywire. Deep down Taurus-Sevens know they should be working hard, when instead they are day dreaming. They know that to spend time painting and writing poetry is unproductive but they enjoy it. They know too that the old ways should be the best because they have stood the test of time; that to philosophize, meditate and search for enlightenment is un-Taurean yet still they continue to break all the rules. People born under this vibration frequently dare to ask the taboo question 'Why?', but do not always understand the answer they get back.

They can be rather weak, confused characters who suffer a great deal from moods and depressions. They are very often plagued with guilt and tend to escape into fantasy land whenever life gets difficult. They often use their partner as an emotional crutch and guard them jealously in case someone else comes along and takes their prop away.

KEYWORDS
Positive: artistic, philosophical, questioning, rebellious
Negative: weak, clinging, unconventional, escapist

TAURUS-EIGHT

Planetary combination: Venus/Saturn

This is probably the most ambitious and go-getting of all the Taurus combinations. Success should be within the grasp of anyone born under this vibration although they should not set their sights too high at first — these things take time and that is where patience is a useful asset.

Taureans are practical, hard-working and reliable and the number Eight should inject just the right amount of strength, determination and ruthlessness to give them a head start. Taurus-Eights are disciplined, self-controlled and economical. They have unflagging energy, a way of applying themselves relentlessly to the job in hand and a healthy respect for money.

Eight is a tricky number which can bring about unexpected reversals of fortune but this combination should have sufficient courage and tenacity to overcome even the worst setbacks which life can throw in its path.

When viewed in an unfavourable light these characters appear rather sober and humourless which is not strictly true: it is just that they tend to keep their feelings to themselves. They are also a bit mean and money-grabbing which will not endear them to everyone and many of them are, in fact, intensely lonely people who find it difficult to make any lasting friendships.

KEYWORDS
Positive: ambitious, strong, determined, patient, tenacious
Negative: ill-fated, humourless, mean, lonely

TAURUS-NINE

Planetary combination: Venus/Mars

The planetary rulers of this combination are also planetary opposites which can make life rather difficult for Taurus-Nines. Venus is passive, receptive, feminine and placating while Mars is aggressive, assertive, masculine and purposeful. People born under this vibration like to give their services voluntarily or not at all and any attempt to bully or coerce will only be met with a display of stubborn defiance. Their hearts are in the right place, it is actually getting to them that is the difficulty.

Taurus-Nines are practical, hard-working and persistent. They are very good at giving orders and organizing others but not so good at being on the receiving end. They resist interference, resent criticism and find rules and regulations far too confining and restrictive. They have a natural caution combined with an impulsive streak so it is anyone's guess which way they will jump in some situations although they will always stand their ground and fight when they believe they are in the right.

They are not the most patient of people and it does not take much to make them irritable. They also harbour grudges and will go to great lengths to get their own back on someone who has wronged them no matter how long ago the incident happened.

KEYWORDS
Positive: practical, well-organized, cautious, hard-working
Negative: irritable, impatient, impulsive, stubborn, revengeful

GEMINI-ONE

Planetary combination: Mercury/Sun

People born under this vibration are extremely capable, highly intelligent and very ingenious. They are versatile, quick-witted and lively. They tend to pick things up as they go along because they are fast learners who absorb facts and information like blotting paper.

Variety is what they like best and their innate curiosity can lead them down all sorts of paths. They thrive on change and excitement, love to travel and have a marked flair for languages. They are charming, well-informed and make great company. They are born communicators who converse easily and fluently and are also articulate and witty. In fact they would talk the hind legs off a donkey given half a chance.

However, they are not always 100 per cent reliable and tend to spend a great deal of their time torn between various different courses of action, all of which they find equally attractive. Their lives often lack continuity and their restlessness can be intensely irritating at times. They can also be a touch two-faced and will frequently say one thing when everyone knows that they really mean something entirely different.

KEYWORDS
Positive: intelligent, lively, versatile, communicative
Negative: indecisive, restless, inconsistent, jumpy

GEMINI-TWO

Planetary combination: Mercury/Moon

Gemini-Twos are intelligent, intuitive, multi-faceted individuals who have quick minds and even livelier imaginations. They are energetic in a nervous sort of way and undoubtedly talented especially where business acumen and languages are concerned. Their wit is ready and razor-sharp, their judgement sound and their ideas shrewd and original. In fact they are competent, versatile, useful sort of people to have around.

Unfortunately as anyone influenced by the Moon will already be only too well aware, emotional balance can be difficult to achieve and even more of a problem to maintain. Gemini-Twos are no exception and at certain times will find it almost impossible to be decisive. They are sensitive, sympathetic and understanding to the needs of others because they themselves are hyper-sensitive, often anxious and frequently misunderstood.

All Geminis enjoy variation and variety in their lives and without it they would soon grow dull and lack-lustre but the changeable moods and a tendency to low spirits traditionally associated with number Two is something which they just have to learn to live with as part of the deal.

KEYWORDS
Positive: business acumen, language flair, sound judgement, original ideas
Negative: anxious, touchy, moody, indecisive

GEMINI-THREE

Planetary combination: Mercury/Jupiter

This is a particularly volatile combination of sign and number because the characteristics of both components display marked similarities. In a situation like this it is anyone's guess whether it will be the good or the bad points or both which emerge as the strongest traits.

Gemini-Threes certainly have a lot of potential. They are charming, popular and intelligent. They have fertile minds, a positive wealth of ideas and enough business sense to promote them in the right manner. They are usually well-read, well-educated and well-spoken with an optimistic, broadminded outlook on life. Many have a talent for speaking and writing while others are irresistibly drawn to modern technology and anything scientific, but one thing they all have in common is a love of travel and a willingness to take risks.

Unfortunately people born under this vibration do have a great many faults that can come out. They are jacks of all trades and master of none. They are forgetful, unreliable and lack discipline. They go from frying pan to fire with predictable regularity and never really learn anything positive from their mistakes. They are rather empty and superficial; arrogant, conceited and full of their own importance.

KEYWORDS
Positive: optimistic, love to travel, intelligent, cultured
Negative: undisciplined, superficial, conceited, forgetful

GEMINI-FOUR

Planetary combination: Mercury/Uranus

The number Four brings industry, organization and stability to this unusual combination, while Gemini provides the intellect, energy and quick reactions. The result could be sheer genius because well-planned strategies plus the nerve to carry them out seldom fail.

Gemini-Fours are patient, logical and inventive. Their ideas are always highly original, if a little unconventional, and their field of operation is usually specialized. They are cool, calm and collected, that is until the time comes to make a move when they will swing into action like a well-oiled piece of machinery.

They are shrewd, clever and resourceful. They never seem to be in any particular hurry to get on in life, however, they are not too slow to let an opportunity for advancement slip by unnoticed.

There's something of the 'mad professor' about all of them and they will frequently work far into the night over plans and calculations. Unfortunately their output is very erratic and they tend to work best in short, sharp bursts followed by long periods of inactivity. They are often eccentric, highly-strung and rather restless at times. And their brutal frankness certainly would not win them many votes in a popularity poll. You should never ask the opinion of a Gemini-Four unless you really want to know the truth because they will give it to you straight and your feelings will be the last thing they will take into consideration.

KEYWORDS
Positive: organized, industrious, energetic, inventive, original
Negative: eccentric, erratic, blunt, restless

GEMINI-FIVE

Planetary combination: Mercury/Mercury

Look out, look out — there is a Gemini-Five about, and when this Mercurial combination takes flesh anything could happen and frequently does. They are in love with life and always impatient for change whatever shape or form it may take. They are bright, lively and intelligent; articulate, adventurous and utterly charming. They need constant mental and physical stimulation; new things to do, places to go and people to meet. They are curious, inquiring and move with the times.

They have usually got a whole host of friends and acquaintances with whom they can discuss their interests and swop ideas. They are also well known for talking late into the night when a particularly heated debate gets started. Gemini-Fives are also in love with love and their private lives are colourful to say the least. Variety is the spice they seem to prefer and they sprinkle it liberally and literally on their affairs.

These people need more discipline and consistency in their lives but not necessarily the burdens of responsibility and routine. They are forever changing course and seldom see a project through to the end. Their interest tends to be superficial, their continuity non-existent and their affairs transitory. However if they learned to concentrate and adopted a more serious attitude to life they could undoubtedly move mountains.

KEYWORDS
Positive: bright, lively, curious, sociable, intelligent
Negative: inconsistent, superficial, restless, changeable

GEMINI-SIX

Planetary combination: Mercury/Venus

Gemini-Sixes are the life and soul of any party. They are elegant, refined and cultured; sociable, light-hearted and rather light-headed at times too. They are amusing, agreeable and very witty.

They have a definite leaning towards the arts and many are talented actors and musicians, writers and painters. They have a flair for colour and an eye for line and form which enables them not only to appreciate beauty but also to create it for themselves in their homes and through their work. They are Bohemian in life-style, theatrical in manner and sparkling in company.

Unfortunately they are also vain, conceited and lazy. They are more interested in enjoying themselves than they are in actually achieving anything in life. They tend to be extravagant, superficial and selfish. However, very often behind those masks of charm and sophistication will lie a lonely, vulnerable soul crying out to be loved but going about it in completely the wrong way.

KEYWORDS
Positive: brilliant, witty, amusing, creative, talented
Negative: theatrical, superficial, extravagant, lazy, lonely

GEMINI-SEVEN

Planetary combination: Mercury/Neptune

The Gemini character is restless and fidgety at the best of times but when also subjected to the mysterious Seven influence this really does throw the astrological Twins into chaos. Gemini-Sevens are scatter-brained and vague. They seem to muddle through life in a state of complete and utter confusion. They are sensitive, creative and, at times, inspired; however they can also be totally unrealistic and hopeless at putting their affairs in order.

All Geminis are quick-thinking, adventurous and versatile. They seek variety and change and are constantly on the go, searching for new things to do and fresh places to explore. Unfortunately the number Seven tends to open doors in their minds which were better left closed. They start to develop spiritual longings which they do not really know how to cope with and they take off on weird and wonderful flights of fancy becoming travellers in the realms of the imagination.

Their strange notions and ideas often get them into trouble or make them appear foolish in front of others. They waste a great deal of time and energy on unproductive schemes and their judgement is far from sound. Fortunately they do have a sense of humour and the ability to laugh at their mistakes which at times can be their saving grace.

KEYWORDS
Positive: energetic, creative, imaginative, adventurous
Negative: unrealistic, vague, disorganized, fanciful

GEMINI-EIGHT

Planetary combination: Mercury/Saturn

People ruled by this combination of sign and number are disciplined, hard-working and well-organized. They have clearly defined goals and ambitions in life and although they may never experience a meteoric rise to fame and fortune their advancement is virtually guaranteed because they plan their moves with care and precision.

They are thorough, reliable and very serious. They have tremendous powers of concentration and the ability to take problems and obstacles in their stride without losing momentum for even a second. However their personal lives are often difficult because feelings and emotions are seldom based on logic and do not always run according to plan. Gemini-Eights find it almost impossible to let themselves go and relax. They are either far too shy and awkward, or so aloof and detached that it is impossible to get through to them. They are inhibited, unimaginative and very heavy going.

While their industry is commendable, their application relentless and their reasoning faultless, their warmth and compassion are nowhere to be seen. They are mean, unimaginative, cold and unfeeling.

KEYWORDS
Positive: organized, disciplined, industrious, methodical, deliberate
Negative: mean, unfeeling, unimaginative, inhibited

GEMINI-NINE

Planetary combination: Mercury/Mars

'Mind over matter' is a phrase which aptly describes this combination because Gemini-Nines can achieve anything provided they have sufficient motivation. They are capable of tremendous effort but will accept nothing less than success for their reward.

They are decisive, determined, dangerous people when crossed and so clever and persuasive with words, that they could charm the birds from the trees should it prove necessary to achieve their ends. They are quick, practical, skilful and whatever they do you can be sure they do it well.

Unfortunately they will speak out, usually in anger, before they have had sufficient time to reflect and this can get them into all sorts of trouble especially with superiors. What is more they have to have the last word on any subject which often only serves to make matters worse. They are rash, tactless, and sarcastic; obstinate, critical and impulsive. Their tempers are hasty and hair-triggered and although it does not take much to set them off it can be an eternity before they finally calm down again.

KEYWORDS
Positive: determined, quick-witted, skilful, ambitious
Negative: unreflective, tactless, obstinate, impulsive

CANCER-ONE

Planetary combination: Moon/Sun

Emotion tends to colour the thoughts and actions of all Cancer-Ones to a greater or lesser degree and although they are ambitious individuals they occasionally find that they are feeling indecisive, fresh out of confidence, or both, at precisely the wrong moment. But generally speaking they have a well-balanced, optimistic approach to life and the ability to adapt to changing circumstances or to cope with difficulties without panicking or becoming hysterical.

They all crave domestic comfort and personal security and perhaps for this reason alone, set great store by their homes and families. Their parental ties are strong and they would move heaven and earth to help a loved one in trouble. They are loyal, fiercely protective and very sentimental.

Cancer-Ones may appear tough and strong on the surface but deep down they are shy, sensitive and easily hurt. Many have inferiority complexes which they try hard to conceal, others fall easy prey to flattery and a few wallow in private moments of doubt and self-pity. They really are very vulnerable individuals but their thick outward veneer usually forms an adequate layer of protection from all but the worst traumas of life.

KEYWORDS
Positive: ambitious, loyal, homeloving, optimistic
Negative: emotional, insecure, sensitive, easily-hurt

CANCER-TWO

Planetary combination: Moon/Moon

This combination of sign and number is exclusively ruled by the Moon and the lunar influence is possibly one of the most difficult to live under, because not only is it changeable it also has a great effect upon the emotions.

Cancer-Twos are undoubtedly hyper-sensitive individuals and, like still waters, their sentiments and feelings run very deep indeed. They are homeloving, domesticated and parental. They care passionately about others less fortunate than themselves, and have an overwhelming desire to ease their burdens in any way they can. They are soulful, spiritual and often too soft and sentimental for their own good. They find pain and suffering almost impossible to bear and are easily moved to tears in emotionally charged situations.

Moon subjects often find that their unconscious minds are very active and that their awareness, intuition and powers of ESP are more pronounced than those of other people. Many choose to develop their gifts further and go on to become fine mediums and clairvoyants while others find that faith and religion play a strong supporting role in their lives.

Moodiness and depression are the greatest problems they have to overcome and rampant jealousy coupled with possessiveness is certainly their worst fault.

KEYWORDS
Positive: caring, sentimental, spiritual, sensitive, mediumistic
Negative: changeable, over-emotional, moody, jealous

CANCER-THREE

Planetary combination: Moon/Jupiter

Cancer-Threes have just the right amount of ambition and energy, humility and feeling within their make-up to give them balance. They are kind, understanding and helpful. They make friends easily because they are tolerant and understanding and are loved and respected for their good-natured common sense which they are always willing to share — but only on request.

They are sane, and intelligent with fertile brains, lively imaginations and a flair for languages. Socially they are popular, businesswise they're astute and well-organized and in private they can be tender and romantic without going over the top. In fact they are a very likeable, inoffensive blend of characteristics and talent.

Their faults are few and really rather innocuous when compared with those of other combinations. Occasionally their judgement can be a little faulty, at times they lack drive and seem to be functioning on a low voltage and the odd bout of over-indulgence can upset their delicate digestive systems laying them low for several days before they fully recover.

KEYWORDS
Positive: well-balanced, intelligent, popular, tolerant
Negative: at times inefficient, lack lustre and over-indulgent

CANCER-FOUR

Planetary combination: Moon/Uranus

Once an insecure, homeloving, emotional Cancerian comes under the calm, steady influence of the number Four the transformation that takes place is really quite astonishing. Ambition, confidence and will-power come to the fore while the delicate ego becomes less fragile and the feelings not quite so easy to hurt.

Cancer-Fours are hard-working and progressive. They know where they are going and are quite prepared to make sacrifices to achieve their goals. They are practical and efficient, determined and tenacious. Security is something they will build for themselves, brick by brick, one step at a time until the structure is complete.

These honest, sincere individuals make devoted, faithful partners, fiercely protective parents and loyal, lifelong friends. They may not move through life at supersonic speed but whatever moves they do make will be well thought out and intended to last. It's permanence and stability they crave, not constant challenge and change.

Unfortunately these willing workers never know when to call it a day and frequently drive themselves far too hard for long periods at a time without a break. Consequently, tiredness and over-strained nerves are often the legacy of their unremitting application to work. Their stubborn desire for total independence can make them seem insular and stand-offish to others, particularly when they flatly refuse to accept well-meant offers of help.

KEYWORDS
Positive: hard-working, independent, practical, slow but sure
Negative: workaholic, stubborn, insular, clannish

CANCER-FIVE

Planetary combination: Moon/Mercury

The last thing a Cancerian needs is to be co-ruled by the number Five. It tends to highlight existing problems and does little, if anything, to boost morale. Cancerians have a hard enough time as it is trying to appear confident and self-assured for unfortunately restlessness, impulsive urges plus a generous helping of latent sexuality are all part and parcel of the Five package that people of this vibration have to learn to live with.

Cancer-Fives are intelligent, imaginative and highly-strung. They are lively, talkative individuals who usually display a marked flair for languages. However, their thought patterns are always strongly influenced by their personal feelings and for this reason their judgement can at times be faulty because they will allow emotion to creep into the picture and cloud the issue.

Anxiety and indecision are two of their main faults while feelings of insecurity and low self-esteem are their greatest problems.

KEYWORDS
Positive: imaginative, articulate, intelligent, language ability
Negative: anxious, fretful, insecure, over-emotional

CANCER-SIX

Planetary combination: Moon/Venus

Cancer-Sixes are always seen at their best when in their natural habitat and whether they dwell in castles or attics, high-rise flats or country cottages, home is most definitely where their heart lies and where they prefer to be. They are creative, artistic, gentle people who have an eye for beauty and a way with colours and furnishings that has to be seen to be appreciated. They are talented, cultured and refined. They are also avid collectors and like to surround themselves with a whole array of personal treasures and sentimental little trinkets.

People born under this vibration are sociable and popular; attractive, easy-going and full of life. They're romantics who set great store by their personal relationships. As they are tender and affectionate by nature, they ask nothing more than to love and be loved in return. They are champions of the family cause and are fiercely protective of their loved ones. Blood-ties form strong bonds and certainly ones which they won't want to break in a hurry.

Unfortunately with Cancer-Sixes moodiness tends to mar the picture slightly from time to time. What's more they become very tight-lipped and silent when their efforts go unnoticed. Their fear of poverty and destitution occasionally reaches manic proportions particularly when the quarterly household bills come flooding in onto the mat. They need to feel secure, emotionally and financially, or their normal sunny smiles will disappear behind clouds of gloom and foreboding.

KEYWORDS
Positive: homeloving, parental, creative, artistic, romantic
Negative: moody, insecure, touchy, crave affection

CANCER-SEVEN

Planetary combination: Moon/Neptune

Those ruled by this particular combination of sign and number often find the harsh realities of life almost impossible to bear. They need to grow thicker skins and harden their hearts if they ever hope to survive. Unfortunately they seldom adopt these tactics, preferring instead to seek solace elsewhere. Many turn to religion for comfort, others prefer to sustain themselves on self-deception and fantasy and sadly the odd handful will turn to alcohol and drugs in search of salvation.

Cancer-Sevens are much too good for this world. They are sensitive, gentle and refined. Their imaginations are colourful and over-active, their perception delicate and finely tuned, and their thoughts mystical and frequently misunderstood. They are tender and compassionate; quiet, sympathetic and totally selfless.

Their feelings are deep and sincere. Love to them is an ideal to be cherished. They lean to the platonic in matters of the heart, preferring to worship from afar rather than coming to grips with their passion. They are solitary, insular people who know only too well the true meaning of the word loneliness. They long for the impossible which they won't find in this lifetime but who knows about the next?

KEYWORDS
Positive: sensitive, gentle, imaginative, perceptive, selfless
Negative: vulnerable, unrealistic, solitary, unworldly

CANCER-EIGHT

Planetary combination: Moon/Saturn

All Cancer-Eights have a strong sense of duty and tend to take responsibilities seriously, especially family ones. They are reliable, hard-working and well-organized. They are also very ambitious. They have a healthy respect for money, never live beyond their means and would sooner cut off their right arms than run the risk of getting into debt. They are serious and conservative with a strong sense of values, good business acumen and the ability to concentrate for long periods at a time.

Emotionally, however, they are a disaster area. Their self-control is so rigid that they don't know how to turn it off. They bottle everything up inside and won't relax their stiff upper lips for even a second. They are jealous, suspicious and possessive. Passion terrifies them; they are frightened to let themselves go and after years of suppressing their feelings its small wonder that they are cold and frigid.

They are not particularly successful in parental roles either. Admittedly they know only too well how to provide all the material requirements of a family but when it comes to giving out love and affection they are non-starters.

KEYWORDS
Positive: ambitious, hard-working, responsible, conservative
Negative: unemotional, cold, jealous, possessive

CANCER-NINE

Planetary combination: Moon/Mars

Once Cancer-Nines have set their sights on a target they are virtually impossible to deflect. They will hang on in there to the bitter end. They have tremendous will-power, fighting spirit and never do anything by halves. They are vigorous, energetic and determined.

People ruled by this combination are refreshingly straight-forward. They are independent, unpretentious and sincere. They like nothing better than something to get their teeth into when their enthusiasm becomes positively infectious. Their opinions, when sought, are always candid, their courage is undeniable and their output when working flat out, as they usually do, is phenomenal.

Unfortunately they are so head-strong and impetuous that they won't take advice even when it's offered. They rebel against restrictions which threaten to impede their progress and are well known for acting rashly once they have lost their tempers. They are excitable, quarrelsome and intolerant. Anyone who dares to poke their nose into a Cancer-Nine's private affairs is really asking for trouble in a big way.

KEYWORDS
Positive: energetic, enthusiastic, independent, purposeful
Negative: excitable, rebellious, head-strong, aggressive

LEO-ONE

Planetary combination: Sun/Sun

Leo-Ones are positive, decisive and very self-assured. Centre stage is where they like to be so that everyone has a chance to admire them and can see just how wonderful they are. They are confident, energetic and irrepressible. They have sunny dispositions, larger than life personalities and masses of charm which they turn on and off at the drop of a hat. Adulation is what they seek and they will show off shamelessly at times to get it.

They are powerful, ambitious people; good organizers, born leaders and capable of great achievement. They have a wealth of ideas, a flair for organization and the knack of getting other people to run around doing all the work while they sit back and wait for the applause.

When viewed in an unfavourable light they are pushy, self-seeking and conceited. They have fixed opinions, strong likes and dislikes and a patronizing way of addressing anyone who they consider to be inferior. They are pompous, intolerant snobs but, for all that, very difficult to actually dislike.

KEYWORDS
Positive: dynamic, powerful, ambitious, confident
Negative: pushy, conceited, intolerant, snobbish

LEO-TWO

Planetary combination: Sun/Moon

People ruled by this particular combination of sign and number are confident, generous and popular; vital, optimistic and forthright in expression. They like to do eveything on a grand scale and always in a dramatic, theatrical manner. When entertaining friends they turn a simple meal into a banquet, they dress to kill even when casual clothes are the order of the day, and birth control is something they have probably never heard of if the size of their families is anything to go by. There is no doubt about it, they're spontaneous, well-meaning, larger than life and, at times, well over the top.

A strong, happy marriage and a large, luxurious home are the most important features of a Leo-Two's life and they will work very hard to achieve both. Career-wise they are ambitious but success in this direction is merely an optional extra. In private they are demonstrative, passionate and impulsive; fiercely loyal, whole-heartedly sincere and very possessive.

Their faults are many and noticeable. They are domineering, intolerant and bossy. They are also jealous, suspicious and vindictive. Beneath that mask of self-assurance they are secretly terrified of physical pain and ill health. Permanent youth is ideally what they would like because the prospect of old-age and infirmity appauls them.

KEYWORDS
Positive: generous, popular, theatrical, passionate
Negative: bossy, jealous, possessive, cowardly

LEO-THREE

Planetary combination: Sun/Jupiter

Big ideas, tremendous self-confidence and the luck of the Devil are all undoubtedly attributes of the Leo-Three. They are generous, optimistic and well-liked. They want to get on in life and their ambition drives them to seek positions of prominence and power.

Social climbing is a game they all know how to play and they will use any means to achieve their ends. They tend to seek out and befriend people who can be useful to them as they know and understand the value of good contacts. They will pick people's brains, gain experience wherever they can and push themselves on until they reach the top. Money talks and their aim is to accumulate enough to hold a long conversation.

They are shrewd, original and observant. Often they're artistically talented but seldom put these gifts to good use preferring to channel their creative energy in a more profitable direction.

Leo-Threes can't bear to be in subordinate positions. They know how to give orders but unfortunately don't like taking them. They are also very good at manipulating people but easily angered when the boot appears to be on the other foot. They are pretentious, ostentatious and sycophantic.

KEYWORDS
Positive: ambitious, lucky, social climbing, materialistic
Negative: insubordinate, ostentatious, pushy

LEO-FOUR

Planetary combination: Sun/Uranus

All Leo-Fours are superb organizers. They are hard-working, enthusiastic and efficient. They have strong, forceful personalities and will leave their mark on everyone and everything they touch in one way or another. They are energetic, original and definitely command respect.

They are never content when things remain the way they are for too long. They need change, excitement and the odd adventure or two to keep life interesting. They are progressive, compulsive reformers who think big and usually along rather unconventional lines. They are unusual, unorthodox and very volatile.

People born under this vibration tend to be rebellious and revolutionary. They are meddlesome, head-strong and determined. They never act without thinking, always plan ahead and seldom overlook even the smallest of details. They may take their time but when they move their actions bear all the hallmarks of a carefully executed military campaign.

KEYWORDS
Positive: organized, efficient, adventurous, energetic
Negative: head-strong, determined, calculating, unorthodox

LEO-FIVE

Planetary combination: Sun/Mercury

Leo's are confident, spontaneous and assertive; Five adds an adventurous, 'Devil may care' attitude and people influenced by them both have the nerve to attempt just about anything.

Leo-Fives are quick-witted, curious and resilient. They are life's stuntmen who will try anything once just to see what it feels like. However they do like a good audience to witness their daring deeds. They love to travel because it keeps them from getting bored, they love to gamble because it gives them a thrill and they take risks simply because they can't resist a challenge. Not all their endeavours meet with success but fortunately they have sufficient stamina, natural buoyancy and strength of character to come bouncing back even after the worst of set-backs. They are born survivors and never down for long.

This combination also has strong sexual overtones and Leo-Fives tend to exhibit rather more than a healthy interest in their personal lives. They are passionate, earthy and demonstrative; unconventional, impulsive and, at times, rather aggressive. This is one area of life that they experience to the full and one in which they like plenty of variety.

KEYWORDS
Positive: adventurous, resilient, daring, curious
Negative: sensual, restless, easily bored, reckless

LEO-SIX

Planetary combination: Sun/Venus

Leo-Sixes are jointly ruled by the Sun and the planet Venus. The former gives them their spirit and energy while the latter bestows upon them peace, love and an appreciation of beauty. They are confident, generous individuals with creative ability and strong artistic leanings.

They are ambitious in a quiet, unaggressive sort of way. In fact they would very much like to succeed in life and will work hard to do so but never at the expense of anyone else. They don't have a single devious or underhand bone in their bodies, so they will play by the rules or not at all.

A happy home and family life is of paramount importance to these kindly, warm-hearted people. They have many friends, a great capacity for fun and enjoyment and lead hectic social lives. They are amusing and generous; free and easy; spontaneous when it comes to giving invitations but not quite so enthusiastic when it comes to clearing up.

Apart from being fussy and a tiny bit selfish they really have no other faults at all worth noting.

KEYWORDS
Positive: generous, warm-hearted, loving, spontaneous
Negative: fussy, trivial, selfish

LEO-SEVEN

Planetary combination: Sun/Neptune

This is a strange combination of sign and number because both components are so very different having few if any qualities in common. It is small wonder that Leo-Sevens are always something of an enigma and very often a contradiction in terms. They have all the usual Leonine qualities of self-assurance, dignity and a strong sense of drama but these change and modify when coupled with spirituality, inner-vision and a desire for the truth.

Leo-Sevens are sensitive, receptive and imaginative. They are magical and very mysterious. Many have undoubted psychic ability but they need to spend time alone in order to develop these gifts. They seem to be continually torn between the material world of ambitions, possessions and desires and the weird and wonderful realms of the supernatural. This is definitely not an easy vibration to live under.

A frail and delicate constitution is often part and parcel of this particular package and although its recipients seldom enjoy robust good health their spirit and courage are indomitable.

KEYWORDS
Positive: self-assured, dignified, courageous, psychic
Negative: sickly, sensitive, confused, unrealistic

LEO-EIGHT

Planetary combination: Sun/Saturn

Leo-Eights are a bunch of megalomaniacs. They think big, act big — in fact everything they do is on a magnificent, larger than life scale. Unfortunately this is a disease for which there is no known cure, although the causes have been identified and the symptoms are easy to recognize. Ambition and a desire to succeed coupled with a strong craving for power, recognition and social standing are definitely at the root of it all.

The signs to look out for are tremendous self-confidence and high self-esteem followed by relentless application to work, a determined set of the jaw and a well-organized plan of attack. Unpleasant side effects can manifest themselves in the form of obstinacy, ruthlessness and conceit while behaviour patterns start to become hard and unscrupulous. Brief remissions can sometimes occur and they usually come about when promotion has just taken place, salary has been raised or a title has been conferred.

Certainly not all Leo-Eights will make it to the top as fate has a nasty way of turning the tables on them at just the wrong moment. Indeed, those that are successful very often pay a high price of loneliness or a broken marriage for their achievements.

KEYWORDS
Positive: mega-ambitious, tough, determined, materialistic
Negative: hard, unscrupulous, power-mad, ruthless

LEO-NINE

Planetary combination: Sun/Mars

Force and energy are the two main ingredients of a Leo-Nine and they can be served up in a variety of ways. People born under this vibration are courageous, enterprising and fired with innate ambition. They are positive, forceful and decisive. They thrive on competition, know how to assert themselves and will stop at nothing to get what they want.

What is it they want? The answer is power. They are hungry for it and won't be content until their appetite has been satisfied. They laugh in the face of danger, perform feats of endurance which no mortal man should be capable of and boldly go where even angels fear to tread. They are ardent, hot-blooded, human dynamos.

To list all their shortcomings would be an impossible task as they have so many faults. They are hyper-active and can't relax for even five minutes; they take on far too much and then wonder why they're feeling exhausted and their hasty temper can get them into all sorts of trouble. In fact quarrels and arguments are a normal part of their daily round. They are head-strong, intolerant, ruthless and enormously conceited.

KEYWORDS
Positive: ambitious, forceful, energetic, decisive
Negative: hyper-active, power-mad, aggressive, conceited

VIRGO-ONE

Planetary combination: Mercury/Sun

This is a nicely balanced combination because the number One not only compliments the Virgoan character it also highlights its good points. Virgo-Ones are intelligent, capable and well-organized. They are disciplined, well-informed and precise. They have a place for everything and everything has to be in its place. Even their computer-like minds are neat and tidy, their thoughts follow conventional patterns and their approach is always practical rather than abstract. They deal in facts, figures and logic and tend to analyse everything in minute detail, sifting, dissecting and criticizing any faults they happen to come across.

Thanks to the One influence they are ambitious and independent. They show a healthy curiosity when anything new presents itself upon the scene, particularly if it is of a technical or scientific nature. They are pioneering, innovative and tenacious. They learn fast and they learn well.

As to their bad points these are easy to list because everything about a Virgo-

One is orderly. They are fussy, fastidious and intense; pedantic, censorious know it alls. They rarely show their feelings because there's a time as well as a place for everything and the two seldom coincide.

KEYWORDS
Positive: intelligent, well-organized, logical, independent
Negative: fussy, critical, pedantic, unemotional

VIRGO-TWO

Planetary combination: Mercury/Moon

Virgo-Twos are good humoured, optimistic and reasonably adaptable, although they don't always take too kindly to having things sprung on them at the last minute. They have fine minds, fertile imaginations and quick wits. Their judgement is sound, their thoughts logical and collected and their conversation interesting and practically non-stop. They are compulsive talkers who can usually make themselves understood in at least three different languages besides their own.

They have astute business brains and a positive flair for organization and administration which they always seem to put to good use. At work or at play they do everything in a precise, orderly fashion.

Virgo-Twos are fuelled by nervous energy and tend to get over excited when under pressure. They are highly-strung and occasionally indecision makes their behaviour erratic until they know which way they are going. They have sharp tongues, a tendency to low spirits and definite problems with their emotions because they regard any show of feeling as a sign of weakness. Also they are all hypochondriacs. They worry incessantly over their health, even when they are well, as they're terrified of catching something unpleasant. When they are actually ill, they bury their noses in medical dictionaries and surround themselves with enough pills, potions and poultices to cover every conceivable contingency from bubonic plague to an ingrowing toe-nail.

KEYWORDS
Positive: logical, organized, talkative, good-humoured
Negative: nervous, highly-strung, excitable, health-conscious

VIRGO-THREE

Planetary combination: Mercury/Jupiter

Three is the number of brilliance and versatility which when 'earthed' by Virgoan reserve and shrewdness makes this combination something really rather special. Virgo-Threes are broadminded, good-natured and well-balanced. They have a lively sense of humour and although they are hard-working they do know when to call it a day and take a breather.

They are not particularly good with their hands but when it comes to brainpower and intelligence they are in a class of their own. They have fertile minds which are full to overflowing with good ideas plus a great deal of common sense. Their business acumen is sound, their actions are always constructive and they learn quickly. They write with flair, have a talent for public speaking and a yen to travel. They are cultured, well-read and socially popular.

Unfortunately the Three vibration will occasionally get out of hand and at such times they are likely to become negligent, frivolous and rather too outspoken.

KEYWORDS
Positive: highly intelligent, well-balanced, hard-working, humorous
Negative: negligent, frivolous, outspoken

VIRGO-FOUR

Planetary combination: Mercury/Uranus

If only they would take life a little less seriously and would learn to smile, Virgo-Fours would be far more attractive individuals. But all work and no play makes them very dull indeed. They are mechanical, robotic and more like machines than human beings. They are precise, methodical and conscientious. They live to work and wouldn't know how to enjoy themselves if they tried.

Their lives are orderly, well-organized and planned right down to the last little detail. They are undoubtedly intelligent and usually well-read but they wouldn't recognize an original thought if they had one. Career-wise they tend to specialize and their work is very often of a technical or scientific nature.

What little spare time they have is usually devoted to their slavish, self-imposed routine of ensuring that everything around them is neat, tidy, spotlessly clean and as near perfect as they can get it.

Virgo-Fours are not much fun. They are dull, gloomy and joyless. Their personal lives are much the same because although they are capable of feeling love they simply don't know how to show it. They lack the passion and spontaneity which would make their relationships come to life.

KEYWORDS
Positive: precise, methodical, orderly, conscientious
Negative: dull, joyless, fastidious, emotionally-repressed

VIRGO-FIVE

Planetary combination: Mercury/Mercury

People born under this vibration have hidden depths thanks to the number Five. On the surface, particularly at work, they are typical Virgoans — rational and analytical; shrewd and intelligent; conscientious and rather reserved. But when the time comes to down tools for the day, a Jekyll and Hyde type transformation seems to take place, for out from behind that prim and proper facade steps a witty, charming socialite.

Virgo-Fives certainly know how to enjoy themselves. They are attractive, popular and talkative; graceful, elegant and always immaculately dressed. They love to exchange ideas, discuss current affairs and debate a wide variety of topics. They have a host of friends and acquaintances and never seem to be at a loss for something to do or somewhere to go.

Now here's the rub. Five is also the number of rampant sexuality which, as a rule, Virgoans show no particular interest in. Some feel genuinely ashamed of the feelings this combination awakens in them, others are modestly curious while those that have got any sense go into the matter with their usual thoroughness paying great attention to every little detail.

KEYWORDS
Positive: conscientious, articulate, rational, popular
Negative: emotionally confused, multi-faceted, changeable

VIRGO-SIX

Planetary combination: Mercury/Venus

Virgo-Sixes are delightful people who seem to have discovered the formula for both happiness and success. They have all the Virgo shrewdness and intelligence plus Six warmth and creativity. They are charming, amusing and cheerful; well-organized, artistic and refined. On first acquaintance they may appear light-hearted and carefree but they are nobody's fools. Their heads are very definitely screwed on the right way even if they do tilt them coquettishly to one side from time to time.

People ruled by this combination are loving, affectionate and fiercely loyal. Domesticity suits them, but when cast in a parental role they tend to be a little too strict and over-critical where their offspring are concerned. They are perfectionists who like everything to be just right; the mess, muddle and chaos that a growing family leaves in its wake nearly drives them to destraction especially at holiday times and week-ends.

Virgo-Sixes are usually so well balanced that their faults tend to be very few and far between. They are all guilty of the odd extravagance every now and again especially where life's little luxuries are concerned. Vanity and conceit can occasionally be detected while fussiness often appears on the menu. None of these character blemishes is particularly serious and all of them are containable.

KEYWORDS
Positive: cheerful, friendly, domesticated, competent
Negative: conceited, extravagant, fussy, intolerant

VIRGO-SEVEN

Planetary combination: Mercury/Neptune

This is really rather a strange combination because the number Seven seems to put all sorts of weird, wonderful and definitely uncharacteristic ideas into Virgoan heads. It opens up doors in their minds which most of them never even notice, let alone bother to investigate.

Virgo-Sevens are erratic. They go in fits and starts. One minute they are miles away in another world and the next they are galvanized into action pushing themselves far too hard as if trying to make up for lost time.

They are imaginative, open-minded and inquisitive; analytical, critical and shrewd. Although practical by nature they find abstract ideas particularly fascinating. Logic is their trusty yardstick but unfortunately its not always one which can be applied to the terrain they try to explore. They like to get to the bottom of everything and become extremely irritated and annoyed when their attempts occasionally fail.

On an off-day they can be boring and pedantic and at such times are best left alone to get on with it. Like all Virgoans they fuss too much over trivial little details and because of their ruling number they are rather moody, sarcastic and inclined to fantacize.

KEYWORDS
Positive: inquisitive, logical, imaginative, critical
Negative: erratic, moody, boring, pedantic

VIRGO-EIGHT

Planetary combination: Mercury/Saturn

Virgo-Eights are loners. They seem to find hard work not only stimulating but also rather pleasurable. Moreover, tedium never seems to irritate them possibly because they are rather unimaginative themselves. They are quiet, thorough and reliable. They do everything at a snail's pace always erring on the side of caution. 'Slow but sure' is their motto and their progress certainly reflects this tenet.

They are methodical, organized and serious; quiet, disciplined and extremely earnest. Their powers of concentration are highly developed so much so that they often don't realize when they are being spoken to, or fail to notice that someone is trying to attract their attention. They become completely lost in thought and their trance-like state is frequently mistaken for churlishness or disdain.

Emotionally they are awkward and extremely inhibited which tends to make them appear rather cold and humourless. They are also narrow-minded, conservative to a ridiculous degree and obstinate. Change and modernization are two evils which they actively resist, while communication is something they experience problems with at any level. In fact a surprisingly high percentage of Virgo-Eights have some form of speech impediment or difficulty.

KEYWORDS
Positive: thorough, methodical, reliable, good powers of concentration
Negative: solitary, inhibited, uncommunicative, obstinate

VIRGO-NINE

Planetary combination: Mercury/Mars

People ruled by this combination of sign and number are easy to identify because not only are they eye-catching and dynamic, they are also alert, quick-thinking and decisive. Their manner of speech is fluent and persuasive however they tend to lack two vital ingredients, namely tact and discretion. They are frank, outspoken and argumentative. They love nothing better than a good heated debate plus, of course, a worthy adversary to pit their wits against.

Virgo-Nines are practical, competent individuals who can turn their hands to most things given sufficient motivation. They are adaptable, dexterous and efficient. They always approach matters in a logical, orderly manner while at the same time paying great attention to detail and presentation. Everything has to look just right and be just right before they feel satisfied. They are hard-working, imaginative and skilful as well as being determined.

Unfortunately they also happen to be exceptionally restless and highly-strung. Their edginess can be intensely irritating. It is highly contagious too, as anyone who has spent time in their company will jerkily testify. They are rash and impulsive; nervous and jumpy; sarcastic and critical. And while clever and intelligent they undoubtedly are, patience is most definitely not one of their virtues.

KEYWORDS
Positive: alert, decisive, adaptable, efficient
Negative: highly-strung, rash, impatient, argumentative

LIBRA-ONE

Planetary combination: Venus/Sun

When charm, intelligence and diplomacy are coupled with ambition, confidence and a slight touch of aggression, the result is a Libra-One. People ruled by this combination are easy-going, adaptable and co-operative but no matter how involved they become with joint efforts, other people's affairs or group projects they somehow always manage to retain their own independence and identity. They are public-spirited, well-mannered and socially much sought after.

Libra-Ones are romantic, sentimental and warm-hearted. At work, play or in earnest, they find the opposite sex far easier to get along with than their own. Men ruled by this combination will almost certainly have several close women friends, whom they can confide in or turn to for comfort when life gets difficult, while the females of the species find that they work best in a predominantly male environment.

Personal relationships play an important role in all their lives because they are in love with love and it's a game which they find most intriguing. They are amorous, demonstrative although occasionally rather shallow and flirtatious. They dislike arguments and will go to great lengths to keep the peace, although this isn't always easy, particularly when they have more than one string to their bows. However what's sauce for the goose is certainly forbidden fruit for the gander. They are not particularly jealous as such but they can be utterly ruthless should they find out that their partner's attention has been wandering elsewhere.

KEYWORDS
Positive: charming, popular, easy-going, affectionate
Negative: shallow, flirtatious, fickle, promiscuous

LIBRA-TWO

Planetary combination: Venus/Moon

There's nothing forceful or at all aggressive about Libra-Twos. They are much too quiet and unassuming for that sort of behaviour. They are kind and gentle; imaginative and creative; receptive and refined. Unfortunately they also tend to lack confidence and find it almost impossible to be decisive — they will keep changing their minds.

People born under this vibration ask nothing more from life than a little peace and quiet and they will go to great lengths to achieve it. Many are artistically talented while others are collectors and connoisseurs who certainly know how to appreciate fine lines and beauty. But no matter what their gifts or interests may be, they all crave affection and what they need more than anything is a strong partner to look up to and lean on in times of trouble because emotionally they are very insecure. Libra-Twos are romantic, sentimental and easily hurt. They need constant demonstrations of affection, much reassurance and enormous amounts of encouragement to feel truly loved and wanted.

However, when this vital back-up isn't forthcoming they allow their colourful imaginations to run riot often with disastrous consequences. They create problems where none actually exists and just like Frankenstein and his monster they often lose control of the situation. They are jealous, suspicious and possessive; moody, complaining and, at times, unnecessarily spiteful.

KEYWORDS
Positive: gentle, imaginative, artistic, affectionate
Negative: insecure, indecisive, shy, clinging

LIBRA-THREE

Planetary combination: Venus/Jupiter

Libra-Threes have an almost insatiable appetite for enjoyment. They are sociable, fun-loving and tremendously popular — the solitary, reclusive life is certainly not for them. They like pleasure, amusement and the bright lights. They are extravagant, flamboyant and really rather fascinating characters. They like to be constantly surrounded by people because they find social contact stimulating and exciting. They are given to lavish entertainments, move in theatrical, arty circles and when they throw a party extravagance is always the watchword.

However, there's more to a Libra-Three than immediately meets the eye. Not only do they know how to enjoy themselves they are also versatile, artistic and highly intelligent; cultured, charitable and philanthropic. They will often go out of their way to help others less fortunate than themselves and although they make no secret of their amorous conquests or financial successes they prefer to keep their good deeds very much to themselves.

People born under this vibration seem to have more than their fair share of weak points. They are wasteful, lazy and terrified of growing old. Vanity often drives them to take desperate measures to preserve their youth, but at the end of the day the only person they're kidding is themselves. Quality and quantity go together in their private lives as well as in their eating habits and an excess of both often leaves them not only all alone in their later years but also coping with illness caused by over-indulgence. Libra-Threes may live now but they have to pay sooner or later.

KEYWORDS
Positive: sociable, extravagant, flamboyant, amorous
Negative: lazy, over-indulgent, wasteful, lascivious

LIBRA-FOUR

Planetary combination: Venus/Uranus

The Libran symbol is a pair of scales which the number Four in this particular combination does its level best to keep balanced. Libra-Fours are easy-going but never careless, decisive but never impulsive, co-operative but never interfering. They tackle matters one step at a time in a calm and practical manner and will always see a project through to completion no matter how tedious it may be. They are perfectionists who won't give up until everything is just right.

People ruled by this combination don't like surprises. They lead honest, respectable, orderly lives and anything which threatens to disrupt their routine is usually given a wide berth. They are calm, practical and industrious. They like peace, quiet and a settled environment. They look upon marriage as a union of minds as well as bodies and it is a commitment which they take very seriously indeed. When they tie the knot it is for keeps. Having offered their love, loyalty and a lifetime of devotion, they expect to receive nothing less in return. Rows and arguments will be avoided if at all possible even if it means sitting up half the night to reach a working compromise.

The Four vibration can sometimes have an adverse effect on the Libran personality. Too much caution can so easily be mistaken for indecision or a lack of confidence and continually playing safe will eventually stifle creativity. What's more, when life is always predictable and perfectly organized it can become very dull and boring. While this number can undoubtedly balance this combination it can also tip the scales in the wrong direction if allowed too much free rein.

KEYWORDS
Positive: calm, practical, loyal, peace-loving
Negative: over-cautious, predictable, dull, unexciting

LIBRA-FIVE

Planetary combination: Venus/Mercury

When they are good Libra-Fives are very, very good but when they are bad, they go well over the top. People ruled by this vibration have two distinct sides to their character — the public one and the private one. Most of the time they seem to be friendly, understanding and co-operative; charming, artistic and talented. They appear to care more about other people than themselves, are always willing to lend a helping hand and will go to great lengths to make everyone around them happy. They are cheerful and easy-going; sociable and amusing; tactful and diplomatic. Problems seldom seem to worry them for long and their natural resilience helps to keep them afloat even after the worst of set-backs. On the face of it they are kind, caring human beings.

But in private Libra-Fives are a very different kettle of fish. They are secretly afraid of failure and this fear constantly preys on their minds. Their fertile brains dream up all sorts of unusual, adventurous ideas which they lack the nerve and confidence to put to the test, and although they smile sweetly and appear to like everyone their thoughts are not always so charitable. They rarely voice their true feelings but on the occasions that they do give vent, they can be sarcastic, hurtful and most unpleasant.

Fortunately Libra-Fives have one sure and pleasurable way of letting off steam. They are sensual, earthy individuals with strong sexual drives and in the heat of passion they seem able to rid themselves of all their physical and mental frustrations. Here they can be adventurous, their imaginations can run wild and their hang-ups can temporarily be forgotten. They are demanding, demonstrative and dynamic. Anyone who partners them will need plenty of stamina to stand the pace.

KEYWORDS
Positive: charming, helpful, cheerful, talented, sensual
Negative: frustrated, fearful, sarcastic, lustful, restless

LIBRA-SIX

Planetary combination: Venus/Venus

Libra-Sixes are the salt of the earth. They are peace-makers whose role in life is always one of selfless service to others. They are gentle, good-natured and tactful; warm-hearted, even-tempered and sincere. Their friendliness and generosity are genuine, their patience endless and their kindness goes beyond words. They are cheerful, uncomplaining and worth their weight in gold for all the good work they do in the community. They never expect payment or seek fame and recognition for their endeavours, because their reward comes from knowing that they have somehow been able to help and assist another fellow human being.

Libra-Sixes are also strongly drawn to the arts and many are gifted painters, writers or musicians. They have tremendous personal style, excellent taste and an eye for colour. They are creative, imaginative and original. While in private they are loyal, affectionate and faithful, make loving parents and devoted, lifelong partners.

They don't really have any major faults although they certainly have one or two minor flaws in their characters. Occasionally their desire to help can be mistaken for nosiness or interference, and because they will put others first this often means that they have little time to spare for their own needs. The excessive care they show for their own children can backfire on them when they are accused of being over-protective. Everyone has to learn to stand on their own two feet at some time and Libra-Sixes don't always realize this soon enough with their own offspring.

KEYWORDS
Positive: caring, generous, kind, selfless, loyal
Negative: over-protective, smothering, too helpful

LIBRA-SEVEN

Planetary combination: Venus/Neptune

Venus is the planet of love and beauty while Neptune governs dreams, fantasies and awakens the subconscious. Ruled by such a combination it's small wonder that Libra-Sevens are not only creative, artistic and peace-loving but also highly receptive, imaginative and intuitive. They are idealists and dreamers who see the world through rose-coloured spectacles, as they would like it to be, but not always necessarily as it actually is.

Libra-Sevens are gentle, kind and considerate. They lean towards the romantic in all matters of the heart and look upon love as the ultimate communion of mind, body and spirit. They are sensitive, sympathetic and sentimental; tender, poetic and highly emotional. They are easily moved by soft words and even more easily hurt by harsh ones.

People born under this vibration certainly don't find life easy to cope with. Their health is usually rather delicate and they fall easy prey to almost every bug and virus that happens to be going around. They tend to find the cut and thrust of trade and industry rather unnerving, as they prefer to work at a steady pace dictated by their own flow of inspiration and not by deadlines or tight budgets.

Their personal relationships are also traumatic, possibly because they expect more from them than it is humanly possible to give. They are weak and unrealistic. They long for the impossible and then escape into fantasy when it doesn't materialize. Libra-Sevens undoubtedly have much to offer but few of them have the necessary stamina and determination to realize their full potential personally or commercially.

KEYWORDS
Positive: creative, artistic, imaginative, intuitive
Negative: delicate, easily-hurt, weak, unrealistic

LIBRA-EIGHT

Planetary combination: Venus/Saturn

Libra-Eights are honest, sober, respectable citizens. There's something almost Victorian about their strong morals, rigid code of conduct and tremendous sense of duty. They are quiet, hard-working and very straight-laced. What's more, they practise what they preach — self-control, self-denial and self-sacrifice. They are far too reserved to ever exude any spontaneity, much too responsible to ever do anything just for a laugh and terribly prudish as far as risqué jokes and ribald humour are concerned.

People born under this vibration are rather cold, joyless individuals. They're so inhibited that they wouldn't know how to let themselves go if they tried. Many devote their lives to looking after elderly parents while others marry partners much older than themselves. They seem to almost enjoy the role of martyr. They will deprive themselves of things unnecessarily, go without when there's no need and repress their own feelings for the sake of someone else. They are faithful, reliable and honourable while their loyalty certainly goes well above and beyond the call of duty.

Sadly many, of their own freewill, seem to choose a more difficult path through life than is really necessary. Much of their emotional torment is self-inflicted and their loneliness is hardly surprising because they don't exactly go out of their way to endear themselves to others. A sense of humour is what they lack and unfortunately it's not something which they find easy to acquire.

KEYWORDS
Positive: honest, respectable, dutiful, self-controlled
Negative: joyless, cold, inhibited, prudish

LIBRA-NINE

Planetary combination: Venus/Mars

This combination produces a high proportion of very lusty characters indeed. Libra's planet is Venus which represents love while martial fiery Mars rules the number Nine. The old sixties slogan 'make love not war' could almost, in this instance, be rewritten as 'make love fiercely'. Libra-Nines are not only attractive to but also irresistably attracted by the opposite sex. They are passionate, sensual, magnetic and easily aroused. They have a strong, healthy sex drive which will never miss an opportunity to exercise itself. They love the thrill of the chase, the excitement of battle and, of course, the victors spoils. They are athletic, red-blooded and very single-minded.

However, there is rather more to Libra-Nines than their immediate physical needs. They are also creative, artistic and co-operative, particularly when working as part of a team. Their opinions are frank, their ideas original and their output is prolific and always highly professional. They work hard, they play hard and they sample everything that life has to offer.

When it comes to getting themselves into difficult situations Libra-Nines are past masters at this art. Their action packed personal lives often cause problems, especially when they have several strings to their bows or when they decide to invade someone else's territory. They are not particularly known for tact or patience either and impetuosity is probably their worst fault and their greatest danger. They are fickle, fast-living and fun while it lasts.

KEYWORDS
Positive: passionate, professional, prolific, physical
Negative: impulsive, tactless, sensual, impatient

SCORPIO-ONE

Planetary combination: Pluto/Sun

Scorpio-Ones desire only one thing from life — to be more successful than everyone else and until such time they will neither rest nor be satisfied. They crave power, dominion and absolute sovereignty and, what's more, it is quite within their capabilities to achieve just that. They are ruthless, determined and virtually indestructible.

They are born leaders, brilliant strategists and superb organizers. They believe wholeheartedly and exclusively in themselves having that same 'never say die' attitude as the old pioneers. They will boldly go where no man has ever dreamed of going before, let alone tried, and on the way they'll inspire others to follow their banners and fight for their cause. They are magnetic, charismatic and very persuasive. These characters are life's super men and women. They are dynamic, energetic, tenacious and insanely ambitious.

However life doesn't always play ball with Scorpio-Ones. Fate has a funny way of intervening in their plans at precisely the wrong moment. They take enormous risks that don't always pay off, their cold-blooded calculations don't always add up and other people's loyalty can't always be guaranteed. Unfortunately anyone who lives by the sword must be aware of the dangers which can be anything from a broken marriage to complete, utter, total defeat.

KEYWORDS
Positive: ambitious, powerful, determined, tenacious
Negative: ruthless, ill-fated, cold-blooded, calculating

SCORPIO-TWO

Planetary combination: Pluto/Moon

Still waters run deep and beneath those calm Scorpio-Two exteriors run feelings so strong and intense that at times they seem almost impossible to control. They have eyes which look right through you and expressions which give no clue as to their thoughts. They are secretive, enigmatic and mysterious; dramatic, dynamic and demanding.

People ruled by this combination tend to have obsessions rather than interests like everyone else. Their concentration is unbreakable, their commitment borders on the fanatic and their passions often reach volcanic proportions. They are compulsive, compelling and, most of the time, extremely self-controlled. Many are instinctively drawn to the occult, for this is an area which they find stimulating and intriguing. Some devote a great deal of time to researching and sifting through the wealth of literature which abounds on the subject while those gifted with ESP waste little time in developing their talent further.

Unfortunately there is rather a cruel, sadistic streak which threads its way through the Scorpio-Two character. They are possessive, jealous and dangerous when crossed. Even within a close relationship they always seem to hold something of themselves back as if afraid that by laying bare their true identity this will somehow weaken their position. They demand the impossible from their partners but are prepared to give very little in return. They also have violent tempers which fortunately don't often erupt, but when they do it is a memorable and frightening experience.

KEYWORDS
Positive: intense, mysterious, deep, dramatic
Negative: secretive, jealous, demanding, menacing

SCORPIO-THREE

Planetary combination: Pluto/Jupiter

Scorpio-Threes have a keen understanding of human nature which they find comes in useful when engineering their rise to power. They know instinctively how to play upon the feelings and weaknesses of others, what motivates them and, of course, how best and most advantageously they can be manipulated. These people know all the tricks and they won't hesitate to use them if it's in their best interests to do so.

They are overtly ambitious, confident and enterprising. They do everything on a grand scale and nothing seems to daunt them. They are determined, courageous and virtually unstoppable. They know how to lead, to organize and to delegate; and the more people they have under their control the better they like it. Strategy is their game and they're first division players.

When viewed from a less charitable angle Scorpio-Threes show up in a harsher light. They are hard, tough and utterly ruthless. They are only out for themselves and don't spare much thought for who they use or who gets hurt in the process. They are quite prepared to cross swords with anyone who stands in their way and they will take the most alarming risks when circumstances dictate. If you're on their side don't expect any thanks for your help and if you are on the opposite side don't expect any mercy.

KEYWORDS
Positive: ambitious, strong, calculating, determined
Negative: hard, unscrupulous, cold, ruthless

SCORPIO-FOUR

Planetary combination: Pluto/Uranus

When Scorpio passion, intensity and will-power are combined with the efficiency, organization and doggedness associated with the number Four, the resultant energy, capacity for hard-work and sense of purpose such a merger produces often reach superhuman proportions.

Scorpio-Fours are pioneers, reformers and revolutionaries. They are bold, progressive and daring. They dream of creating a new world which will one day rise like a phoenix out of the ashes of the old, decaying system. They crusade vehemently on behalf of endangered species and the starving millions in Africa and Asia, they fight against political oppression and the dangers of pollution and they actively protest against the threat of nuclear war. They want to set the world to rights and they firmly believe that they can do it somehow.

Unfortunately most of their efforts are doomed to failure right from the start because what resources and help they do manage to muster are scattered and rather thin on the ground. Impatience and frustration are daily problems they have to cope with while some of their more subversive activities often land them in hot water with the police and local authorities. Their hearts are in the right place; it is just their heads that are in the clouds.

KEYWORDS
Positive: pioneering, reformative, revolutionary, active
Negative: subversive, fanatical, impatient, unrealistic

SCORPIO-FIVE

Planetary combination: Pluto/Mercury

Intellectually Scorpio-Fives are razor-sharp. They always seem to know far more than everyone else and never miss an opportunity to prove it — usually in a rather arrogant and condescending manner. They certainly don't suffer fools gladly and make little or no attempt to disguise the fact.

Their minds are agile and active, their perception is quick and acute while their powers of persuasion/argument are faultless. They make fine orators and writers whose use of the spoken and written word often borders on brilliance. They are strong, dynamic, imposing figures who command respect wherever they go. They have acid tongues, a biting wit, sparkling repartee and always a ready answer to any question.

There is a very thin dividing line between genius and insanity which a few Scorpio-Fives will unfortunately cross. They push themselves far too hard and overtax their strength depleting their reserves of nervous energy in the process. Mental breakdowns and bouts of depression and anxiety are part of the legacy that comes with this package unless adequate time is allowed for rest and relaxation in between bouts of intense concentration. Scorpio-Fives need to keep their batteries topped up to full strength in order to perform at their best.

KEYWORDS
Positive: intellectual, brilliant, sharp, intelligent
Negative: sarcastic, nervous, condescending, arrogant

SCORPIO-SIX

Planetary combination: Pluto/Venus

Scorpio-Sixes are artistic, creative and highly imaginative thanks to the planet Venus which partially rules them. Unfortunately Pluto, their other heavenly guardian, does nothing to make life simple. In fact it complicates the issue considerably by putting all sorts of strange and revolutionary ideas into their heads. So instead of towing the line and following convention they do the exact opposite and fight against it.

Change is stability to a Scorpio-Six and this is particularly noticeable in their work. They are forever seeking new ways of doing things, flying in the face of tradition and crossing swords with the establishment. Gifted they undoubtedly are but their paintings, poetry and music all bear the same unmistakeable hallmarks of the rebel. These people are dramatic, fascinating and more than a little unusual.

They are square pegs who deliberately try to alter the square holes they've been put in.

This combination of sign and number also heightens the already strong Scorpio passion and sexuality. People born under this vibration are lusty, sensual and lead tempestuous private lives. Surprisingly for ones so sensitive and intelligent they can be very coarse and vulgar while some of their ideas, to put it politely, border on the obscene. They are a weird and wonderful amalgam of talents and temperament which will undoubtedly shock the world if not actually change it.

KEYWORDS
Positive: creative, imaginative, artistic, progressive
Negative: rebellious, shocking, sensual, coarse

SCORPIO-SEVEN

Planetary combination: Pluto/Neptune

When it comes to unusual interests Scorpio-Sevens certainly have them. Their minds are databanks full of strange theories and unorthodox concepts. They are philosophical and contemplative; intellectual and intuitive; solitary and secretive. Their lives are one long quest for spiritual development and enlightenment. They delve into mysticism and the occult, study religion, investigate all things paranormal with an almost fanatical zeal, always in the hope of finding some hitherto undiscovered clue to one of life's great mysteries.

A very large proportion of Scorpio-Sevens possess psychic powers. Many have second-sight and are first-class mediums and clairvoyants while others are clairaudient, natural dowsers and psychometrists. They are on a subconscious wavelength all of their own which they seem able to tune into at will.

People ruled by this particularly sensitive vibration usually have to pay a high price for the privilege. They are often regarded as odd and peculiar by their contemporaries, treated like outcasts and misfits by society and accused of trickery and fraud when demonstrating their talents. Occasionally their lonely dabblings in the supernatural get out of hand causing them to become confused and unbalanced. They are also very tempted to experiment with drugs in order to reach heightened states of awareness. It is a foolish, dangerous pastime and one they should avoid at all costs.

KEYWORDS
Positive: philosophical, spiritual, unorthodox, psychic
Negative: solitary, misunderstood, obsessive, unbalanced

SCORPIO-EIGHT

Planetary combination: Pluto/Saturn

Scorpio-Eights have undoubtedly got what it takes to be enormous, resounding successes. They are ambitious, hard-working and single-minded. Their discipline is rigid and of the self-imposed variety, their approach is thorough and well-planned, always with 100 per cent effort put in. Nothing will ever deflect them from their goals and no sacrifice is ever too great because they believe that the ends well and truly justify the means. They are shrewd, resourceful and persistent; self-motivated, self-propelled and eventually self-made.

They may well have all the right ingredients to break records and achieve miracles but the milk of human kindness is noticeably missing from the Scorpio-Eight character. People ruled by this combination tend to work in seclusion, regarding the presence of others as irritating and unnecessary. They become so totally obsessed with their undertakings that pleasure, relaxation and social contact are allowed to go by the board. They are insular, cold-hearted and down-right offensive at times, especially when they feel their privacy has been invaded.

Scorpio-Eights are utterly ruthless and will often drive themselves to the point of mental and physical collapse. It is almost as if they have built-in self-destruct mechanisms. They can be unfeeling, uncaring and unscrupulous. It's difficult to say anything complimentary about them because they are virtually impossible to get through to on a personal level. Their tempers are akin to winter weather forecasts — 'violent storms and thundry outbreaks can be expected with no possibility of sunny periods or a break in the prevailing pattern'.

KEYWORDS
Positive: ambitious, disciplined, hard-working, persistent
Negative: insular, ruthless, unscrupulous, cold

SCORPIO-NINE

Planetary combination: Pluto/Mars

This particular combination of sign and number governs some very tough characters. They are so well-disciplined, active and courageous that they're more like members of a specialist military squad than anything else and they're capable of almost superhuman achievements.

They are fearless, danger-loving and indestructible. Confidence surrounds them like a force field, their energy is boundless and their output is phenomenal. By comparison everyone else appears sluggish and lazy. They will rise with the birds, come home with the milk and never show even the slightest trace of fatigue.

Unfortunately they do have some major faults which need to be remedied. They have strong wills which they exert on others, they will get what they want by fair means or foul and they don't care who gets hurt in the process. This applies to all areas of their existence. Their sexual appetites are voracious and their passionate feelings aren't always under tight enough control. In extreme cases they're capable of great cruelty, acts of violence and physical assault. They really ought to be stamped with a government health warning, because unless they're handled with care and respect they could seriously damage someone's health.

KEYWORDS
Positive: active, energetic, fearless, superhuman
Negative: ruthless, violent, strong-willed, explosive

SAGITTARIUS-ONE

Planetary combination: Jupiter/Sun

Personal freedom, of mind, body and spirit, is imperative for all Sagittarius-Ones. They just can't be doing with restrictions in any shape, size or form. In fact, to get stuck in a rut is the worst possible misfortune that could befall them. They have adventurous minds and athletic bodies. The world is an oyster they love to explore. They are nomads at heart and for many success lies abroad, while others move around from place to place in search of stimulating company and a change of scenery.

Sagittarius-Ones are mobile, imaginative and intelligent; foot-loose and fancy free. They are quick on the uptake and learn fast. They have powerful intellects, cheerful dispositions and positive attitudes. They are generous, capable and well-informed. They have the curiosity of a cat, the energy of a beaver and, given half a chance, could talk the hind legs off a dozen donkeys.

Unfortunately people born under this vibration are almost impossible to pin down. They are undisciplined and unreliable. They like to come and go as they please, not as someone else dictates. They are honest, open and kind, but not really marriageable material. With Sagittarius-Ones it's usually a case of love them and leave them long before the trap can spring shut. This is probably the best way because, like wild beasts in captivity, they soon grow dull and lose their sparkle when kept in one place for too long.

KEYWORDS
Positive: mobile, intelligent, freedom-loving, adventurous
Negative: restless, unreliable, undisciplined, fidgety

SAGITTARIUS-TWO

Planetary combination: Jupiter/Moon

Basically Sagittarius-Twos are inconsistent. They are restless and changeable, blowing hot one minute and cold the next. They never seem able to decide whether they're coming or going and often try to do both at once. But despite all their contrary ways they are likeable, sociable characters.

Sagittarius-Twos are generous, tolerant and obliging. They are kind-hearted, responsive and understanding. Like all true archers they are fun-loving free spirits but because the Two influence is also strong they often find it difficult to keep their emotions under control or to put their private lives in order. They enjoy good food, good wine and good company in any order but most of all they love to travel. Anytime, anyplace, anywhere — it's immaterial, just so long as they don't have to rough it too much. They like to do things in comfort and with style.

People ruled by this vibration are often extravagant and wasteful. They are impulse buyers, compulsive eaters and prone to bouts of deep depression. They are either on a tremendous high or a devastating low and never quite manage to strike a happy medium. They have something of the gypsy in their souls and once they've grown bored with the job they're doing or the place they live in, nothing bar a major change around, will suffice to snap them out of it.

KEYWORDS
Positive: sociable, responsive, generous, stylish
Negative: impulsive, moody, restless, indecisive

SAGITTARIUS-THREE

Planetary combination: Jupiter/Jupiter

When the intelligence, foresight and sound judgement of the Sagittarian character are combined with the brilliance, versatility and energy of the number Three the result can be sheer magic. But when the restlessness, impetuosity and wanderlust of the former join forces with the restlessness, frivolity and quick-temper of the latter the outcome could be quite dreadful. This is one of those combinations that can be either exceptionally good or disastrously bad, but certainly never mediocre.

From a positive point of view Sagittarian-Threes are calm, agreeable and expansive. They are generous, even-tempered and relaxed. They have fine minds, deep penetrating intellects, the ability to learn fast and the luck of the devil. They are original, observant and shrewd. It appears that they have got everything it takes to be happy, successful and content if they put their talents to good use.

Unfortunately the other side of this coin bears an entirely different set of markings, because Sagittarian-Threes also possess some highly undesirable ingredients which could turn their lives into an empty, synthetic charade. They can be tactless, boastful and inconsiderate. They want to be important but for all the wrong reasons. They're materialistic and social climbing with over inflated opinions of their own worth. In fact they are loud, flashy and vulgar. They can take one of two roads through life and the guidebooks recommend the scenic route every time.

KEYWORDS
Positive: intelligent, versatile, even-tempered, expansive
Negative: materialistic, restless, conceited, flashy

SAGITTARIUS-FOUR

Planetary combination: Jupiter/Uranus

Sagittarius-Fours are unusual, unorthodox and unconventional but never impulsive. They are steady, calm and practical. They always look before they leap and are so far-sighted that they anticipate and make allowances for possible problems long before they materialize. They are original, inventive and intelligent. They lead tidy, well-organized lives which, on the surface, appear to be the models of respectability.

But all is never quite as it seems. The minds of Sagittarius-Fours are seething with activity. Their views are non-conformist, their political opinions are extreme and their thoughts are on a reformative, rebellious wavelength. Freedom and independence are their battlecries and they are front line campaigners. They tend to have many like-minded friends and associates with whom they exchange ideas, their homes often become used as the forum and meeting place for members of their movement.

People ruled by this combination of sign and number are adventurous, progressive thinkers who are certainly not averse to taking the odd calculated risk or two. They are argumentative, rousing and subversive. They often find themselves at odds with the authorities and at times unwisely voice their opinions in the wrong places. They are self-appointed champions of the underdog and even when a cause has already been well and truly lost, they'll still fight on regardless.

KEYWORDS
Positive: unconventional, well-organized, steady, intelligent
Negative: argumentative, subversive, political, rebellious

SAGITTARIUS-FIVE

Planetary combination: Jupiter/Mercury

This is one of the more volatile combinations of sign and number because when the active, assertive spontaneity of the Sagittarian is coupled with the elasticity of character, spirit adventure and resourcefulness traditionally associated with the number Five, the effect is certainly catalytic. Sagittarius-Fives have fertile brains, quick wits and plenty of original ideas. They are lively, restless and versatile; garrulous, gregarious and game for anything. They need space around them, plenty of room to breathe and the opportunity to develop themselves to the full at all levels.

People born under this vibration are positive, outspoken and intelligent. They are good natured, popular and humorous. Many are intellectually and academically inclined while others are athletic, sporty types who are constantly on the go, trying to burn off some of their excess energy.

Five is an earthy, sensual number and those influenced by it in any way tend to display more than just a passing interest in members of the opposite sex — indeed Sagittarius-Fives are no exception. They are hot blooded, passionate and demonstrative. They are whole-heartedly into natural pursuits and are experts in this particular field. They are students of life who specialize in the pleasures of the flesh and they all hold honours degrees in carnal knowledge.

Unfortunately, these mercurial individuals do have a great many faults. They are unreliable, inconsistent and lustful. They take the most alarming risks without even a moment's hesitation, have over-inflated opinions of their own worth and seldom remain in one place for very long. They're jumpy, careless and very quick-tempered.

KEYWORDS
Positive: versatile, adventurous, intelligent, athletic
Negative: unreliable, restless, sensual, conceited

SAGITTARIUS-SIX

Planetary combination: Jupiter/Venus

Sagittarian-Sixes are flamboyant, fun-loving and fascinating. They are larger than life characters who do everything on a lavish, magnificent scale. They love to entertain, to seek new dimensions of thought and to travel. But no matter how far they may wander or how many adventures they may have along the way, home is undoubtedly where their hearts lie and perhaps the only place where they can feel really comfortable and able to relax.

Socially these characters are in great demand. They are amusing, warm-hearted and generous. They have boundless energy, brilliant, unusual ideas and a voracious appetite for enjoyment. They are charming, intelligent and physically exciting. They like to play the field, fall in and out of love with predictable regularity and seldom remain with one particular partner for long. They are pleasure-seeking, spontaneous and restless. They need variety, change and constant stimulation or their minds become dull and their sparkle quickly vanishes.

Sagittarius-Sixes are inclined to be lazy especially where mundane household chores are concerned. They are also wasteful, vain and over-indulgent. They seldom remember to take adequate exercise, rarely refuse second or even third helpings of rich food and, as a result, their health often suffers. Their personal lives are complex and colourful to say the least. They are promiscuous and lustful and occasionally their infidelities catch up with them in a spectacular manner.

KEYWORDS
Positive: charming, sociable, entertaining, generous
Negative: sensual, lazy, over-indulgent, fickle

SAGITTARIUS-SEVEN

Planetary combination: Jupiter/Neptune

'Bohemian' is a word which succinctly describes Sagittarius-Sevens, as they have a unique and unorthodox code of conduct all of their own. Their manners, habits, and sometimes their morals too, are free, easy and flexible. They are generous to a fault, extremely tolerant and very broadminded.

People ruled by this combination of sign and number tend to have unusual interests and hold unconventional views. They are dreamy, romantic and phil-osophical. They have colourful imaginations, tremendous perception and creative flair. In fact, many aspiring artists, writers and craftsmen fall into this particular category. They are irresistibly drawn to all things magical, mystical and mysterious, especially religion and the occult. They love to travel and explore but it's within their own minds that they make their greatest breakthroughs and discoveries.

They are deep-thinkers; mental adventurers who probe, question and analyse a diversity of subjects in the hope of discovering some small vestige of the truth. They often experience vivid, prophetic dreams; those brief, fleeting glimpses of the future which can be both exhilarating and strangely disturbing. Clairvoyance is a frequent gift among members of this clain which a few will take steps to develop further. By and large they are expansive, lucky, free-spirited people who somehow manage to get by without making too much of an effort.

Unfortunately they are rather inclined to push their luck and will occasionally find that its not running in their favour. They are vague, unrealistic, muddlers who leave far too much in life to chance.

KEYWORDS
Positive: Bohemian, lucky, flexible, easy-going
Negative: vague, unrealistic, disorganized, dreamy

SAGITTARIUS-EIGHT

Planetary combination: Jupiter/Saturn

Sagittarius-Eights are dignified, responsible and determined. They are patient, persevering and conscientious. They move at a steady, deliberate pace and although their advancement may be rather on the slow side it's always sure. They would rather be safe than sorry any day. They are hard-working, serious and quietly confident that they'll eventually meet with success.

Where marriage and family ties are concerned, Sagittarius-Eights are quite prepared to do their duty and stand by their commitments. They are conventional, respectable and conservative. But as far as love, gentleness and understanding are concerned they are non-starters. They find it just about as difficult to show affection as they do to receive it. They're not easy people to live with because emotionally they are a mess. They seem to suffer all the agonizing pangs of jealousy and possessiveness without any of the real pleasures of passion. They are inhibited, repressed, undemonstrative and moody. As breadwinners or housekeepers they are unrivalled but as lovers they are useless.

Sagittarius-Eights are gloomy, unimaginative and far too formal. They have stiff upper lips and even straighter laces. They are plodding, cautious and predictable. Once entrenched in their deep, comfortable ruts that's probably where they'll remain for the rest of their lives unless something pretty cataclysmic happens to them in the meantime.

KEYWORDS
Positive: patient, responsible, cautious, conservative
Negative: dull, moody, inhibited, unimaginative

SAGITTARIUS-NINE

Planetary combination: Jupiter/Mars

It's small wonder that people born under this vibration are expansive and irrepressible when they have Jupiter and Mars for their ruling planets. They are energetic, ambitious and very independent. They seem to know instinctively what they want from life and they will cut corners and take all sorts of risks to achieve their ends. They are enterprising, resourceful and spirited; capable, courageous and bold.

However they do realize how important it is to set aside a certain amount of time for relaxation and enjoyment. Unfortunately they play just as hard as they work and even when involved in a quiet card game only for matchstick stakes, or a friendly spot of tennis in the local park that competitive streak of theirs won't lie dormant. They still have to win at all costs. The thrill of the contest plus the need to prove themselves time and again seems to drive them on, even when there's no real call for an all-out effort. But when there is, and they are playing for real, they can be utterly ruthless.

Sagittarius-Nines have one great fault. They simply cannot abide rules and regulations in any size, shape or form. Their right to personal freedom, on all levels, must never be violated for even a second. Figures of authority make them see red and only serve to bring out the worst in them. From early infancy right through to old age they rebel at the slightest petty restriction which threatens their liberty and they'll use violence if necessary to make the point clear.

KEYWORDS
Positive: ambitious, irrepressible, competitive, spirited
Negative: insubordinate, rebellious, aggressive, ruthless

CAPRICORN-ONE

Planetary combination: Saturn/Sun

'Softly, softly catchee monkey' really must be the Capricorn-One motto as anyone who has ever watched them coolly, deliberately and methodically laying their plans must surely agree. They are self-contained, self-disciplined and self-motivated. They seem able to bear hardships and frustrations in a stoical manner and are capable of making tremendous personal sacrifices just so long as their target remains within reach.

They are ambitious, tenacious and goal conscious; hard-working, objective and materialistic. They will never give up even when the odds are stacked heavily against them — defeat is something they won't even consider let alone accept.

Capricorn-Ones are difficult people to get to know because they are sober, conservative and reserved. They take life very seriously and tend to put business before pleasure every time. Work always comes first with them. They are innately cautious and take a long time to weigh people up and even when involved in a permanent relationship they still don't make a great show of their affections. Yet no matter how much they may hide their feelings or how detached they appear, deep down they are loyal, faithful and utterly reliable. They make responsible parents, trusty friends but rather cold, unimaginative lovers.

It is surprising how many of those ruled by this vibration have inferiority complexes. Their self-esteem is a fragile commodity which they try to bolster up by being self-contained and disciplined. They believe that by doing everything for themselves no one can possibly hurt or let them down. When in a negative frame of mind they become over-anxious, indecisive and fretful, while the little confidence they do have flies right out of the window.

KEYWORDS
Positive: deliberate, methodical, objective, ambitious
Negative: cold, cautious, unaffectionate, insecure

CAPRICORN-TWO

Planetary combination: Saturn/Moon

Capricorn-Twos are cautious and reserved, sometimes suspicious for no particular reason, but always ambitious and materialistic in their outlook. They need to know what's in it for them before making any sort of commitment, but having once agreed on a course of action nothing will ever persuade them to go back on their word. Their careers are of paramount importance possibly because their emotional involvements are usually stressful, problem areas which they would sooner not discuss. They are practical, patient and professional; rational, serious and self-contained.

The private life of a Capricorn-Two almost defies description and they have only got themselves to blame. Basically they have two main problems. The first is that emotionally they are insecure. The second is that they want to be loved and needed but they are so afraid of rejection or getting hurt, that they bottle everything up and hide their feelings to such an extent that potential partners practically have to be mind-readers to grasp the situation at all. They are emotionally repressive, dour and prudish; much too self-controlled and lacking in imagination, and to make matters even worse, they can also be jealous, possessive and selfish.

Capricorn-Twos are all in all an odd kettle of fish. They plod deliberately on through life come what may, taking problems and set-backs in their stride and although they usually score business goals their arrows of love either misfire completely or miss the target by a mile. They just don't seem to have what it takes to get the best out of both worlds.

KEYWORDS
Positive: career-minded, professional, ambitious, materialistic
Negative: emotionally-insecure, unimaginative, jealous, inhibited

CAPRICORN-THREE

Planetary combination: Saturn/Jupiter

Capricorn-Threes are clever but cautious and that's why they seldom make mistakes. People born under the sign of the goat are naturally practical and enterprising although perhaps a little too conventional and conservative in their approach. However, when Three energy, originality and versatility are added then a more balanced picture is created.

Those ruled by this combination are hard-working, shrewd and observant. They are ambitious, modestly confident and very quick-witted. They calculate, plot and plan, then they will swing into action like a carefully programmed machine which is so well designed that it can't possibly malfunction. Lady Luck also seems to smile benevolently on these particular individuals so when careful groundwork and good fortune unite, the outcome can't conceivably be anything else but a resounding success.

However, Capricorn-Threes do have one or two problems to cope with, the main one being their inability to relax. They are workaholics who seldom go off duty and enjoy themselves. They seem to be afraid that someone will creep up and steal a march on them, if they take their minds off work for even a second. They are also prone to gloomy moods when they view everything pessimistically, expecting the worst to happen at any moment. Even with the number Three working overtime they can still be far too brooding and serious on occasion.

KEYWORDS
Positive: clever, shrewd, careful, hard-working
Negative: pessimistic, gloomy, workaholic, uptight

CAPRICORN-FOUR

Planetary combination: Saturn/Uranus

With this particular combination both sign and number have a great deal in common which means that character strengths are doubly endorsed; unfortunately the same applies to weaknesses. Capricorn-Fours are models of respectability. They are conservative, conscientious and conventional. They never live beyond their means, always look before they leap and never do anything reckless or impulsive. They are cool, calm and calculating.

People born under this vibration are practical, hard-working and industrious. They have a strong sense of duty, a sound sense of values and a serious, responsible outlook on life. They are honest, trustworthy and reliable. They are virtually impossible to upset, nothing ever seems to ruffle their feathers and when everyone else is in a state of uproar and panicking it is these stoic individuals who will knuckle down and deal with the problem carefully and systematically until it has been resolved. They are pillars of strength, ports in a storm and life-savers in an emergency.

Capricorn-Fours are undoubtedly, strong, stolid and stentorian but they are not exactly a barrel of laughs. They are dull, boring and about as exciting as cold rice pudding. They are irritatingly modest, desperately cautious and infuriatingly slow.

KEYWORDS
Positive: cautious, conservative, unflappable, reliable
Negative: dull, boring, unexciting, predictable

CAPRICORN-FIVE

Planetary combination: Saturn/Mercury

Capricorn-Fives are an odd amalgam of talents and temperament. They have two very distinct and separate sides to their character which don't always co-exist harmoniously in the same body. They are Jekyll and Hyde characters; hard to analyse because they're such a contradiction in terms.

Side one of the Capricorn-Five personality tends to manifest itself at work or in polite company when they appear honest, respectable and very down to earth. They give the impression of being conservative, conventional, respectable citizens and, indeed, they are capable of sustained bouts of hard-work, deep concentration and displays of tremendous patience. They seem disciplined, responsible and well-organized; cautious, industrious and punctillious.

However, side two of their personality is far more Fivish than Capricorn and bears absolutely no resemblance whatsoever to their nine to five appearance. When night falls and their time is their own Capricorn-Fives are restless, inquisitive and adventurous. They love to gamble and take risks which would not go down well at work should anyone ever find out. They like a flutter on the horses, a game of cards where the stakes are worth playing for; a trip to bingo or a go on the fruit machines. Their minds are seething with strange ideas and secret longings. They would love to drop out of society and travel the world but something always seems to stop them. And sexually they are earthy, lustful and promiscuous given half a chance. They dress formally by day but in the evening they wear casual, fashionable clothes, which form an essential part of their private image.

They are sober but sensual, thrifty but speculative, ordinary but unusual. Just so long as they don't allow their two personalities to overlap all will be well. But come the fateful day that an office romance is allowed to blossom or business combines with pleasure then the truth will out with disastrous consequences.

KEYWORDS
Positive: honest, respectable, responsible, hard-working
Negative: restless, adventurous, sensual, schizophrenic

CAPRICORN-SIX

Planetary combination: Saturn/Venus

People born under this vibration often fail to achieve anything tangible in life because their emotions are dominated by an inordinately strong sense of duty. They are devoted to their families and all too often will put the needs of others before their own. They will willingly sacrifice their time and personal desires to give help and support to their loved ones thus, of their own volition, becoming martyrs to a cause which can not only be very selfish and demanding but which will also place them last in the pecking order every time. They are rather like a doormat which, although it bears the inscription 'Welcome' allows everyone to wipe their feet and trample all over it.

Capricorn-Sixes are responsible, conscientious and caring. They are capable of bearing hardships and frustrations with cheerful optimism. They have the patience of a saint and the self-control and personal discipline of a well-trained soldier. They are affectionate, loyal and faithful. They are also imaginative, artistic and creative but because they give up so much of their time to other people they seldom put these gifts to constructive use. Their homes, which although they are usually comfortable and tastefully furnished, will often bear some discreet hallmarks of their latent talent.

Most people ruled by this combination lead unnecessarily hard and unfulfilled lives, because they never seem to want anything badly enough to fight for it. They take second place so naturally that they don't know how to act in a starring role. They are self-effacing, self-denying and only have themselves to blame as most of their problems are self-inflicted.

KEYWORDS
Positive: conscientious, caring, dutiful, patient
Negative: sacrificial, unambitious, self-effacing, unfulfilled

CAPRICORN-SEVEN

Planetary combination: Saturn/Neptune

Capricorn-Sevens are extraordinary characters who seem able to divide their time equally between the pursuit of material status, personal pleasure and practical idealism. They are out to get the best of all worlds and have just the right sort of qualifications required for the task. They are methodical, disciplined and exacting. They have times, places and compartments for everything in their minds and provided that career stays in one pigeon-hole, feelings and emotions remain isolated in another and thoughts and ideas are segregated from the rest they function with precision and ease. They are neat, tidy and very logical.

At work they are serious, responsible and conscientious. They never take risks and they seldom make mistakes. They can concentrate under any conditions, remain calm in a crisis and never make a move without firstly carefully calculating the odds in favour of its success. Within a personal relationship they are capable of showing great passion, depth of feeling and understanding but they always keep someone of themselves back as if afraid of becoming too dependent on something else for their happiness. However, it is only in times of complete solitude and total privacy that their intellect and imagination are taken out and given an airing. They are secret philosophers and mystics whose thoughts are on higher things and whose existence is on a higher plane. The mind, body and spirit are all important components of the Capricorn-Seven way of life. They will already have taken care of today's needs, and are preparing for tomorrow but are more concerned with the hereafter.

Unfortunately their normally tidy minds do, on occasion, become confused and cluttered. They tend to worry too much over unlikely contingencies and are prone to moodiness and depression coupled with bouts of laziness. They also set too much store by routine and organization because when something unexpected crops up they find it difficult to be flexible and accommodating.

KEYWORDS
Positive: materialistic, idealistic, intellectual, imaginative
Negative: inflexible, solitary, private, over-organized

CAPRICORN-EIGHT

Planetary combination: Saturn/Saturn

This particular combination of sign and number is ruled exclusively by the planet Saturn whose influence is always heavy, restrictive and severe. Capricorn-Eights reflect this by being reserved and serious in their ways. They are innately ambitious but so patient that they are prepared to wait if necessary for what they want even if it takes a lifetime. These people are old beyond their years, they give the impression of having seen it all at least a dozen times before. Even the children and adolescents ruled by this vibration seem to have wise heads on their youthful shoulders.

Capricorn-Eights are tenacious, materialistic and determined. They leave nothing to chance and plan carefully, coolly and deliberately to achieve their aims and desires. They are cautious, calculating and disciplined; adaptable, tough and capable of making a superhuman effort should circumstances so dictate. They will get what they want eventually, come hell or high water, and nothing will ever deflect them from their goal.

Unfortunately they have no soul, no finer feelings and the little affection which they are capable of feeling is meted out almost grudgingly. They are offhand, detached and undemonstrative. There is nothing gentle or understanding about any of them. They find it almost impossible to show their feelings, are difficult to live with and, to crown it all, they are also jealous and possessive. They are goal conscious, hard-working but totally devoid of love, compassion or simple human kindness.

KEYWORDS
Positive: ambitious, patient, tenacious, determined
Negative: cold, detached, unemotional, unfeeling

CAPRICORN-NINE

Planetary combination: Saturn/Mars

Capricorn-Nines are very career-minded. They are courageous, persistent and tough. They have strong survival instincts and always put their innate wit and native cunning to good use. They are street-wise, clued-in and determined to succeed. They have such a pioneering spirit that they find it difficult to function in a subordinate position under any form of restraint or supervision. They will work hard and with a will, but at their own pace and by their own set of rules. Under the right conditions their output can be prolific and their ideas shrewd and original. However, when their style is cramped and the scope restricted they become restless, impatient and soon lose interest altogether.

Their personal lives are usually fairly conventional. They tend to marry, settle down and have children in that order making loyal partners and responsible parents into the bargain. In private they can be surprisingly passionate and demonstrative. They try hard to please and seldom stray from the straight and narrow path into the forbidden realms of infidelity.

Provided no one, and that means friends, neighbours or relatives, interferes in the affairs of a Capricorn-Nine then all is well. But once a hint of criticism reaches their ears or someone tries to give unsolicited advice then it becomes a different story altogether. Their reaction is immediate, occasionally violent and always directed straight at the guilty party. They abhor and detest meddlesome people and will never let an infringement of their privacy go by with just a shrug of their shoulders. Action is what is called for and action there will be.

KEYWORDS
Positive: tough, street-wise, pioneering, hard-working
Negative: impulsive, insubordinate, direct, private

AQUARIUS-ONE

Planetary combination: Uranus/Sun

Aquarians have strong, reformative ideas. They are original, intelligent and unorthodox. The number One bestows an independent, pioneering spirit on those it rules. When these two come together and unite, as they do in this particular combination, the result is progress.

Aquarian-Ones are born leaders. They could change the world if they had a mind to and many will in fact try to do just that. They are intensely individual with overpowering personalities, tremendous energy and a nervous restlessness that's highly contagious. They are popular, dynamic and very determined.

People born under this vibration are idealistic and humanitarian. They have a fine understanding of human nature and a keen grasp of politics. Power is what they seek, not purely for self-aggrandisement although it has to be said that they do like the feel of it. They try to help others, to put mankind back on the right track and to make the earth a better place to live in. They undoubtedly have charisma and are capable of achieving great things.

Unfortunately their views are often regarded as being cranky, impractical and eccentric. They are frequently branded as rebels and trouble-makers or treated like social outcasts. The life-style they chose is never easy and seldom peaceful. Excitement and upheaval are commonplace, readjustments are often necessary and occasionally they receive the cold-shoulder treatment from neighbours and workmates. Their mission is a perilous one to accomplish but they usually have sufficient courage and confidence to see them through.

KEYWORDS
Positive: original, reformative, progressive, charismatic
Negative: unorthodox, impractical, eccentric, rebellious

AQUARIUS-TWO

Planetary combination: Uranus/Moon

Aquarian-Twos are emotional and highly-strung. They are gentle, understanding and easily hurt. Their prime concern is to feel secure both personally and financially because a growing fear of loneliness and isolation is never far from their minds. They are sociable, gregarious and at their best when fully employed and surrounded by people. Their mannerisms are colourful, their thoughts imaginative and progressive and their convictions backed one hundred per cent with courage.

There is nothing commonplace or run of the mill about anyone ruled by this combination of sign and number. They're intelligent, intellectual and unpredictable. They tend to have curious interests and unparalleled accomplishments. What's more they like to specialize and often develop expertise in unusual fields. They are independent, original and totally fascinated by science and technology especially when it comes to breaking new ground. Many become involved in politics and local government, albeit on the fringes, while others show their concern for humanity by organizing self-help schemes, community welfare projects and pressure groups. There is so much they'd like to do, and see done, during their lifetimes, that their main problem is fitting everything in. They are continually on the go from dawn till dusk, never allowing even one precious second of their time to go to waste.

Unfortunately, for this reason, their personal lives are often difficult. They require not only support from their partners but also constant reassurance and a non-stop show of affection. However, they don't always give their loved ones the same VIP treatment in return. Often second class, third class or even standby has to suffice in order to fit in with their hectic schedules. It is quite in order for them to go gadding about all over the place expecting to be made a fuss of when they return, but at times when the boot is on the other foot and they are the ones left at home on their own then this situation becomes unforgivable. Aquarian-Twos want to have their cake and eat it and this sort of attitude won't help them to build a happy relationship.

KEYWORDS
Positive: progressive, imaginative, independent, original
Negative: unpredictable, insecure, emotional, selfish

AQUARIUS-THREE

Planetary combination: Uranus/Jupiter

Freedom and independence are the watchwords for this particular combination. People born under this vibration are original, adventurous and progressive. They're curious, inquisitive and often brilliant. They want to get to the bottom of everything but that's only for starters. They like to take ideas a stage further and explore possible new variations on old themes. In fact, they like to take everything back to square one and then start again from scratch.

Aquarius-Threes are intuitive, imaginative and inventive. They are restless, energetic and intensely individual. They absorb facts and figures like blotting paper due to their amazingly retentive memories. They have novel ideas and unorthodox opinions because their thought patterns are unconventional, not always governed by logic, and their sudden flashes of inspiration can be positively inspired. They are remarkable, unusual and highly intelligent.

Non-conformity can be both an asset and a liability as many Aquarius-Threes find out to their cost. They can certainly see things from a different angle, never allowing existing beliefs to blinker their views and frequently come up with exciting new solutions to perennial problems. However this won't necessarily gain them friends or influence people in their favour. In fact, quite the reverse. They are often drawn into heated arguments and disputes, 'rebel' is the nametag that society chooses to pin on them and they are frequently regarded as cranky and eccentric by their contemporaries. Progress is necessarily a slow process and its pioneers often only gain their recognition and respect posthumously.

KEYWORDS
Positive: original, progressive, curious, unconventional
Negative: rebellious, eccentric, unorthodox, non-conformist

AQUARIUS-FOUR

Planetary combination: Uranus/Uranus

With this particular combination both sign and number are ruled by the planet Uranus, governor of intuition and idiosyncracy which together form the basis for all invention and independence. It bestows originality, imagination and eccentricity upon its Aquarian subjects, manifesting its influence in the form of practicality, organization and a healthy suspicion through the number Four. Aquarius-Fours are therefore not only individual, creative and highly original but also capable, efficient and certainly nobody's fools.

People born under this vibration are broadminded, energetic and unpredictable. They go their own sweet way through life, refusing to be shackled by convention or dictated to by other people. They are assertive, decisive and really rather lucky. Their choice of profession is generally dictated by their interest in modern technology and all things scientific. But whatever the field of endeavour one factor remains constant, they always seem to end up working on unusual, specialist projects which call for someone with novel ideas, unorthodox methods who isn't hidebound or blinkered by tradition.

Only a small handful of Aquarius-Fours will manage to stay in one place doing the same job for the whole of their working lives. Most will have chequered careers while a few will change horses just the once, but in mid-stream which is always a hazardous undertaking. Whether they move once or a dozen times they are usually only left with themselves and their stubbornness, haste and irritability to blame at the end of the day. They respond far too quickly, leaping before they look, rising to the bait long before they have ascertained whether or not its palatable. By which time their fates are already sealed and its much too late to make amends.

KEYWORDS
Positive: original, creative, independent, unorthodox
Negative: hasty, stubborn, impulsive, irritable

AQUARIUS-FIVE

Planetary combination: Uranus/Mercury

Aquarian-Fives don't conform to any existing standard, pattern or model, they are a law unto themselves — unique. They are inventive, intuitive and imaginative. Their reactions are fast, their brains like quicksilver and their ideas unconventional and positively inspired. They are independent, resourceful and incredibly shrewd; brilliant, intellectual and more highly-strung than any thoroughbred horse.

People born under this vibration are also sexually adventurous due entirely to the influence of the number Five. They are physically active, restless and sensual, drawn like a magnet to anything new or exciting. They like to take risks and push their luck. And when their gambles misfire, as is bound to happen from time to time, they simply pick themselves up and start again because they are buoyant, resilient and never down for long.

Unfortunately Aquarian-Fives often behave erratically when unsure of themselves or when they have no fixed course to follow, while their opinions, habits and conduct can all be a little odd and eccentric at times. They are over-excitable, hyper-active and cranky. Once they have a bee in their bonnet about something they won't rest until they've got to the bottom of the matter. The dividing line between genius and insanity is very fine and one which these amazing individuals are in danger of crossing should they omit to take some form of mental safety precautions.

KEYWORDS
Positive: brilliant, imaginative, active, daring
Negative: erratic, restless, exciteable, eccentric

AQUARIUS-SIX

Planetary combination: Uranus/Venus

When Aquarian inventiveness, intellect and unpredictability are coupled with the dreamy, ethereal qualities attributed to the Venusian number Six the result is frequently unusual but never, ever mundane. Aquarian-Sixes are charming and witty. They have a wealth of talent literally at their fingertips. Many are fine artists, sculptors and musicians while others are writers and poets who wield their pens with great imagination and tremendous perception. They have an eye for beauty, good colour sense and creative flair. Originality is one of the keywords for this combination and all those ruled by it are guaranteed to be unconventional in their life-styles, unorthodox in their methods and outstanding in their achievements. They have a distinctive, individual style of their own which others will attempt to copy, but few will ever duplicate.

These people are sociable, easy-going and amenable. The Aquarian side of their nature makes them very broadminded and their attitude towards love, sex and marriage tends to be flexible verging rather on the permissive side. The number Six provides all the flowery speeches, meaningful glances and stolen kisses of the true romantic. Within their personal relationships it is usually a case of anything goes provided both adults are attracted, consenting and physically able. Fidelity and total commitment are not prerequisites here, although discretion is always called for.

These are the men and women who dare to be different — they are non-conformists. But people who refuse to behave in an accepted way often have to pay a high price for the privilege.

KEYWORDS
Positive: original, artistic, creative, unconventional
Negative: permissive, individual, inconsistent, unorthodox

AQUARIUS-SEVEN

Planetary combination: Uranus/Neptune

Aquarian-Sevens exist on an entirely different plane to everyone else; they function on a wavelength all of their own concerning themselves with matters which lesser mortals have never even heard of, let alone understand. They often go unnoticed and unrecognized during their lifetimes, yet their extraordinary abilities and visionary ideas could put them amongst the intellectual elite if only they were more ambitious and forthcoming about their findings.

People born under this vibration have progressive minds, adventurous spirits and restless bodies. They tend to intersperse their long periods of unbroken concentration with journeys to the far flung corners of the globe. Package deals to Spain or Greece are not for them, they like to trace lost civilizations, explore dense jungles and study the habits of primitive peoples always in the hope of making some amazing discovery or startling anthropological breakthrough.

Emotionally they are cool and calm. Their self-control is rigid, their approach dispassionate and their intent well hidden but mentally they are active, intuitive and brilliant. They are spiritual, humanitarian and religious in an unorthodox sort of way. Anything unusual fascinates them, particularly the occult, and many will experience strange phenomena, states of trance or flashes of clairvoyant premonition during their lifetimes.

Unfortunately Aquarian-Sevens tend to operate in a state of organized chaos. They live in such a muddle that they often temporarily mislay items or lose them altogether on occasion. They are not only confused with themselves at times, but also very confusing to others who find their conversation hard to follow. They have strange interests, work in fits of wild enthusiasm followed by total exhaustion and their odd brushes with the supernatural sometimes completely unnerve them. They are weird, wonderful and decidedly different.

KEYWORDS
Positive: spiritual, self-controlled, mentally active, psychic
Negative: disorganized, confusing, over-enthusiastic, strange

AQUARIUS-EIGHT

Planetary combination: Uranus/Saturn

Like all true Aquarians, people ruled by this combination are original, intelligent and shrewd but with the extra bonus of traditionally Eight qualities such as ambition, tenacity and a healthy respect for money, they've got it made.

Aquarian-Eights are fuelled entirely by their own nervous energy. They are capable, practical and determined. These self-willed, powerful individuals will stop at nothing to achieve their goals. They take hardships and set-backs in their stride; problems and obstacles are never allowed to block their way for long and so gradually month by month, year after year as their strength increases and their position improves they fight their way doggedly to the top. They can be hard, tough and unyielding; virtually indestructible and utterly ruthless.

Their staying power and gutsy attitude are useful assets in a competitive environment but off duty not many people want to partner a steam roller. In private, Aquarian-Eights are difficult men and women to get through to. They are affable enough but in a detached sort of way. They prefer to remain cool and aloof because they regard any visible display of emotion as a sign of weakness. They are inclined to keep everyone at arm's length and that way no one can get close enough to do them any harm. They are charming, polite, well-mannered and absolutely terrified of letting themselves go and becoming totally committed to anyone other than their career.

KEYWORDS
Positive: strong, tough, ambitious, determined
Negative: ruthless, cold, unemotional, calculating

AQUARIUS-NINE

Planetary combination: Uranus/Mars

Aquarian-Nines have such tremendous fixity of purpose that they can crystallize hope into belief and convert dreams into realities. They are courageous, independent and decisive with superhuman energy and an unswervable determination to succeed come hell or high water. These people will work till they drop because they're impatient for results, totally dedicated to the task in hand and unable to relax until something concrete has been achieved, and even then they're not satisfied for long.

Unfortunately many Aquarius-Nines have hasty tempers and their fighting spirit often lands them in trouble when it gets out of control. They are impulsive, obstinate and aggressive. Their survival instincts are particularly strong and when the going gets tough and circumstances call for drastic action, they're capable of being absolutely ruthless and totally unscrupulous. In a 'him or me' situation they'll act first and ask questions or face the consequences later.

In private life they will give their all to their partners and expect nothing less than love, honesty and loyalty in return. They are passionate, demonstrative and fiercely protective of their loved ones — woe betide anyone who tries to interfere or offers unsolicited advice on family matters. A certain amount of tension is the norm and only to be expected within any Aquarius-Nine relationships, but it pales into insignificance when compared with the way that they treat, or perhaps more accurately 'mistreat', busybodies or rivals!

KEYWORDS
Positive: independent, ambitious, energetic, determined
Negative: impulsive, obstinate, ruthless, aggressive

PISCES-ONE

Planetary combination: Neptune/Sun

Pisceans have never had a reputation for being the most decisive of people. They are usually sensitive, over-emotional and rather inept at handling their affairs. However, this particular combination is an exception to the rule because the number One provides them with sufficient ambition and confidence to make a world of difference.

Pisces-Ones are reasonably positive and actually manage to get things done all by themselves without having to rely on other people for support or encouragement. They are hard-working, energetic and surprisingly well-organized.

Within relationships they prove to be loyal and sincere. They are compassionate, understanding and very, very affectionate. The thought of responsibility undoubtedly frightens them but as far as their families are concerned no one could possibly criticize the care and affection they shower on them. They may well be a little too soft and easy going at times but their hearts are most definitely in the right place. In fact they have so much love to give that even the goldfish and the pot plants receive their share.

Unfortunately, like all people ruled by the Fishes, Pisces-Ones do have their off-days when life gets them down and they wonder whether they can cope any more. They try to hide these negative feelings as best they can, but to those who know them well it is always transparently obvious that something's wrong. On such occasions they are likely to be tearful, clumsy and uptight. There isn't really much anyone can do to help except to make them a cup of sweet tea and wait for them to snap out of it.

KEYWORDS
Positive: confident, decisive, responsible, mildly ambitious
Negative: emotional, tearful, moody, tense

PISCES-TWO

Planetary combination: Neptune/Moon

Pisces-Twos always seem to get a raw deal from life because they are totally unrealistic. They see the world through rose-coloured spectacles, as they would like it to be — never as it actually is. They are quiet, gentle and sensitive and can't understand why everyone else isn't the same. They recoil from suffering, abhor violence and brutality, refusing to acknowledge the presence of the distasteful aspects of society. Like ostriches they bury their heads in the sand in the hope that all the unpleasantness will magically disappear.

People ruled by this combination are bewildered refugees from a bygone age of refinement and culture. They are idealistic, romantic and imaginative. The vast majority of them are poetically inclined while others are talented painters and musicians. But always in the old traditional style; they never produce anything loud or dischordant. They have such heightened feelings and instincts that they are able to tune into and sense things which other people might miss. They are often psychic, mediumistic and clairvoyant. These spiritual men and women usually chose the solitary, reclusive life because they need room to breathe, time to think and as few distractions and disturbances as is humanly possible.

Most Pisces-Twos have delicate health with constitutions that could certainly never be described as robust. They suffer from a whole range of real or imaginary ailments and their medicine chests are usually better stocked than the shelves of the local chemist shop. They are highly-strung, over-anxious and will worry themselves sick over the slightest little thing. Their bodies seem to frighten them, always afraid that something terrible will go wrong. Yet, at the same time as they strive to improve their diet, they will quite happily smoke and take the odd glass or two of spirits to calm their nerves. These individuals seldom leave their mark on life except perhaps as a brief case history in a medical journal.

KEYWORDS
Positive: poetic, artistic, sensitive, refined
Negative: unrealistic, anxious, hypochondriac, delicate

PISCES-THREE

Planetary combination: Neptune/Jupiter

There's something decidedly Bohemian about Pisces-Threes. They are so free and easy-going. They show compassion for those who deserve it, understanding to those with problems, and tolerance to those who try their patience. They are warm and generous; caring and kind-hearted; humane and helpful. They have strong religious convictions, romantic notions and great expectations.

Pisces-Threes have many abilities all of which come under that vast umbrella of 'the arts'. They can paint, write, draw, play, sculpt and act — the list is endless and their main problem is deciding which of their talents to concentrate on and develop. Although people ruled by this combination admittedly put a great deal of time and energy into their endeavours Fortune also strongly favours them. Many of their breaks happen more by luck than judgement. Opportunities are handed to them on a plate, friends put in a good word or they just happen to be in the right place at the right time.

Their personal lives tend to be very casual affairs. They have strong feelings and emotions which they can express dramatically under the right circumstances but with them it's a case of out of sight out of mind when their partner is not around. They are neither possessive nor jealous and once the heat of the moment has passed not particularly bothered one way of the other.

If anything, they are too easy come, easy go about their lives, living for today and leaving tomorrow to take care of itself. They are inclined to daydream, never taking anything very seriously and would give their last penny to a stranger if they felt his need was greater. However somehow they always seem to survive, in spite of their many shortcomings.

KEYWORDS
Positive: warm, generous, tolerant, arty
Negative: casual, unrealistic, disorganized, foolhardy

PISCES-FOUR

Planetary combination: Neptune/Uranus

Pisces-Fours hide behind a mask of respectability. They go through all the right motions of being practical, efficient and hard-working and generally they convince everyone, bar themselves, quite successfully that they are rather ordinary. On the surface they appear solid, reliable and down-to-earth but still waters can run very deep at times. Inside their material bodies dwells an entirely different entity which is sensitive, receptive and self-willed — their subconscious.

People born under this vibration undoubtedly have psychic gifts which they prefer to keep to themselves. They often experience flashes of clairvoyance, premonitory dreams and strange occurrences which have no rational explanation.

They have second sight, the ability to experience altered states of consciousness and a way of sensing what is going on many miles from where they actually are. They find all this both disturbing and incomprehensible and it's hardly surprising they keep quiet about it in case people think they're mad. This is an ability they didn't ask for and they don't always know how best to handle it.

Pisces-Fours put a great deal of time and effort into their relationships. They make loyal partners and conscientious parents. A stable home environment is what they try to create and they usually manage to achieve just that. They tend not to go gadding about to pubs and discos, never living beyond their means and if it wasn't for their little secret they would be no different from the average man or woman in the street.

KEYWORDS
Positive: practical, efficient, respectable, homeloving
Negative: receptive, sensitive, psychic, deceptive

PISCES-FIVE

Planetary combination: Neptune/Mercury

Most of the people born under this vibration are a pretty woolly-minded bunch. They never seem to know whether they're coming or going. They are credulous, totally unrealistic and vague. Their heads are always high up among the clouds and their feet are rarely on the ground. They daydream, they theorize, they take off on the most incredible flights of fancy but never actually get anything done. They deal in concepts, lacking in originality to produce their own ideas. They see themselves as poets, mystics and highly-evolved spiritual beings, when in reality they are nothing more than an idle, lazy crowd of good for nothings.

The number Five has a disastrous influence in this particular combination because it can put all sorts of crazy ideas into Piscean heads. Many feel the urge to travel and decide to take off to India to sit at the feet of a Guru, while others prefer to search for lost cities in China or Peru. It also creates havoc by giving their intensely emotional characters extra strong sexual drives and desires to cope with, thus making them not only temperamental and moody but also restless, earthy and promiscuous.

When seen at their worst Pisces-Fives are weak-minded, weak-willed and feather-brained. They are impractical, disorganized and indecisive. Most of their efforts are a complete and utter waste of time and when they finally come to their senses and realize what a mess they've made, usually it is far too late to make amends.

KEYWORDS
Positive: vague, indecisive, dreamy, unrealistic
Negative: promiscuous, restless, weak-willed, time-wasters

PISCES-SIX

Planetary combination: Neptune/Venus

Pisces-Sixes can't help but be dreamy, sentimental and artistic with Venus as one of their planetary rulers. They have a great love of music and art, good colour sense and an eye for beauty. They are kind-hearted, sympathetic and sensitive; natural, spontaneous and gentle. Not only do they like to attend concerts and visit galleries they also have considerable talent of their own. Many have fine, strong voices while others are gifted artists who seem positively inspired at times in their way of creating depths of light and shade.

People ruled by this combination desperately need to feel loved preferably in a romantic, fairy-tale way (and if they're lucky enough to be worshipped and adored, then they could ask for nothing more from life!). Unfortunately they are so trusting and innocent that they leave themselves wide open to trickery, exploitation and seduction. In the hands of an unscrupulous lover who will use their feelings in a manipulative way, their lives can be misery and should the object of their affections ever become cool or distant they act as though the end of the world was nigh. They are also mad about animals and usually keep several pets at a time which they pamper outrageously, spoil wickedly and treat like their own children because fate often cruelly denies them the experience of parenthood.

Pisces-Sixes sometimes overdo the sugary sweetness bit and allow their need to be loved to get the better of them, becoming clinging, possessive and stifling. To be smothered with affection may be what they want but slow suffocation is certainly not everyone else's cup of tea. They often set their hearts at impossible targets, tend to hero-worship others and although love as a concept appeals to them they are not always very good at coping with passion at close quarters.

KEYWORDS
Positive: musical, artistic, romantic, loving
Negative: cloying, possessive, unrealistic, over-sweet

PISCES-SEVEN

Planetary combination: Neptune/Neptune

This is a unique combination of sign and number ruled exclusively by the planet Neptune, governor of psychic activities such as precognition, clairvoyance and prophetic dreams as well as the higher levels of perception which can be assisted and enhanced by the use of certain hallucigenic drugs. This is definitely not a good or an easy vibration to live under as many of its subjects will find to their cost.

Pisces-Sevens are contemplative, sensitive and responsive to external stimuli. Their interests are unusual and generally centred around their fascination for mysticism, the occult and the supernatural. They are seekers of spiritual enlightenment and their search often takes them along some strange, unconventional and, all too often, dangerous pathways. They have vivid imaginations, enquiring minds and remarkably accurate intuition. Most have powers of ESP in one form or another which they exploit and develop to the full.

Unfortunately many Pisces-Sevens tend to be rather weak and impressionable characters. They are escapists who make plans and then lack the nerve to execute them. Their objectives are vague, their notions unrealistic and their results are usually disappointing. Bad luck seems to follow them around and generally they lack the confidence and mental stability that is a prerequisite for the sort of dabblings they become involved in. They are also inclined to use any available crutch to bolster their flagging egos, calm their tattered nerves or snap them out of periodic bouts of depression. Alcohol and tobacco usually come first but many will be tempted to experiment further with stronger substances. Sadly, time and again, they fall easy prey to the unscrupulous because they lack the strength and will power to say no and mean it.

KEYWORDS
Positive: sensitive, imaginative, intuitive, curious
Negative: vague, escapist, weak-willed, prone to addiction

PISCES-EIGHT

Planetary combination: Neptune/Saturn

Pisces-Eights have a dual nature. They like to hedge their bets by keeping a foot in both camps whenever possible which is basically why they are materialists with colourful imaginations and idealistic tendencies. They have lofty thoughts and a keen grasp of finance and business practice. With this sort of outlook they really shouldn't go wrong, but all too often their ambitions are thwarted and their hopes dashed due to their own indecision and lack of confidence at the critical moment. On paper they appear to have what it takes to do very well, but in reality any modicum of success they do achieve is generally a long time coming and when it does arrive their hold on it is usually tenuous to say the least.

People ruled by this combination are methodical, hard-working and precise. They can add up endless columns of figures in their heads, calculate difficult mathematical problems in seconds and at any given time will know, to the exact penny, their financial standing — or lack of it. However, when it comes to charm, humour and a sense of fun, they can be totally lacking. They have none of the social graces and very little feeling for anyone other than themselves.

Pisces-Eights seem to be permanently tense, worried and uptight about something. In fact they tend to suffer from a whole range of stress related ailments and problems. They take a morbid interest in their health and even when enjoying good health they imagine that all sorts of things are wrong with them which have yet to be detected. Self-torment is the name of their game, requiring only one player. They have a whole host of fears and phobias which range from the sublime to the utterly ridiculous. They are fanatical about personal hygiene, never walk under ladders and will go to almost any lengths to avoid treading on cracks in the pavement in case they see a bear!

KEYWORDS
Positive: materialistic, idealistic, mathematical, precise
Negative: tense, insecure, unfeeling, paranoid

PISCES-NINE

Planetary combination: Neptune/Mars

This is the last but certainly not the least of all the possible combinations of sign and number. Pisces-Nines are imaginative, creative and artistic, albeit in a modern sort of way. They have all manner of original ideas and unusual hobbies which they pursue avidly in their spare time. Although they may never attract media attention or win public acclaim, these interests nevertheless assume a role of considerable importance in their lives. They will work silently and without hope of recognition far into the night with never a thought for how late the hour, how tired they're feeling or what anyone else is up to. They become completely engrossed and totally absorbed in what they are doing which is all to the good because it takes their minds off other matters which they really shouldn't dwell on over long.

Pisces-Nines have a seamy side to their nature which they try hard, but often unsuccessfully, to repress. They turn to escapism in a big way which is why they need to keep busy and occupied at all times. When they are not usefully employed their drinking habits get out of control, they gamble for higher stakes than they can really afford and their strange private fantasies spill over into their everyday lives becoming realities of nightmare proportions. They are easily led, prone to bouts of depravity and find temptation almost impossible to resist particularly when it's staring them in the face.

Emotionally they are a mess. They find the opposite sex extremely attractive but difficult to attract and that is really the root cause of all their problems. Because they are unable to establish the right kind of relationships they tend to seek out other more dubious means of relieving their frustrations and this can lead them into bad company, introduce them to bad habits and eventually land them in serious trouble.

KEYWORDS
Positive: imaginative, creative, artistic, hard-working
Negative: unattractive, emotionally confused, easily-led, seamy

CHAPTER FOUR

The Initial Letter

It is thought by many that your choice of forename is no accident. A whole variety of circumstances, environmental and social conditions as well as spiritual considerations are brought to bear on that choice. Indeed forenames themselves have specific meanings such as the French 'Odette' which means homelover, the Greek 'Christopher' meaning bearer of Christ or the Teutonic 'Emily' meaning industrious.

For the purposes of *The Wheel of Fortune* the most important letter in your forename is the initial. This letter can be converted into a number using the simple correspondence chart shown below:

1	2	3	4	5	6	7	8	9
A	B	C	D	E	F	G	H	I
J	K	L	M	N	O	P	Q	R
S	T	U	V	W	X	Y	Z	

So if your name is Gillian your initial number will be 7, Deirdre will be 4 and Leonie will be 3.

Now move on to the section in this chapter which gives insight into the meanings of your initial number.

THE ONE LETTERS — A J S

A — The Head
A is the first letter of the alphabet and quite rightly ruled by the number One. It is traditionally associated with the head and such phrases as 'head-strong',

'headman' and 'headmost' aptly describe its independent, forceful influence. People with A for their first initial are determined not only to succeed but also to make it to the top. They are strong, purposeful and resolute always making their intentions crystal clear. Hard work never daunts them, in fact they put a tremendous amount of effort into everything they do. There is nothing half-hearted or mediocre about any of them.

A's are also courageous and daring. They rely entirely upon their own judgement when making decisions, organizing projects or taking risks. That way if things go well they take all the praise but if their schemes misfire they have only themselves to blame. Some people think them rather pushy but they firmly believe that you only get what you ask for in this life and are certainly not slow at coming forward.

They have a spirit of adventure and boundless energy to back it up. They take things much as they come but usually manage somehow to turn them to their own advantage. They are level-headed, ambitious and confident.

Unfortunately they can be very selfish at times, putting themselves first when perhaps they should give someone else a chance. They are cautious and sceptical which means that they take a lot of convincing when they're unsure about something. They also make hard taskmasters. Everything has to be just so and woe betide anyone who doesn't come up to the high standards they demand.

KEYWORDS
Positive: determined, courageous, bold
Negative: selfish, sceptical, demanding

J — Aspiration
J is the tenth letter of the alphabet and vibrates to the number One. It is associated with aspiration, desire and action. J's are bright and intelligent. They are talented, creative individuals who can do many things well and a few brilliantly. They have shrewd, inventive minds, colourful imaginations and highly original ideas.

People with J as their first initial are fair, honest and reliable. There is nothing false or pretentious about any of them. They are genuine in their concern for others, correct in all they do and loyal and faithful to those they love or serve. They know exactly what they want from life and what they must do to achieve it. They are active, independent and purposeful.

J's have warm-hearts and sunny dispositions. They are generous, kind and helpful. Their word is their bond and once given they will never go back on it come what may.

However, a J with nothing in particular to do or, worse still, no goal to aim at is a sorry sight. When they are not usefully engaged and fully occupied they soon lose their sparkle. They seem dull and lifeless, everything is too much of an effort and they can't even be bothered to busy themselves with what few chores there are to be done. At such times they can be infuriatingly lazy, listless and lackadaisical about everything.

KEYWORDS
Positive: creative, original, shrewd
Negative: dull, lazy, lack-lustre

S — Beginnings

S is the nineteenth letter, traditionally associated with beginnings and ruled by the number One. This is a strong, positive vibration which knows where it is going and what route to take. The shape suggests flexibility rather than deviation and its message is clear — go for it even if you can only see as far as the first bend clearly.

S's have strong, intense feelings. They are ardent, passionate and capable of superhuman efforts. But like the snake, which the letter resembles, they will lash out at anyone who gets in their way or poses any kind of threat to their life and liberty.

They have a sound sense of values and are experts when it comes to handling money. Business acumen they acquire through experience, capital they build up over the years but their undeniable powers of leadership were born with them. They thrive on challenge, pioneer new schemes and ideas and never flinch when faced with the unknown or the unexpected. They are innovators and inaugurators; adventurers, creators and explorers. S's are daring, dynamic and bold.

People ruled by this vibration have all the social graces. They are charming, attractive and amusing. Their manners are impeccable, their dress sense is perfect and their appearance is usually smart but casual. They make tender, loving partners, responsible parents and loyal friends. But should anyone ever cross them, they make dangerous enemies.

They tend to experience many ups and downs during the course of their lives and not all their efforts meet with the success they deserve. They have one main fault — they act on impulse. When they start following up hunches or entering into deals without sufficient time for reflection they usually come unstuck.

KEYWORDS
Positive: ardent, charming, materialistic
Negative: impulsive, unreflective, vengeful

OVERALL KEYWORDS FOR THE ONE LETTERS
Positive: independent, determined, original, creative, strong, dynamic
Negative: lazy, sceptical, selfish, impulsive, indecisive

THE TWO LETTERS — B K T

B — Emotions

The letter B vibrates to the lunar number Two. It is traditionally associated with the emotions but because these are so often of a changeable nature it is not a particularly strong letter, easily influenced by prevailing circumstances.

People with B as their first initial are homelovers. They like peace, quiet and familiar surroundings. They find meeting new people rather daunting and when faced with a crisis they retreat into their shells hoping fervently that someone else will step in and sort the problem out for them. Male B's are countrymen. They love the wild open spaces, the beauty of Nature and the simple life, whereas females of the species tend to be motherly and domesticated with a whole brood of children and an assortment of pets of various shapes, sizes and descriptions all vying for their attention.

B's are undoubtedly highly-strung. They panic easily and have nerves of jelly rather than steel. They get over-excited, over-wrought and worry over everything and nothing. They are also very stubborn and once they've dug their heels in, it would take rather more than a small charge of dynamite to get them to change their minds. They are possessive and jealous within their relationships, greedy when it comes to things they like and selfish when it comes to sharing them.

KEYWORDS
Positive: homeloving, emotional, domesticated
Negative: highly-strung, jealous, possessive

K — Extremes

The letter K is ruled by the number Two and traditionally associated with extremes. There is certainly nothing moderate or predictable about the emotions, actions or measures taken by anyone under it's influence. A K will be either for or against, never neutral as they are all or nothing people, while emotionally they are either up or down. They seem to have no happy medium to strike in between.

When their emotional pendulum is swinging in a positive direction then all is well. K's are energetic, optimistic and completely in command of not only themselves but also the situation they are in. They feel well disposed to everyone and particularly loving and responsive towards their partners. They are receptive and imaginative, versatile and creative, good all-rounders who work with a will and can turn their hands to most things at a moments notice.

However, when their pendulum is behaving negatively the picture alters completely. The strong, decisive K is replaced by a timid, mouse-like creature which seems afraid of its own shadow. They appear dejected and miserable, fed up with themselves and dissatisfied with their relationships in particular and life in general. Instead of looking on the bright side they tend to expect the worst and then wait for it to happen.

KEYWORDS
Positive: strong, optimistic, responsive
Negative: timid, pessimistic, unresponsive

T — Growth

T is associated with the number Two and represents growth which is synonymous for development, cultivation and expansion. People influenced by this letter are always trying to improve themselves both mentally and spiritually. They are creative, inventive and original but it doesn't stop there. T's like to take things a step further. They'll find ways to develop their ideas, broaden their minds and build on their existing talents. They are progressive, energetic and purposeful. Even the shape of the letter itself suggests a branching out once a certain point has been reached.

This vibration also has a higher side which effects the deep inner reaches of the soul, the finer feelings. In quiet moments of reflection T's can be very solemn and reverent. Their thoughts turn to God and they wonder what life is really all about. Although they may not actually attend services on a regular basis they certainly give their maker rather more than just a cursory nod every now and again. They are moral, virtuous people who go out of their way to set a good example whenever they can.

Unfortunately T's do have one or two flaws in their character. They are easily influenced by the opinions of others and they often cause problems within their relationships because their feelings of insecurity make them behave over-emotionally. They are moody, jealous and possessive. They need to work on their self-confidence and build it up more and at the same time acquire just a shade more self-control.

KEYWORDS
Positive: creative, progressive, spiritual
Negative: moody, insecure, over-emotional

OVERALL KEYWORDS FOR THE TWO LETTERS
Positive: emotional, receptive, creative, responsive, imaginative
Negative: over-emotional, insecure, moody, jealous, possessive

THE THREE LETTERS — C L U

C — Energy
Three is a get up and go vibration and the letter C, representing energy, certainly echoes these sentiments. People with C for their first initial can't sit still for five minutes. They are impatient and impulsive, spontaneous and restless. They tend to do everything on the spur of the moment. They are over-generous and have quite a reputation for extravagant living. They are light-hearted, liberal and spirited. They have a cheerful disposition, a carefree attitude and a willing nature. They are talkative, outspoken and extrovert. They seem able to do almost anything, usually much better than everyone else, and with the greatest of ease. They are versatile, intelligent and very clever with their hands.

C's are great organizers. They are experts when it comes to telling other people what to do but not always quite so good at buckling down to things themselves, particularly when the task in hand is boring or repetitive. They could charm the birds from the trees and frequently exploit this ability when dealing with members of the opposite sex. Male C's only have to smile to set a woman's heart beating faster while their female counterparts simply flutter their eyelashes and look helpless to get a man dancing to their tune.

Unfortunately a few C's tend to be unscrupulous and unprincipled. They will manipulate people shamelessly and take advantage whenever they can. They don't always keep their minds on what they're doing, often seem inattentive and neglectful and in their private lives some of their goings on are immoral to say the least. 'Naughty but nice' to coin their phrase.

KEYWORDS
Positive: carefree, versatile, impulsive
Negative: shameless, inattentive, unscrupulous

L — Action
L is a typical Three letter representing action. People influenced by this vibration

are bright, intelligent and usually at least one jump ahead of everyone else. They are genuine characters who mean what they say and are, in fact, what they seem. They don't go in for ulterior motives and underhand plotting — it is simply not their style. They are honest, fair and unbiased; well-adjusted, even-tempered and reliable. These truthful men and women have undeniable management potential because they know how to handle people. They deal with problems dispassionately, remain calm in times of crisis and cool when placed under pressure. They don't just command respect, they earn it.

In private life they rarely indulge in anything which would rock the boat. They are loyal and devoted to those they care for, generous with their friends and charitable towards other people. Their one great love is travel and perhaps their greatest ambition is to see the world — all of it. They enjoy meeting new people and visiting foreign parts. Whether they journey first class or tourist it's all the same to them just so long as they go. The experience is the important part, not the fancy trappings that are all too often part of the package.

L's don't really have any major flaws or character deficiencies but they do seem to be particularly accident prone. They're usually in such a thundering hurry to get things done or to be first on the scene that in their haste they don't always notice where they are going or pay full attention to what they are doing. They should always remember to look before they leap especially when racing against the clock.

KEYWORDS
Positive: intelligent, honest, even-tempered
Negative: accident-prone, inattentive, hasty

U — Accumulation
The twenty-first letter of the alphabet U is ruled by the versatile number Three and traditionally associated with accumulation of either the mental or material variety. Even the shape of the letter suggests a vessel emminently suitable for storage. U's have retentive memories, heads crammed full of useful facts and information, brains like computer banks and total recall. They never forget a thing. They are well-read, well-informed and well above average when it comes to intelligence quotient. Fortune favours these talented individuals because they seem to experience rather more than their fair share of lucky breaks. Accidental occurences have a way of turning out well for them and they have the happy knack of always being in the right place at the appropriate, fortuitous time.

U's are not only bright and clever, they are also acquisitive. They collect all manner of strange and exotic items which they guard jealously and view with pride. What is more, they seem to have the Midas touch. Whatever they handle turns to gold and it certainly doesn't take two guesses to know who will win the office sweepstake or the jackpot on the fruit machine!

Unfortunately U's sometimes find it hard to be decisive, probably because they have so many interesting channels open to them from which to make a choice. They are also rather greedy and avaricious, particularly when it comes to hoarding things, and selfishness is something they have perfected to a fine art. There are some areas of life which they regard as sacrosanct and which they refuse to share with another living soul.

KEYWORDS
Positive: intelligent, acquisitive, lucky
Negative: greedy, selfish, indecisive

OVERALL KEYWORDS FOR THE THREE LETTERS
Positive: versatile, intelligent, impulsive, lucky, carefree
Negative: greedy, selfish, indecisive, hasty, inattentive

THE FOUR LETTERS — D M V

D — Balance

D is the fourth letter of the alphabet and ruled by the number Four. Traditionally it represents balance and has all the necessary qualities to create just that. D's have will-power and authority. They are determined, powerful and superbly well-organized. They plan their campaigns with all the skill and strategy of a military commander, are prepared to bide their time patiently until the odds are running in their favour at which time they show their hand and bring their power and influence into play. They are empire builders who not only know where they are going but also have the necessary business acumen to get there.

D's have phenomenal powers of concentration. They are born leaders and shrewd judges of character who can endure hardship, withstand competition and achieve miracles. They are perceptive, persevering and purposeful.

However when viewed in an unfavourable light some of their strengths become distorted. Stubbornness replaces resolution, pig-headedness prevents them from reaching a working compromise and obstinacy could be their undoing. As commanders they will never regiment their forces successfully unless they learn to become a little more flexible and a little less unyielding in the face of progress or opposition.

KEYWORDS
Positive: determined, purposeful, shrewd
Negative: stubborn, pig-headed, inflexible

M — Industry

M is the thirteenth letter of the alphabet and despite popular superstition not an unlucky vibration. It is ruled by the number Four and associated with industry in all its myriad forms. M's are hard-working, active and efficient. They are self-reliant, courageous and bold. Nothing ever seems to get them down for long and even when progress is slow their tolerance and endless patience stands them in good stead. They rarely complain, seldom tire and never, ever throw in the towel without a fight.

Most M's are homeloving and domesticated. They have a strong need for material security and simply cannot relax when there are any outstanding bills to be paid or unexpected expenses to meet. They live within their means, seldom splash out on unnecessary luxuries and usually have a little nest egg tucked away somewhere for a rainy day. They are thrifty and frugal with a tremendous respect for money and a morbid fear of one day discovering that they don't have any themselves.

Unfortunately an M on an off day is like a bear with a sore head. They are grouchy, grumpy and bad-tempered. The slightest little thing gets on their nerves, they fly off the handle at everyone and are generally irritable and unpleasant. On the rare occasions that they do something rash or hasty they usually have ample reason to regret their impulsiveness later.

KEYWORDS
Positive: hard-working, patient, homeloving
Negative: insecure, quick-tempered, irritable

V — Construction
The letter V comes under the umbrella of the number Four. In numerology it represents construction rather than victory although people with V for their first initial have all the necessary qualities to produce outstanding results. V's are practical, hard-working and industrious. They are energetic, capable and particularly good with their hands. Their word is their bond. They make loyal, efficient employees and fair, honest employers.

Off duty V's are sociable, gregarious and fond of company. They are good mixers, entertaining conversationalists and very often the life and soul of the party. In private they are passionate, emotional and responsive towards their partners but, unfortunately, possessive and insanely jealous too. They have over-active imaginations, suspicious natures and are easily hurt. Most of their personal problems are of the self-inflicted variety and could be so easily avoided with just a little more trust on their part.

V's have fixed views and inflexible opinions. Nothing will ever persuade them to change either their minds or the habits of a lifetime. They are set in their ways, which is how they are going to stay. What's more they are totally unpredictable and it is anyone's guess which way they'll jump in a given situation.

KEYWORDS
Positive: industrious, practical, sociable
Negative: inflexible, unpredictable, suspicious

OVERALL KEYWORDS FOR THE FOUR LETTERS
Positive: hard-working, industrious, practical, patient, determined
Negative: stubborn, inflexible, suspicious, insecure

THE FIVE LETTERS — E N W

E — Communication
E is ruled by the restless number Five and linked with communication. Not in the technical sense via news satellites, reference books and the media but in its day to day application through a one to one exchange of views, opinions and information. E's are delightful, diverting and entertaining. Their conversation is interesting, their company amusing and their ideas imaginative and original. They are inventive, creative and, at times, positively inspired.

People influenced by this letter are independent. They need plenty of space to breathe, room to manoeuvre and the freedom to come and go as they please.

They are skilful, talented individuals who, like a chameleon, will adapt themselves to blend in with the prevailing circumstances and situation. They tend to live exciting and eventful lifes, opportunity seems to know where to find them and luck certainly smiles in their direction.

The main disadvantage when dealing with an E is their irresponsibility. They just don't take things seriously and because of their temperamental and changeable nature they can't be relied upon. Within relationships they are fickle and flirtatious and when left in charge they are liable to go off somewhere leaving things to run themselves. These characters are impulsive, almost impossible to pin down and very definitely a law unto themselves.

KEYWORDS
Positive: independent, impulsive, freedom-loving
Negative: unreliable, irresponsible, fickle

N — Imagination

The letter N vibrates to the number Five and represents imagination. It has a remarkably positive influence on those it rules giving them courage, self-assurance and masses of confidence. N's are not only creative, talented individuals they are also persuasive orators and imaginative writers. They make first class spokesmen skilled in the field of public relations and well versed in the ways of the world. They are ambassadors; go-betweens who know how to get their message across, and when wielding their pens they keep accurate records, detailed notes and present their reports in an interesting yet accessible style.

N's are inventive, intuitive and intelligent. Their beliefs are unshakable and their ideas brilliant and original. These competent men and women undoubtedly work hard but they play even harder. They are sensual, demonstrative and sexually adventurous. Pleasure, enjoyment and satisfaction are what they seek and more often than not they find all three within their relationships. They are passionate and earthy. They like to experiment, tend to fantacize and will try anything at least once if it promises to be fun.

Envy is a sin they commit almost daily. They can't bear to see someone else enjoying themselves when they are having to work. They can't stand it when their friends earn higher salaries, get better perks or have more luxurious homes and although they don't actually covet their neighbours' oxen and asses, their wives or husbands are a different matter. Jealousy eats away at them like a worm in an apple and it needs to be nipped in the bud before it can do any serious damage.

KEYWORDS
Positive: confident, creative, pleasure-loving
Negative: envious, covetous, jealous

W — Self-Expression

Self-expression is the characteristic traditionally associated with the letter W and Five is the number which rules it. W's are original, creative and intelligent. They have quick, razor-sharp minds, active imaginations and a whole host of talents. They are thoughtful, purposeful and very determined once they've identified and set their sights on a particular target. They have boundless energy, adventurous spirits and the natural buoyancy of a piece of cork. They are versatile, resourceful and persistent.

W's often surround themselves with an air of mystery and secrecy which serves to make them all the more interesting and fascinating. They are charming, sociable and attractive, mix well, are fond of company and have a strong, personal magnetism which draws people to them. They are fun to be with, nice to know but virtually impossible to fathom out. Many people try to discover what makes them tick but their attempts rarely meet with any success. They are intriguing, baffling and enigmatic.

Unfortunately one thing which occasionally does motivate them is greed. They never know when they have had enough and they have great difficulty in saying no and meaning it. They are also selfish and much too fond of taking risks. They cut corners, take chances and one day they will come unstuck, however until such time nothing will persuade them to mend their ways.

KEYWORDS
Positive: original, determined, magnetic
Negative: greedy, selfish, risky

OVERALL KEYWORDS FOR THE FIVE LETTERS
Positive: independent, confident, pleasure-loving, creative, original
Negative: impulsive, unreliable, irresponsible, greedy, sensual

THE SIX LETTERS — F O X

F — Love
F comes under the rulership of the Venusian number Six so it's hardly surprising that it is traditionally associated with love. F's are homeloving and domesticated. They make model parents because they take responsibility seriously, never neglect their duties and care for their children conscientiously and unselfishly. They make dedicated, devoted husbands and wives as they are affectionate, faithful and loyal.

F's are friendly, kind-hearted individuals who are always ready to lend a helping hand, show consideration to others and offer comfort to those in trouble. They are gentle, sympathetic and understanding with kind faces, warm smiles and broad shoulders to cry on. They are the salt of the earth and a rare commodity in this changeable modern world. Most people ruled by this vibration are also good organizers. They plan carefully, never leave anything to chance and if anyone can work miracles on a shoe-string budget they certainly can.

From time to time F's will get down in the dumps and miserable. They give willingly to others but don't always receive the thanks or consideration they deserve in return. They are prone to bouts of depression when they become anxious and uneasy about everything and everyone, but fortunately these don't last for long and don't occur all that often.

KEYWORDS
Positive: friendly, sympathetic, helpful
Negative: unhappy, anxious, depressed

O — Patience

Patience is a virtue which O's have in boundless supply thanks to the number Six which rules them. They are never in a hurry, take life at their own sweet pace and are quite prepared to wait, until kingdom come if necessary, to harvest the fruits of their labours. People influenced by this vibration are studious, scholarly and intellectual. They are well-informed, well-read and knowledgeable on a great many subjects.

O's have strong moral convictions, religious beliefs and spiritual yearnings. They long for enlightenment and will explore every path open to them to achieve just such a heightened state of awareness. They are soulful, pious and God-fearing. In their work they are methodical and painstaking, in their dealings with others they are frank and honest and they are respectful of law and order. They long for a balanced society where all men are equal and where disease and poverty no longer exist.

However, the emotions of an O are not always so calm and serene as their outward appearance would belie and their thoughts don't always reflect that other special virtue — charity. They tend to wear their hearts on their sleeves which should be green to match the jealousy which lurks within them. They are insecure, easily hurt and dangerous when cast aside for another.

KEYWORDS
Postive: scholarly, intellectual, spiritual
Negative: emotional, insecure, jealous

X — Sexuality

The letter X is ruled by the number Six in a most unusual and perhaps not always desirable way. Instead of bringing out the higher self and the finer feelings here it plays upon the base instincts and seamier side of life hence its association with sexuality and all that it implies. X's are hedonists. They are self-indulgent, pleasure loving and out to enjoy themselves. As pupils they are willing and eager to learn but because they're also easily led some of the subjects they consider worthy of study won't be found on the curriculum of any reputable school, training college or university.

X's are thrill-seekers. They are earthy, sensual and adventurous; intemperate, unrestrained and excessive in their behaviour and habits. They like to live the high life, will burn the candle at both ends and in the middle too preferably in comfortable, luxurious surroundings. Although judging by some of the haunts they frequest they are not particularly fussy about where they are seen or the company they chose to keep.

People influenced by this vibration seldom make satisfactory marriage partners because they are extremely promiscuous. These characters are not only unfaithful in their promises but in their affections too. And as far as drugs, alcohol and tobacco are concerned they're a push-over. They'll experiment with these just like they do with people, but the consequences are likely to be more far reaching than they could ever have imagined possible.

KEYWORDS
Positive: receptive, luxury-loving, sensual
Negative: hedonistic, unrestrained, easily-led

OVERALL KEYWORDS FOR THE SIX LETTERS
Positive: loving, patient, helpful, friendly, intelligent
Negative: emotional, insecure, selfish, sensual, moody

THE SEVEN LETTERS — G P Y

G — Mystery

The magical, mysterious Seven vibration influences the letter G. People who have it as their first initial are sympathetic, methodical and tidy. They also have orderly, disciplined minds which hopefully will keep them in touch with reality. They are strong-willed, purposeful, individuals whose characters are etched into their very faces for all to see. They have determined expressions, brows which bear the furrows of deep thought and concentration and strong, determined jaw lines. They do everything in their own inimitable way using some highly unorthodox methods and they'll tolerate no interference in their affairs however well-meaning or well-intentioned the motives behind it may be.

G's are irresistibly attracted to all things weird, wonderful and yet to be explained. Mysticism, religion and the occult are all subjects which they touch upon in their studies. They tend to rely heavily on their instincts rather than reason or logic, their ideas are original and unconventional and one of their most precious gifts is clairvoyance. They often experience flashes of inspiration, brief, disturbing glimpses of the future and strange, precognitive dreams. These men and women operate on a wavelength all of their own and their numbers are private and unlisted by request.

Occasionally G's will cross swords with the Church especially when they cast doubt upon existing beliefs. They are stubborn, critical and hard to convince which doesn't always win them friends. Unfortunately, the odd handful will risk their sanity when dabbling in dangerous regions of the unknown.

KEYWORDS
Positive: determined, mysterious, secretive
Negative: stubborn, disbelieving, unorthodox

P — Power

The letter P stands for power but because it pays allegiance to the number Seven the word is not used here in its conventional sense as a means of government or upholding authority but is applied strictly to the mind: and an exceptional one at that. P's are shrewd, perceptive and intellectual. They have above average IQ's, memories like a computer and are programmed for outstanding achievement. They are knowledgeable, well-informed and impressive.

P's are level-headed and thoughtful. They are spiritual, enlightened individuals who have the knowledge, wisdom and foresight so often associated with true genius. They also have the innate ability of being able to express themselves in a way which not only makes sense but that can also be understood by the layman. The influence their ideas can have is enormous, their presence commands attention and the respect they receive is certainly no more than they deserve.

Now here's the rub. In private P's just don't know how to switch their brains off and their feelings on. They treat their partners like possessions which can be picked up and put down at will. They are totally selfish and very often so deeply engrossed in their work, which they frequently take home with them, that they have neither the time nor the sympathy to spare for other people and their needs. They often earn phenomenal salaries but money isn't everything and it certainly can't buy them happiness or domestic tranquility.

KEYWORDS
Positive: wise, intellectual, enlightened
Negative: selfish, possessive, unsympathetic

Y — Freedom

Y is the penultimate letter of the alphabet, ruled by the number Seven and traditionally associated with freedom of which there are many kinds. Y's are independent, go-ahead, progressive and pioneering. They need time to think, to meditate and to imagine. They need the opportunity to study, to learn and to amass knowledge. They need room to breathe, to do their own thing and to make their own mistakes. They also need some time off to relax, to enjoy themselves and to travel which they love.

Y's lead busy, active lives and provided their freedom isn't curtailed in any way then they're perfectly happy with their lot. They simply can't bear to feel restricted and restraint in any guise will bring out the rebel in them. People influenced by this vibration are free spirits who ask for nothing more than to come and go as they please.

Although control is a dirty word to a Y they certainly aren't trouble-makers or timewasters. They have good manners, exquisite taste and a flair for design. Their surroundings must be aesthetically pleasing, their work must conform to their own high standards and their aspirations are always ambitious. They know exactly what they want and so long as nobody tries to stop them they should succeed.

KEYWORDS
Positive: freedom-loving, independent, active
Negative: dislikes restraint, uncontrollable, rebellious

OVERALL KEYWORDS FOR THE SEVEN LETTERS
Positive: wise, intellectual, enlightened, mysterious, independent
Negative: stubborn, rebellious, unorthodox, selfish, disbelieving

THE EIGHT LETTERS — H Q Z

H — Authority

The number Eight rules the letter H and in a roundabout way it bestows authority upon it. H's are extremely self-contained. They're self-sufficient, independent and very fond of their own company. People influenced by this vibration tend to be successful at whatever they do because they are born winners. They also have the Midas touch; their endeavours usually show a handsome profit, they are always solvent and occasionally rather well-off. In fact, they attract money and the more they make the more it comes rolling in. Money undoubtedly talks, it has its own kind of authority, but the person who controls it is the real power behind the golden throne — and more often than not it will be an H.

Surprisingly these materialistic individuals have another side to their character which they tend to play down in public. They are nature lovers; ecologists and conservationists who often donate their time and money freely to help preserve our living world. They have a deep and sincere concern for the earth and its endangered flora and fauna. The white rhino, the wild orchid, the vanishing rainforests all need to be saved and in their own small way they do all they can to help.

However, conservation aside, H's can be greedy, possessive and selfish. They care about themselves first, foremost and exclusively. They are loners by choice, or so they profess, but perhaps in truth they simply can't find anyone who will put up with their churlishness for long.

KEYWORDS
Positive: independent, materialistic, nature-loving
Negative: greedy, selfish, self-centred

Q — Command

Eight is a strongly materialistic number which rules the letter Q. Traditionally this letter is associated with command and Q's have undeniable powers of leadership. They are tough, determined and capable. Positions of authority suit them and they wield power and influence wisely. They are eloquent, outspoken and persuasive. They have a clever way with words, could charm the birds from the trees and are so persuasive that they can soon sway anyone round to their point of view should they so desire.

Q's are intelligent, clever and shrewd. They are overtly ambitious, confident and self-motivated. Their ideas are brilliant, their schemes daring and their commitment always one hundred per cent. They are ardent, intense and utterly ruthless in the pursuit of their objectives. However, people influenced by this vibration are always something of an enigma: deep, mysterious and puzzling. They tend to keep everyone at arm's length and even in the company of loved ones and close friends they still hold back to a certain extent.

Not only are Q's difficult to fathom, their reactions are also hard to gauge. They have fiery tempers which operate on a hair trigger, moods which can change in the blinking of an eyelid and a mean streak which puts in an appearance from time to time. They can be obstinate, demanding, angry and unscrupulous in any order and sometimes all at once which is an awesome sight to behold.

KEYWORDS
Positive: ambitious, determined, powerful
Negative: obstinate, ruthless, aggressive

Z — Confidence

Z is the last letter of the alphabet but certainly not the least, ruled as it is by the dynamic number Eight and traditionally associated with confidence. Z's have great expectations. They are hopeful, optimistic and very, very positive. They are also wise, discreet and level-headed. They know instinctively when to keep a low profile and are past masters at handling difficult people or tricky situations with skill and diplomacy. They make first-class negotiators because they know how to clinch a deal without appearing to have been pushy or demanding. They always have their own, or their employers, interests at heart but because they're so charming this is seldom apparent at the time. Behind that beaming smile, warm handshake and friendly expression lies a calculating brain which is well aware not only of the odds but also how to manipulate them in the most beneficial direction.

Z's are capable, quick-thinking and practical. They have a great deal of common sense, a down to earth attitude and always know the most expedient way to deal with problems. They have fine minds, clever hands and level heads. In private, where they can afford to relax, they are different people; gentle, tender and considerate. They really are great, big softies at heart who, for working purposes, find it necessary to wear an extra thick layer of skin for protection.

Impatience is a Z's worst fault and one which they find difficult to remedy. They can't bear to be kept hanging around waiting, want everything to be done in record time and suspense is something which nearly kills them. They are headstrong, inclined to be over hasty and need to think before they act a little more often than they do normally.

KEYWORDS
Positive: confident, positive, optimistic
Negative: hasty, head-strong, impatient

OVERALL KEYWORDS FOR THE EIGHT LETTERS
Positive: materialistic, determined, ambitious, confident, independent
Negative: obstinate, ruthless, head-strong, impatient, greedy, selfish

THE NINE LETTERS — I R

I — Compassion

There are only two letters ruled by the number Nine and I is one of them. This is a gentle, sensitive vibration traditionally associated with compassion. I's are humane, caring and considerate. They have warm hearts, kind thoughts and helpful natures. They are shy, loving and utterly unselfish.

People influenced by this letter are artistic and stylish but never in a loud or unconventional way. They like to wear elegant clothes and tend to furnish their homes tastefully with the emphasis falling mainly on dark rich colour schemes and subdued, hidden lighting. They like to draw, to paint and to write. They enjoy going to the theatre, attending concerts or visiting galleries and one-man shows.

I's rely heavily on their instincts and intuition when making decisions. When pushed for ideas, inspiration more often than not will come to their assistance and when short of company they are always more than happy to settle down with a good book because they belong to that rare breed of people who can amuse themselves.

Unfortunately I's do tend to lack confidence. They are highly-strung, timid, fearful — in fact, they are a bundle of nerves. The slightest little noise will make them jump and, like children, they are afraid of the dark. They are easily hurt or offended and even more easily moved to tears because they are very sentimental.

KEYWORDS
Positive: tasteful, compassionate, kind
Negative: shy, nervous, timid

R — Possibilities

All things are possible particularly where the letter R is concerned because it is ruled by the visionary number Nine. R's are gentle, tender and kind. They show genuine concern for fellow human beings in trouble or going through a bad patch no matter who they happen to be. They are always ready to lend a helping hand, to listen and to give advice when asked. They are warm-hearted, broad-minded and not in the least bit selfish with either their time or their affections. They have a lot of love to give and are only too happy to share it.

R's are virtually bomb-proof. Nothing ever seems to shake, upset or worry them for even a second. They are placid, even-tempered and tolerant. They always appear calm and composed, their mental stability is unquestionable and their patience is of saintly proportions. But for all their virtues there is certainly nothing dull or goody-goody about any of them. They are active, lively and alert. Their enthusiasm is positively infectious and their capacity for hard work is enormous. They are energetic, entertaining and fun people to be with.

The only things which ever seem to annoy R's are their own short-comings. They get irritable with themselves when they mess things up, are a bit touchy if someone suggests they are putting on weight and when they mislay or lose their own possessions, which they are rather apt to do, they get very niggly indeed. Perfection is what they would like to achieve and on the odd occasions that they fall short of the mark they find such minor failures extremely aggravating.

KEYWORDS
Positive: even-tempered, helpful, considerate
Negative: touchy, irritable, niggly

OVERALL KEYWORDS FOR THE NINE LETTERS
Positive: selfless, compassionate, kind, helpful, humane, intuitive
Negative: impulsive, impatient, touchy, irritable, hasty

CHAPTER FIVE

The Triple Combination

We have now established the major components in your Wheel of Fortune — Birth sign, Date of birth number and Initial letter number. To make things easier, these can be expressed in a shortened form, for example: Aries/3/9 or Leo/8/2. The meanings applied to the combinations in this chapter are by necessity brief and concentrate on the major reinforcements or oppositions in order to achieve a general picture. It may be that other influences are brought to bear about which only you can know. This is where you will have to interpret the results accordingly.

Now turn to your appropriate section, listed below:

ARIES/ONE/ONE

You might think that you're leading the foray in all you want to do but watch out for the pitfalls that could trip you up. You need to think more about the people around you and less about your own role. While you are keen to get things done and see your goal through to the end you may need to compromise to win the confidence of those around you.

ARIES/ONE/TWO

Changing moods could cause you to swing between submissiveness and aggression, and while you try to achieve a balance these emotional see-saws could result in your becoming deceitful and, even cruel. Look for those around you who can bolster your self-confidence. Then you will be able to use your own personality to get things done.

ARIES/ONE/THREE

Your inflated sense of your own importance could upset those around you. Whilst few would deny your shrewd and quick-witted ability to cope with life in general, guard against your tendency to be too outspoken and too intolerant. While you might be naturally lucky your own thoughtlessness and short-temper could lose you many friends and allies.

ARIES/ONE/FOUR

Your unique combination of ambition, efficiency and practical ability means you are likely to go far in your chosen field. But while you might be enterprising and even aggressive when needs demand, that lack of humour and occasional suspicion of other people's motives could hold you back. Avoid letting your own problems destroy important friendships.

ARIES/ONE/FIVE

You might get members of the opposite sex swarming around you like bees around a honey pot but once they get to know you better, the unfortunate sides of your character could force them away just as quickly. That combination of conceit, driving ambition and resourcefulness which goes hand in hand with a short temper and occasional feelings of insecurity could result in hurtful and sarcastic comments about those around you.

ARIES/ONE/SIX

Your keenness to get on in the world yet still need to help those around you is likely to result in great satisfaction if not wealth or power. You tend to get on with most people but beware your tendency for idle gossip. While you appreciate the good things in life there are times when that sneaking urge to live dangerously could get you into quarrels and arguments which will hurt you more than anyone else.

ARIES/ONE/SEVEN

Great academic achievement is something you either strive for or dream about. But your own inability to deal with things in a down-to-earth way could prevent you achieving any sort of goal. Add to this your tendency to act on the spur of the moment and you could find any achievement you have in mind to be thwarted.

ARIES/ONE/EIGHT

Your obsession with success could be your biggest downfall. As you approach any challenge head on you must remember that your own obstinacy could prevent you seeing the wood for the trees. It's the little things that will trip you up in the end and whether you succeed or fail the results are likely to be spectacular.

ARIES/ONE/NINE

There's little that can stop you achieving whatever you want in almost any field. That combination of ambition, quick-wittedness and imagination could take you to the top in almost any profession — especially those where you need to deal directly with other people. Those around you will respect your views but may not wish to get any closer because of your tendency towards conceit and selfishness.

ARIES/TWO/ONE

Your sense of independence puts all other emotions into the shade. You feel that there is nothing you cannot achieve and at no time do you need the help of others. But this in no way belies the responsibility you feel to those around you. Avoid situations where you are cornered and can only deal with the matter by emotional reaction.

ARIES/TWO/TWO

Your battle is one between independence and deceit, honesty and maliciousness. And the only way out is to recognize the fact that you are competent at your chosen task and honest about your abilities. Avoid any relationship which makes too many demands and try to be less intolerant of those around you. Above all strive to control your temper.

ARIES/TWO/THREE

Your ability to take things at face value will stand you in good stead in both business and personal relationships. You can deal with most situations providing you curb your desire to be outspoken, your independent spirit will see you through most situations if you avoid emotion colouring your actions.

ARIES/TWO/FOUR

Competence is the key word which will see you through most crises. It's that ability to deal logically and practically with almost every problem that life has to offer. But do not allow your sense of humour to get lost in the process — this is a vital weapon in an arsenal which prevents your life becoming dull and joyless.

ARIES/TWO/FIVE

Life has a habit of throwing challenges in your face, very often to do with members of the opposite sex. It is only your independent and basically honest nature which prevents things from getting out of hand. You know how far you can go and to what extent you can take additional problems on board. Let your own sense of what is right and wrong be your guide.

ARIES/TWO/SIX

Your need to be independent very often clouds all thinking to the point of triviality. You can see the problems but frequently you can only express them in relatively unimportant terms. This side of your character leads you into the one thing that you cannot abide and that is argument, and isolation. You must try to think and act in a more harmonious way.

ARIES/TWO/SEVEN

You are always trying to break out of bonds — whether personal, or business. You have high ideals which you often find hard to share with other people. While you find your actions easy to justify to yourself, trying to make sense of them to someone else is a much harder task. Perhaps this is why you often find your temper is on a short fuse.

ARIES/TWO/EIGHT

You are always looking disaster in the face and it comes from being impulsive, and acting at the wrong time in the wrong place. Your greatest weakness is your inability to express what you really think. Providing you can curb your excesses you can succeed through your innate authority and an ability to see wider perspectives.

ARIES/TWO/NINE

Impulsiveness is the key to your character and it can work in your favour or against it. Your reaction to any situation, either in the home or at work will depend on how much planning you do. You cannot always rely upon your ability to talk your way out of a crisis. On the positive side you are sincere, and purposeful and those around you will soon recognize your true value because of this.

ARIES/THREE/ONE

You might be energetic, enterprising and ambitious but that obstinate trait will get you nowhere. You need to be more flexible in your attitudes and more tolerant towards other people and their shortcomings. Leadership is one of your strong points but to achieve maximum performance and earn respect your authority must be wisely used.

ARIES/THREE/TWO

You need to toughen up and grow a thicker skin in order to achieve your goals. If you are going to take offence at every minor criticism or harsh remark then you will never make the grade. You are clever, resourceful and capable so do not let sensitivity spoil your chances. Do not go taking your frustrations out on other people when you have only yourself and your own haste to blame for mistakes.

121 The Triple Combination 121

ARIES/THREE/THREE

You have certainly got what it takes to be a resounding success but with one important proviso - you cannot afford to go throwing in the towel half-way through a project simply because you are getting bored or have lost interest. You need to make a consistent effort in order to reach your goals. You cannot afford to cross swords with those in authority too often.

ARIES/THREE/FOUR

Even though you are always raring to go and ready to rise to almost any challenge, you are certainly nobody's fool. Your latent energy is on tap whenever required but not there to be squandered on useless errands. You have courage, ability and more than your fair share of luck but your greatest asset by far is common sense.

ARIES/THREE/FIVE

Unless you make a concerted effort to relax, slow down and count to ten before doing anything you could end up being your own worst enemy. You are restless and jumpy; in too much of a hurry and far too interested in the opposite sex for your own good. Concentrate more on the job in hand, do not be quite so hasty to ring the changes and never mix business with pleasure.

ARIES/THREE/SIX

Try to ensure that your chosen career allows sufficient scope for your creativity. You will only become restless and frustrated if you have to suppress your artistic talents and if you cannot put your ideas to good use you will soon lose heart. Within a relationship it is important that you learn to say 'no' occasionally and mean it, even if your refusal does spark off an argument.

ARIES/THREE/SEVEN

Provided you always keep both feet firmly on the ground, resist acting on impulse and learn to be more tolerant, then you could do very well for yourself. However, this will be no easy task because you are prone to flights of fancy and some of your schemes are highly impractical. Moodiness could also be a problem you will have to learn to handle.

ARIES/THREE/EIGHT

You have all the right ingredients for success, but luck doesn't always run in your favour. On the positive side you have energy, ambition and confidence to spare, however you also have a large helping of aggression, obstinacy and ruthlessness. At times you will lack concentration and staying power and you tend to set your sights much too high.

ARIES/THREE/NINE

Freedom to do what you please is something you hold in the greatest regard but it can also lead to your downfall. The very act of waving a banner for other people can see you open to attack from all quarters. Think more about the friends you make and their motives and less about setting yourself up to act on their behalf.

ARIES/FOUR/ONE

Extremes of ambition and intolerance might lead you into personal blind alleys. While you are capable of great achievement you are unlikely to reach your ultimate goal unless you learn to curb your temper, think less about yourself and channel your creative energies into both work and play.

ARIES/FOUR/TWO

Your sense of justice and concern for others is often battered by your driving ambition in your chosen career or lifestyle. This conflict must be controlled before it leads to ill health or personal problems. Learn to co-operate with those around you and allow your own intuition to be your guide.

ARIES/FOUR/THREE

You exhibit talent at both home and work making your opinions valuable on both the social and business scene. But while you revel in the limelight do not become flattered into thinking this is a substitute for hard work and dedication. Try to be more honest with those you deal with and remember that all those webs you weave could catch up with you at a later date.

ARIES/FOUR/FOUR

Friends and relations could be forgiven for thinking you dull. Your tendency to take life seriously has blunted your sense of humour. Spend more time being less righteous and learn to relax and enjoy more of the good things in life. Let others benefit from your personal stability and dedication.

ARIES/FOUR/FIVE

You find it hard to operate without an admiring audience who appreciate your wit, and sexuality. But deep down you realize that ultimate success can only come with concerted hard work. This conflicts with your natural desire to look over every horizon and ignore the middle ground in between. It means you can be quite brilliant at seeing the size of problems and challenges but find it hard to deal with the minutiae.

ARIES/FOUR/SIX

You have a few enemies and many of your friends will take you for granted. But while you offer total loyalty in your relationships you must be on your guard against those who fail to return your faithfulness. Do not let complacency lull you into a false sense of security.

ARIES/FOUR/SEVEN

You can hold your own in almost any conversation — and what you may not know at the time you will soon find out. Your apparently superior air is likely to earn you a pompous and arrogant reputation, an image which you must work hard to dispel. Only your closest friends will see that you are dedicated, hard-working and caring.

ARIES/FOUR/EIGHT

You seem to have the best of both worlds, the ability to see things on a grand overall scale and cope with the details at the same time. But your successes and failures are likely to be compounded by this unique faculty. So be prepared to greet the very best and the very worst.

ARIES/FOUR/NINE

You have a tendency to approach life with about as much subtlety as a combine harvester tackling a field of wheat. Remember that the success of a harvest depends upon more than just one machine and its operator. Try to gear your imagination and ability to succeed more towards joint efforts rather than solo performances.

ARIES/FIVE/ONE

No one can deny your originality in work and play — the danger is you will be among the first to endorse your own talents. While you hate arguments your tendency towards sarcasm and tactlessness can often lead you where you do not want to go. Let others enjoy the glory at times, even though you know you can outwit and outshine them.

ARIES/FIVE/TWO

Your tendency to justify physical attraction for someone else as a genuine emotional involvement could lead you into trouble. Not only can you persuade others to do what you want, but you can also talk yourself into things. Let your own intuition become more of a guide and leave the hard selling for your workplace.

ARIES/FIVE/THREE

Most people find you good company and your wit and humour is frequently in demand in your social scene. The risk is that you waste time being clever in unimportant areas and fall back into sarcasm and tactlessness when shrewdness is really called for. The message is a simple one — get your priorities right.

ARIES/FIVE/FOUR

There are few problems you cannot cope with. Behind that calm exterior is an ability to deal quickly and efficiently with all sorts of crises. But your commanding abilities can take their toll which is likely to show up when you are least under pressure. This could mean that your home and social life might suffer from fits of depression, unnecessary stubbornness and unfounded suspicions.

ARIES/FIVE/FIVE

Your potential for sexual athleticism is only bettered by your ability to convince others you are always right. But lurking behind that veneer of worldliness is insecurity, jealousy and conceit. Too often you blame others for your own failures both in and out of bed. Be more realistic with yourself and with those around you.

ARIES/FIVE/SIX

You try to find beauty in all things, particularly in your relationships both at work and home. More often than not you will use your skills and charm on behalf of others rather than yourself. Your greatest weakness is to entangle personal feelings with sound judgement. Try to stand further back from situations and let common sense be your guide.

ARIES/FIVE/SEVEN

You make no secret of your wish to be on your own and while you might convince others of this need, you secretly know you need time to unravel your own confusions. The swings between solitariness and the need to be with others can make you moody, and anti-social. Give others the chance to take you at face value.

ARIES/FIVE/EIGHT

Given the chance you could easily succeed in your chosen career. But it is likely you will be labelled 'ruthless' in the process. You cannot help but use people for your own ends whether in business, socially or sexually and the image you try to portray of strength and wisdom will often be seen as nothing more than obstinacy and unscrupulousness.

ARIES/FIVE/NINE

Your tendency to over-sell yourself could lose you more friends than you can make. Your desire to be liked and respected can be better achieved if you try to become a good listener, less impatient and act upon well-meant criticism. Become tougher with yourself in anything you undertake — use your imagination and abilities but see the job through to the end.

ARIES/SIX/ONE

You have a lot going for you both at work and at home. Your organizational and creative qualities will almost certainly bring rewards in your chosen career and while your private life might be somewhat more traumatic you will never be short of romantic partners.

ARIES/SIX/TWO

You always seem to be waiting for the right person to come along, but unless you take more of a lead you'll never find what you are looking for. Do not let minor set-backs discourage you and avoid acting out of deceit. Take advantage of your understanding nature.

ARIES/SIX/THREE

You generally succeed with any task or challenge but your impatience to achieve instant recognition can sometimes lead you into wasteful and impulsive action. This is especially important in your private life when you want an immediate emotional response and cannot understand why it is not forthcoming. The message is to be patient.

ARIES/SIX/FOUR

While your imagination and energy pull in one direction the need to be a respectable and joyless pillar of society tug in the other. This conflict could lead you into dramatic changes of career and home-life. However, this diversity enables you to get on with people from all walks of life and ensures you will never be short of a wide circle of friends.

ARIES/SIX/FIVE

Decisions you make are likely to be based on whims rather than logic. As a result you run the risk of wasting money and friends. But when you do succeed either at work or at home you can be sure you will reap any benefits straight away. Your ability to bend with the wind means you will rarely be down for long.

ARIES/SIX/SIX

Do not let all the unimportant things in life get on top of you and try not to over-react to minor upsets. Others regard you as a reliable friend, an easy-to-get-on-with workmate and loyal to those you think highly of. While you may not make the top ranks in your career, it is likely you will succeed in leisure activities or social groups.

ARIES/SIX/SEVEN

You are expressive and creative especially if your work or leisure activities are concerned with the arts. Your talents tend to go in fits and starts which means you feel, at times, that you are not achieving all you would like to. You would be definitely advised to keep away from gambling or financial speculation.

ARIES/SIX/EIGHT

Money tends to rule your life. You have the capacity to make it but equally spend it at the same rate. It is your originality and imagination which help you to grasp financial opportunities but you have difficulty in learning from past mistakes.

ARIES/SIX/NINE

Friends sometimes find you difficult to get on with and those closest to you sometimes despair of your impulsiveness and intolerance. At the same time you object loudly to the same traits in others. Attention to matters of etiquette and behaviour will help improve life for you and those around you.

ARIES/SEVEN/ONE

You have a sense of responsibility, know how to compromise and you are not afraid of hard work. But you may need to get a greater grip on reality. Once you have learned to stop wishing for the impossible and are prepared to accept life as it really is, then you could succeed in your chosen field.

ARIES/SEVEN/TWO

You think that life is always playing cruel tricks but have you ever looked at your own role in the process? You have a lot to offer if you can stand up for what you believe and not allow yourself to be bullied and put upon. Look for someone who can genuinely guide you.

ARIES/SEVEN/THREE

Others envy you for your creativity and imagination both in the way you deal with your working life and those closest to you. But your ambitions tend to overtake your abilities and you can only make real progress when you take true stock of yourself. Lean on a close friend for well-found advice.

ARIES/SEVEN/FOUR

That calm and steady exterior often hides self-doubt and weakness. You often find your home becomes a refuge rather than a relaxation. Despite this you have a lot to offer so use your home-life as a redoubt you can expand from. Attempt to learn more from the experiences of those you look up to.

ARIES/SEVEN/FIVE

It takes you a long time to get your act together once you have overcome those early feelings of inadequacy and self-doubt. But in the end, and given the right support, you can cope with almost any problem you encounter in your private or business life. Very often it takes others to recognize your real potential — give them the chance to tell you.

ARIES/SEVEN/SIX

In the right environment you can dictate the fashion of the moment. Your creative talents at home and work are frequently acknowledged but you lack the ability to constrain yourself and need others to offer sound, practical advice. In social circles you will always be warmly welcome but sometimes risk outstaying your welcome.

ARIES/SEVEN/SEVEN

When the going gets tough you tend to take the easy way out and look for solitude. But here you tend to compound your mistakes rather than solve the initial problem. While it is essential for you to have a bolt-hole available you must come to terms with the fact that you can only succeed with the help of others.

ARIES/SEVEN/EIGHT

Your dreams of riches are rarely out of your mind but your chances of achieving them are remote. You rarely accept good advice and deceive yourself into thinking you can go it alone. Often the successes you do achieve are at the cost of friends and family. Allow that deeply bedded sense of understanding and kindness to come to the surface more often.

ARIES/SEVEN/NINE

There is nothing you like more than having your ego bolstered by those close to you. In the right circumstances the support of others can lead you to great achievements but you know that, deep down, you must learn to stand on your own two feet. Remember you will always risk losing good friends by thoughtless words.

ARIES/EIGHT/ONE

There's little you are not capable of, especially when you are asked to build from your own ideas. However, in your climb up the ladder you are likely to leave behind a number of casualties. Despite this you will achieve total loyalty from those closest to you.

ARIES/EIGHT/TWO

You know how to get the best from people and providing you curb your ruthless tendencies you could become a natural leader in almost any walk of life. You demand high standards both at home and in your work place, and will use every means to achieve this.

ARIES/EIGHT/THREE

The stage might not be your chosen profession, but nevertheless you are a born actor. You will play whatever role is needed to get what you want but you must learn to share your successes, otherwise your personal victories will only be hollow ones. In personal relations you gain the most satisfaction as a teacher and guide.

ARIES/EIGHT/FOUR

Behind that calm exterior and respectable image is someone striving for all that life has to offer. You set great store by the most fashionable and expensive possessions but you fail to recognize that the image you are buying will not result in true happiness. Money cannot buy love, friendship and respect.

ARIES/EIGHT/FIVE

You know what other people enjoy and you can often help them achieve their wishes but for you the task is harder. You must try not to take your work home or allow your home life to affect your career. By keeping them separate you will gain both material success and personal happiness.

ARIES/EIGHT/SIX

Involving yourself in other peoples' affairs may bring you temporary acclaim, but in the end you will be the loser. Only offer advice when it is asked for and try to be less dispassionate in the affairs of those closest to you. Do not use gossip to achieve your own ends.

ARIES/EIGHT/SEVEN

You know exactly what you want from life and how best to achieve your ends. Your understanding of financial matters is second to none and you have a natural flair for business. Unfortunately what you lack is compassion and understanding. Relationships are often strained and difficult because you do not really know how to handle people on a personal level.

ARIES/EIGHT/EIGHT

It is all very well being determined and ambitious just so long as you know when to down tools and relax. If you keep up the pressure twenty-four hours a day, seven days a week something will inevitably give way and it could be your health. Allow yourself adequate time to unwind and try to be more sympathetic as far as other people and their needs are concerned.

ARIES/EIGHT/NINE

Impatience and spur of the moment actions could undo all the hard work and effort you put into building your career. Do not be in quite such a hurry to get things done and remember that criticism can sometimes be constructive. You may not like having your faults pointed out but sometimes other people are in a better position to give an unbiased opinion.

ARIES/NINE/ONE

Goal-consciousness is what drives you on through life in such an aggressive and tenacious manner. Once you have set your sights on something you would not give up until the target has been reached. You are single-minded, independent and self-motivated. Unfortunately you might also find that you have become very lonely unless you pay more attention to your family and friends.

ARIES/NINE/TWO

Jealousy is a negative, time-consuming emotion. While you are busy envying other peoples' success and status you could be making progress with your own career. You have the ability to achieve great things but you will never get anywhere with a chip on your shoulder. Be yourself and do not worry about other people and what they are up to.

ARIES/NINE/THREE

Channel your energy wisely and try not to rely too much on luck. It is the amount of effort you make that will dictate your rewards at the end of the day. You must also learn when to keep a still tongue in your head. Outspokenness will neither win you friends nor influence people, particularly those in positions of authority.

ARIES/NINE/FOUR

You are so calm and methodical that it takes a great deal to upset your natural balance but once your feathers become ruffled you are not easy to placate. You are undoubtedly ambitious and want to get on in the world but often find it difficult to make headway, as you tend to err heavily on the side of caution.

ARIES/NINE/FIVE

You are much too fond of taking risks and cutting corners and one day you are going to come unstuck. The opposite sex is also a constant and pleasurable source of distraction. What you need is far more self-discipline if you are ever going to make the grade. Life is not all fun and games and the sooner you realize this the better.

ARIES/NINE/SIX

At work you appear ambitious, reliable and capable of great effort but your colleagues are seldom allowed to see the real you. Deep down you are soft, sentimental and romantic. Provided you never mix business with pleasure, by allowing your feelings to cloud your judgement or aggression to creep into your relationships, then all should be well.

ARIES/NINE/SEVEN

Whether at work or at play you cannot expect those around you to be mind-readers. You need to be more open about your plans and ideas, more forthcoming with facts and information and far less insular. Independence is a commendable quality but not when carried to extremes. It can also be misinterpreted as stubbornness.

ARIES/NINE/EIGHT

Are you really surprised that your relationships are difficult and that colleagues do not seem overly keen to befriend you? You are sensual but lack sympathy and understanding; clever and capable but certainly not modest about your achievements and down-right selfish when it comes to sharing. Try to be less aggressive when dealing with workmates and show a little more affection to loved ones.

ARIES/NINE/NINE

There is no reason why you should not be both happy and successful in life because you are bright, enterprising and determined. However, you will need to watch that hasty temper of yours, remember to think before you speak and learn to be more patient if you do not want to spoil your own chances. You have got everything it takes with the exception perhaps of wisdom and foresight which, hopefully, will both develop with age and experience.

TAURUS/ONE/ONE

You could easily make more progress in both your work or private life if you spent less time dealing with trivia and more with the fundamental issues. Do not be frightened of change for the sake of it — sometimes the grass is greener on the other side. You cannot achieve success without taking risks.

TAURUS/ONE/TWO

Hard work is the only way you will acquire all those luxuries you crave for but you will also need to take a more positive stand if you want to get on top of your home life. Plan ahead more often if you want to ensure that feeling of security which is so important to you.

TAURUS/ONE/THREE

You tend to be a good communicator and it is likely that your career will involve information, entertainment or instruction. Take advantage of your talents because others will rely upon your skills for sound and unbiased judgements, but that rebellious streak you possess could lead you into trouble from time to time.

TAURUS/ONE/FOUR

Friends and colleagues admire your ability to reason and assess situations. However, because you can clearly see two sides of an argument, thus it often means that you cannot make up your mind and take a firm stance. Allow your intuition to guide you more often.

TAURUS/ONE/FIVE

You are often thought to be the life and soul of any party. You enjoy being the centre of attention but that wish to show off could lead you into difficulties. Avoid being labelled flippant and spend more time listening to what others have to say.

TAURUS/ONE/SIX

More often than not you prefer talking about what you can do and what you want, rather than getting on with it. While you relate to most people you will not buy friendship through quixotic gestures and hollow promises. Let your own self-confidence and natural ambition come to the fore.

TAURUS/ONE/SEVEN

You like to think of yourself as a loner. This is most likely because you dislike change and you lack a feeling of security. Until you come to terms with the changing world its likely you will be left behind both at work and at home. Get out and meet more people, enlarge your circle of friends and generally be more flexible.

TAURUS/ONE/EIGHT

You have a natural gift for handling money and while it will rarely be turned to huge profits, you are not likely to run up huge debts either. You admire people who are solid and reliable and prefer that type of company both at home and at work. For you the most important goals in life are safety and financial security.

TAURUS/ONE/NINE

Your ability to think on your feet and cover yourself in almost every crisis is a much admired characteristic. However, it is often your own impulsiveness which leads you into situations of conflict and diffculty. Spend more time in thinking your problems through before you deal with them.

TAURUS/TWO/ONE

You need to push harder, be more independent and use your creativity to the full if you are ever going to get what you want from life. You need to make a concerted effort and there is no time like the present to set the ball rolling. Popularity is one thing but progress and survival demand different methods.

TAURUS/TWO/TWO

Security of both the financial and emotional variety is of paramount importance to you but unless you are prepared to make an effort you will lose out on both scores. At work you need to be more co-operative to achieve even a modicum of success while in private you need to control your emotions and be more loving and giving.

TAURUS/TWO/THREE

Versatility is your greatest asset so milk it for all it is worth. Be prepared to take on any role, however daunting, which could be beneficial to your career. Try to keep one jump ahead of the competition and, at home, try to be less flippant and more demonstrative towards your partner.

TAURUS/TWO/FOUR

Playing safe can be both a strong point and a weakness. You need to learn when to go all out and when to leave well alone. You also need to control your emotions. Wearing your heart on your sleeve will only make you vulnerable. Love may make the world go round but with the wrong partner it can come to a grinding, shuddering halt.

TAURUS/TWO/FIVE

Because of your varying attitudes towards the opposite sex it is difficult to guess what you will make of your private life. However at work, provided that you do not set your sights too high, your future looks good. Try to choose a profession where originality and talent count for more than the ability to work under pressure — working to tight schedules is not one of your strong points.

TAURUS/TWO/SIX

If only you could stay at home all day long then life would be perfect. Unfortunately we all have to earn a living and to get the best results you should keep away from the cut and thrust of commerce. Fall back on your creativity and develop your talents to the full would seem to be your best course of action. That way you can combine business with pleasure.

TAURUS/TWO/SEVEN

Emotionally you are insecure, financially you are hopeless — what you are going to need is a rich partner, a great deal of luck or a change of attitude to see you through. You need to grow a thicker skin, adopt a tougher approach and stop relying so heavily on intuition. There is a niche for you somewhere but finding it will not be easy.

TAURUS/TWO/EIGHT

When life is good to you it is usually very good but when things go wrong they tend to do so in a spectacular fashion. You must learn to take the rough with the smooth and be prepared for any contingency. The same applies to your relationships — you would not get anything worthwhile from them unless you are prepared to make a greater effort.

TAURUS/TWO/NINE

Charity begins at home and unfortunately it is likely to be a rare commodity in your household because of your selfishness. You are also very hard to please even though you give the outward appearance of being easy-going and friendly. Try to be more tolerant, less impatient and generally more lenient with those around you. You will find this makes everyone feel happier — including yourself.

TAURUS/THREE/ONE

Provided you define your goals clearly and always keep them in mind, your life should run relatively smoothly. Unfortunately you tend to get side-tracked much too easily thereby losing sight of your prime objective. You must pull up your socks, stop being irresponsible and learn self-control if you are ever going to get anywhere with your career or private life.

TAURUS/THREE/TWO

Nothing is impossible if you are sufficiently determined but with you its more a case of 'cannot be bothered'. Not only do you lack motivation you are also self-conscious, indecisive and really rather lazy. You need reassurance and encouragement to get you started and your family and friends are just the ones to give you the right kind of support.

TAURUS/THREE/THREE

It is to be hoped that a hedonist like you has a private income to finance the lifestyle you like to lead, otherwise you will have to change your tune drastically. You can be wasteful, extravagant and idle, and none of these qualities will help you with your career or your personal relationships.

TAURUS/THREE/FOUR

What you need to establish is where to draw the line between necessities and life's little luxuries. You do have some common sense so why not use it before you run up debts you cannot repay. At work you are careful, methodical and precise so surely you could apply the same rules to your own affairs without too much difficulty?

TAURUS/THREE/FIVE

It's all very well burning the candle at both ends for short periods at a time, but you are the kind of person who thinks it can be burned in the middle too. You are restless, resourceful and resilient. Living for kicks will not get you anywhere, neither will racy escapades with members of the opposite sex. You need to drop down a few gears or you will burn your engine out long before its time.

TAURUS/THREE/SIX

Home is where the heart lies and that is where you like to be, provided its tastefully decorated, expensively furnished and full of high-tech status symbols. You are into comfort and luxury in a big way but who are you trying to impress? Why not let the *real* you shine through, develop your talents to the full and stop throwing your money around. Remember you cannot buy friendship.

TAURUS/THREE/SEVEN

You could manage to be alone even in a crowd. You enjoy socializing and can be the life and soul of the party but somehow you always seem to keep everyone at arm's length. Very few people are allowed to get too close which is a great pity because you have so much to offer. Try not to be quite so mysterious and secretive, drop your guard a little and see what a difference it makes.

TAURUS/THREE/EIGHT

Leisure, entertainment and the luxury goods market are all perfect areas for you to carve out a career because that way you could mix business with pleasure. You are versatile, flamboyant and like to enjoy yourself but fortunately you also have a head for business and plenty of ambition. You could make quite a name for yourself provided you curb that natural extravagance and do not fritter away the profits.

TAURUS/THREE/NINE

If anyone is likely to go over the top it is you. You are outspoken, over-indulgent and impatient. Your heart may well be in the right place but you have the unfortunate knack of upsetting others. Impulsiveness is your greatest fault, followed closely by impatience, laziness and deceit. What you need to do is to start again from scratch because the formula you are using at present is one for disaster.

TAURUS/FOUR/ONE

Financial security is of paramount importance to you and without it you would panic. What is more you even try to guard against the unforeseen. Each move you make is carefully planned and cautiously executed, you never live beyond your means and you seldom put a foot wrong either at work or in the home. You need to let your hair down occasionally.

TAURUS/FOUR/TWO

You will probably never make it to the top in your chosen career because, although you have ambition, you lack the necessary drive and determination to propel yourself forward. On the home front make sure you do not become too possessive, allow jealousy to jaundice the situation or let your moodiness get out of control. Cultivate your good points and try to develop more self-esteem.

TAURUS/FOUR/THREE

With efficiency, shrewdness and a fair helping of luck there is no reason why you should not succeed. You are versatile, quick-witted and socially in demand as well as being hard-working, ambitious and totally reliable. However, you do need to control your temper and learn to think before you speak.

TAURUS/FOUR/FOUR

'Safe but sure' is your motto, but unfortunately these are not the watchwords for success. Unless you are prepared to be more decisive and to take a few well calculated risks you will neither take full advantage of your potential nor be able to capitalize on your assets. You are honest, hard-working and reliable — in fact, precisely the sort of person that other people build their empires on.

TAURUS/FOUR/FIVE

You are somewhat of a contradiction in terms because one minute you will cut corners, take risks and enjoy living dangerously and then you will play safe. This applies equally to your work and private affairs. Deep down you are secretly afraid of failure and for this reason you do not quite know which attitude to adopt for the best. Fortunately you are also extremely resilient.

TAURUS/FOUR/SIX

When it comes to being responsible, reliable and understanding you are in a class all of your own. Within a relationship you are loyal and faithful. As a parent you are dedicated and conscientious and as an employee you are an asset. However, as far as reaching the top in your profession is concerned you are at a disadvantage because you are too soft. You need drive and aggression to get yourself started.

TAURUS/FOUR/SEVEN

Actions speak louder than words, unfortunately you spend most of your time talking about what you would like to achieve instead of knuckling down and getting on with things. Day-dreaming is your favourite pastime but make sure it does not become a habit. You need to develop a more realistic attitude towards life and leave philosophy to the philosophers.

TAURUS/FOUR/EIGHT

Financially you are a wizard; you have a head for figures, an eye for opportunity and a positive flair for managing your own, and other people's, money. You are materialistic, ambitious and just ruthless enough to fight your way ever upwards and onwards. However, what you fail to understand is that you cannot buy love or friendship, and unless you become more caring and considerate towards others then personal happiness will continue to elude you.

TAURUS/FOUR/NINE

If only you were not quite so quick-tempered and impulsive then you would not make so many silly mistakes. You have a great deal to offer both at work and at home but more often than not you spoil your chances by speaking out of turn or giving up because you lack patience. You need to make a more consistent effort, try a little harder to please, even if it does go against the grain, and learn to accept criticism with good grace.

TAURUS/FIVE/ONE

If it was not for your stubborn single-mindedness you probably would not get anywhere. But provided you work hard and remain goal-conscious you should manage to reach your targets. You are also rather adventurous by nature which means you can take changes in your stride. However too much variety in your personal life could lead to unnecessary complications.

TAURUS/FIVE/TWO

Emotional security and a stable home life are the two things you strive most for and sadly are perhaps the two things you are most unlikely to achieve for many reasons. You are possessive, moody and jealous. You try hard to be faithful but somehow cannot resist the occasional little clandestine assignment. This is hardly a recipe for personal success and unless you mend your ways you are heading for trouble.

TAURUS/FIVE/THREE

Sometimes you can be much too sharp and clever for your own good. Being a know-all would not do much for your popularity ratings either. You can never resist the urge to show off, take great delight in running mental rings around people of slower intellect than yourself, and generally put everyone's back up with your acid tongue. You need to be more thorough and reliable and far less frivolous and flippant.

TAURUS/FIVE/FOUR

Without your practical common sense you would get into some real muddles. Most of your madcap schemes never get past the embryo stage and the only fantasies you ever try to act out are strictly personal. You need to guard against over-indulgence and excess as this will put unnecessary strain on your health which could lead to problems in later life.

TAURUS/FIVE/FIVE

Living on your nerves can be a dangerous pastime for someone as restless and excitable as you. You are talented, clever and original but seldom put these gifts to good use, preferring instead to follow a free-and-easy life style. The opposite sex is a source of constant fascination and attraction to someone with your strong drives and desires. But tread with care and remember to be discreet if you do not want your exploits to become common knowledge.

TAURUS/FIVE/SIX

When viewing career options try to choose a field which offers either scope for personal expression or the opportunity to travel because you do not like to feel cooped up for too long. When selecting a partner try to find someone who is either a sinner, like you, or a saint. You should get on famously with a partner who shares your enthusiasm for life.

TAURUS/FIVE/SEVEN

You are one of those all-or-nothing people who are either full of life and raring to go, or down in the dumps feeling indecisive and depressed. You seem to have no shades of grey. Try to put more method into your madness, a little bit of order into the chaos you create and more sincerity into your personal affairs.

TAURUS/FIVE/EIGHT

Pride comes before a fall – a motto which should be kept firmly in mind all the time. Even the best laid plans of mice, men and Taurus/Five/Eights can go wrong occasionally and when they do it is very spectacular. You tend to see things on a broad, overall scale and really need to spend more time assessing minor details and looking out for tiny flaws before putting your ideas into action.

TAURUS/FIVE/NINE

Accidents will happen and because you are usually in such a hurry to get things done you are a prime candidate. Curb your impatience, think before you act and leave impulse to those who can afford to take the risk. The same holds true with your private life. Give relationships more time to develop and make sure that you are entering into them for the right reasons.

TAURUS/SIX/ONE

Your home life should be a model of peace, harmony and domestic bliss because you are loyal, sincere and prefer compromise to full scale arguments. You would do anything in your power to help those you love, and always lend a sympathetic ear to their problems. At work it is a different picture because although you are ambitious and want to get on, you find working under pressure rather wearing and hate telling others what to do.

TAURUS/SIX/TWO

From a career point of view you need to find a way of marketing your talents in the least stressful way. You work best in a quiet, sheltered environment with someone else to handle the finances, clients and problems, as and when they arise. You are not a commercial animal and never will be. On the home front you are hard to live with because you need constant reassurance, encouragement and demonstrations of affection.

TAURUS/SIX/THREE

Your versatility can be both a blessing and a bind. It certainly means you can turn your hand to most things but when it comes to specializing, the question is – what in? You are a fine artist, a passable musician, an amusing writer and a born communicator. Your home life is bound to be enhanced by these gifts but unfortunately there are not many openings these days for a Jack-of-all-trades.

TAURUS/SIX/FOUR

Why must you always hide your light under a bushel? You do not mind compliments on your organization and efficiency but when they praise your creative prowess you act embarrassed. Do not be so apologetic and do not be tempted to give up an enjoyable hobby for fear of what others might think.

TAURUS/SIX/FIVE

Talented, clever and original you may be, but do not go pushing your luck too often. Everyone has to work hard to achieve results and you are no exception. The world does not owe you a living and the sooner you realize that the better. When it comes to your personal life you cannot have your cake and eat it too.

TAURUS/SIX/SIX

Try not to get too deeply involved in other people's affairs or you will soon find yourself weighed down with problems you had not bargained for. You are kind and understanding; open-minded, helpful and an absolute push-over for hard luck stories. Keep your mind on your job not on your work mates' problems, look after your own family and let the neighbours take care of themselves.

TAURUS/SIX/SEVEN

You need to set a little time aside for yourself each day otherwise your work, family and friends will take over your life. You must also learn to say no and mean it or you will find yourself doing all sorts of jobs you do not really want to do. Being helpful and considerate is one thing, but being a doormat for someone to walk on is another.

TAURUS/SIX/EIGHT

With your talent and business acumen you should not put a foot wrong if you snap up opportunities as and when they arise and do not allow emotion to colour your judgement. But you will need to take a tougher line with your family and friends because you cannot go rushing about at their beck and call when there is work to be done. And you cannot afford to drop everything just because your partner has a day off and wants to spend it with you.

TAURUS/SIX/NINE

If you are at loggerheads with the world then you have only got yourself to blame. You are ambitious, enterprising and determined but you need to rise above personalities and this is something you often seem unable to do. Control your temper, slow down a little and concentrate more on matters in hand rather than those around you.

TAURUS/SEVEN/ONE

You need to keep your mind firmly on the goal you have set yourself otherwise there is a very real danger that you will go off course. Keep business and pleasure in two separate compartments. Always remember that at work you need to be single-minded and purposeful.

TAURUS/SEVEN/TWO

At work you would do better as part of a team rather than trying to go it alone. But in private you need a strong, reliable partner to guide you. Emotional and financial security are important to you although you do very little to earn either. Jealousy often spoils your relationships and your career can be marred by inertia and indecision.

TAURUS/SEVEN/THREE

You cannot go playing the fool all the time unless you decide to take up politics or acting for a career. Why do you always have to do things differently from everyone else? Your non-conformist ways will probably get you into trouble more quickly than they will earn you recognition. You are a rebel without a cause and the sooner you see sense the better.

TAURUS/SEVEN/FOUR

When your common sense dictates a particular course of action you would be best advised to follow it up. It's when you start playing hunches that you run into difficulties. Stick to tried and tested methods both at work and at home because, in your case, these formulae will turn out the best.

TAURUS/SEVEN/FIVE

Running away is no answer to problems. You need to develop more self-confidence, a greater understanding of human nature and stop wishing for the moon. Life is not a bed of roses and once you find you can take the rough with the smooth you will be more than half way towards making something of yourself.

TAURUS/SEVEN/SIX

You are in a rather difficult situation because, although you are talented, that alone is not enough to guarantee you a living. You have known all along what you would like to do with your life but have had to come to terms with the fact that it is not always possible to achieve your ambitions so second best is what you have grudgingly had to accept. Provided you do not let bitterness and resentment spill over into your private life this is one area which you could find particularly rewarding.

TAURUS/SEVEN/SEVEN

Some people simply cannot handle money, responsibility or pressure and you are one of them. You are totally unrealistic, impractical and inclined to be lazy.

You live in a world of your own which you people and furnish with your fantasies. Your best bet is to get yourself a strong partner on whom you can heavily lean at all times.

TAURUS/SEVEN/EIGHT

Although relationships could prove to be frustrating and difficult, mainly because of your changeable moods and possessiveness, your financial prospects look much brighter. You are capable of concentrated effort and relentless application but only for short periods at a time. Once you have learned to take things easy and to work at a steady pace your output should be less erratic, more consistent and much in demand.

TAURUS/SEVEN/NINE

Try not to worry so much about things which may never happen and concentrate more on what you could achieve with just a little more effort. Do not think about acid rain, pollution and nuclear disaster if these things upset you. Live more for today and, just for once, let tomorrow take care of itself.

TAURUS/EIGHT/ONE

With your rigid self-control, tenacity and determination you could achieve just about anything in your chosen field. Try not to be quite so hard and intolerant because, should you ever fall from grace, you may find yourself reaping a bitter harvest, especially when others decide to settle old scores. The same applies to your relationships.

TAURUS/EIGHT/TWO

Never take on more than you can handle! You are fine when things are running smoothly but you tend to crack under pressure. A working partnership might be worth considering especially as you find money difficult to manage. In private you have certainly got to learn to stand on your own two feet. Smile more often, make light of your problems and try not to be quite so moody.

TAURUS/EIGHT/THREE

Hang on to your sense of humour and your hat — you might need one and lose the other the way you carry on. You always want to run before you can walk, start off with good intentions but lose momentum half way through and cut far too many corners for your own safety. Your attitude frightens more customers than it attracts and, in private, you need to be more subtle and less like a bull in a china shop.

TAURUS/EIGHT/FOUR

You are cool, calm and calculating just like Patience on her monument. With you it's discipline, self-control and a stiff upper lip at all times and while you may build yourself a business empire by these methods you're going to get very lonely all by yourself. Let yourself go, relax, learn how to enjoy yourself and don't be quite so mean and penny-pinching.

TAURUS/EIGHT/FIVE

You take the most alarming risks, are always prepared to try something new and exciting and seem to be constantly on the go. You would do almost anything to get on in the world but living on your nerves isn't good for you over long periods of time. What is more, your busy love life takes up all your spare time. If you don't ease up and learn a little self-discipline you won't be fit enough to enjoy the fruits of your labours.

TAURUS/EIGHT/SIX

A point of balance is what you must achieve between your career and your personal commitments. If you take work home you'll have no opportunity to relax and if you allow your private affairs to encroach upon valuable business time you'll soon lose custom. With just a little forward planning this should be an easy exercise for someone of your ability.

TAURUS/EIGHT/SEVEN

Make sure your ideas are feasible before you put them into action. You also need to keep a tight rein on your purse strings as money quickly runs through your fingers. The same could apply to your partner. Give more time and attention to your personal life and don't be quite such a loner, most experiences are better shared.

TAURUS/EIGHT/EIGHT

Mammon has to be your god because all you ever talk about, think about or even dream about is money. You simply want to get rich and you're not always fussy about how you do so. But watch your step because the way down is much quicker than the way up. In the event that you have time for a private life, it's unlikely to be rewarding, because you're rather offhand and undemonstrative by nature.

TAURUS/EIGHT/NINE

You are very ambitious and quite prepared to work all hours if necessary. However, all work and no play not only makes you dull and uninteresting, especially when you will insist upon talking shop, but it can also play havoc with your health in later life. Enjoy your home life and don't be in such a hurry to notch up your first ulcer.

TAURUS/NINE/ONE

Leadership is undoubtedly one of your strong points. You are active, confident and hard-working but you tend to carry your independence to extremes by refusing offers of help when you could truthfully do with some. What's more, you're very good at giving orders and advice but surly and churlish if you happen to be on the receiving end. Try to take the middle path more often.

TAURUS/NINE/TWO

Second in command would be the perfect position for you because it would mean you would have some authority and also someone to whom you could pass the buck. You could make an excellent administrator or mediator but are far too emotional and thin skinned to handle real power. Your basic insecurity is most noticeable in your private life.

TAURUS/NINE/THREE

You are far too hasty to be thorough and too sarcastic to be widely liked. You must also take your personal life more seriously. It's all very well being witty and entertaining just so long as you know when to stop playing the fool. The trouble is — you don't!

TAURUS/NINE/FOUR

While your name may never become a household word or your work world-famous, within your own social circle you're bound to gain respect. You are practical, hard-working and very down-to-earth. However, woe betide anyone who ever dares to cross you. Although you may never cast the first stone you will always have the final word and the last laugh.

TAURUS/NINE/FIVE

Itchy feet is your problem — you always have to see what's round the next corner, or whether the grass is greener somewhere else. Although you may gain valuable experience you never stay anywhere long enough to build up a strong foundation. Your private life follows much the same pattern. You go from one partner to another in rapid succession filling your address book with numbers, your nights with passion but your old age with what?

TAURUS/NINE/SIX

You are what is known as 'a good all rounder'. Natural caution is what holds you back along with stubbornness, complacency and lack of objective. You have all the right qualities to achieve great things but you don't martial your resources properly. Become more demanding and push yourself harder.

TAURUS/NINE/SEVEN

Why is it that you can advise other people, help them with their problems and turn out a good days work, when at home you get yourself into such a muddle? It is probably because you are a loner and with only yourself to fend for you can't be bothered to make an effort. You need to get out and about more, widen your circle of friends and smarten yourself up.

TAURUS/NINE/EIGHT

At work you are certainly on the ball. You know exactly what you want, where you're going and how best to get it. Unfortunately in private, your act is virtually non-existent. Your problem lies in the inconsistent way you express your feelings. You're not an easy person to live with because your moods change so frequently and unless you take steps to resolve this problem your relationships will almost certainly continue to come under pressure.

TAURUS/NINE/NINE

Generally you need to make a greater effort to keep that stubborn streak, a characteristic of many Taureans, better hidden. On the work front you should try to accept criticism without the usual ensuing arguments, while at home every attempt should be made to become a better listener — something which Nines are not well known for.

GEMINI/ONE/ONE

Once you've managed to get the gypsy out of your soul and decide to opt for a particular course of action you should make rapid strides along the pathway to success. But if you continue to act like a butterfly you won't get anywhere at all. You have a wide and varied range of talents all of which should be useful to you in your chosen career, particularly your ability to communicate. The message is clear — settle down and apply yourself.

GEMINI/ONE/TWO

Emotionally you need to get a firm grip on yourself, you're far too sensitive and changeable. Your confidence could also do with some bolstering so try to seek the company of people who will encourage and reassure you. Once you've adopted a more positive attitude and stopped feeling so shy and self-conscious then your life should show an all round improvement.

GEMINI/ONE/THREE

What you need is a safety valve; some safe and harmless way of letting off steam, well away from work or home. A hard, strenuous work-out at the local gymnasium, a game of squash or a trip to the local pool would all fit the bill. That way your restlessness wouldn't irritate those around you.

GEMINI/ONE/FOUR

You could do a lot better in life if you weren't quite so cautious. You are versatile, well-informed and articulate but you lack that vital spark of interest and curiosity.

By the time you've weighed up all the pro's and con's, opportunity has passed you by. Admittedly it is better to be safe than sorry, but equally true is, who dares wins.

GEMINI/ONE/FIVE

It is high time you had your brakes looked at and your eyes tested because you never seem to realize when to stop. You take frightening risks when everyone else can see the dangers, you push yourself far too hard working to the point of physical and mental exhaustion then you stay up half the night in the pursuit of pleasure.

GEMINI/ONE/SIX

Your main problem in life is making decisions. There are so many interesting possibilities open to a person with your abilities that the difficulty lies in making a choice. However, there are also one or two things you should guard against, with conceit heading the list followed closely by complacency, restlessness and inconsistency.

GEMINI/ONE/SEVEN

People are drawn to you like so many moths to a candle flame, and while this can do wonders for your ego it can also be intensely irritating because you seldom seem to get more than a few minutes to yourself each day. It can also make your home life rather difficult when friends and neighbours pop in and out all the time.

GEMINI/ONE/EIGHT

You can't help thinking big but you often forget to pay attention to detail, which could cause your downfall. Small things don't interest you, but they should, because one silly mistake or miscalculation could tip the balance between success and failure. You also need to work harder at your private life. Inconsistency is the main fault here.

GEMINI/ONE/NINE

Don't let your imagination run away with you. Careers and relationships take time to develop and although you can picture yourself being both successful and happy it is never really that simple. At work you're ambitious and impatient to see results and you'll only do that through relentless application not wishful thinking. So too in your private life, there's no instant recipe for harmony and contentment.

GEMINI/TWO/ONE

Your ideas are original, your qualifications and experience impressive but you will let personalities spoil your performance and stand in the way of progress. You can't afford to let other people's opinions influence your decisions and you certainly shouldn't allow emotions to cloud your judgement. Don't worry quite so much about what others think and rely more upon yourself.

GEMINI/TWO/TWO

It has to be said that you are an emotional disaster area and if you don't get a grip on yourself both your business and personal life could end up in ruins. In private you're jealous, possessive and moody, while at work you can be cruel, malicious and deceitful. Perhaps if you had a better opinion of yourself and your worth it would be a different story.

GEMINI/TWO/THREE

Lady Luck certainly smiles on you because you get away with murder and you know it. At work you get everyone else jumping while you swan off to enjoy yourself. In private you expect fidelity and commitment while you do exactly as you please. One of these days your luck's going to run out.

GEMINI/TWO/FOUR

There's not much difference between tenacity and stubbornness as far as you're concerned because once your mind is made up nothing will ever change it. You need to become more versatile and less rigid, otherwise your work will never progress, your relationships will grow stale and you'll remain in the same old rut for the rest of your life.

GEMINI/TWO/FIVE

You are one of those people who is always around but seldom there when wanted. You never sit still for five minutes, seem unable to stay in one place for long and are always looking for something new and exciting to try. You're as restless as a caged lion. The only way you'll ever settle down will be when someone finally locks you up and throws away the key.

GEMINI/TWO/SIX

Although you dislike unpleasantness of any kind more often that not you're the cause of it. At work you seem to spend more time minding other people's business and monitoring their progress than you put in on your own job. You're critical, fussy over detail and rather inclined to gossip. While at home your changeable moods would try the patience of a saint. You ought to count your blessings more often, worry less about other people and get your emotions fully under control.

GEMINI/TWO/SEVEN

There is no real reason why you shouldn't be moderately successful because you are bright and intelligent yet you regard work as nothing more than a means to an end and your relationships as transitory moments of pleasure. The truth of the matter is that you're lazy, impractical and unambitious. If you spent a little more time considering your future and a little less time day-dreaming that would be a good start.

GEMINI/TWO/EIGHT

With your business acumen, sound judgement and flair for finance you've practically got it made as far as your career is concerned. But where you do fall down is when the lights are low and the setting is intimate. Close encounters of any kind tend to intimidate you because you hate getting into situations you can't handle.

GEMINI/TWO/NINE

Variety is the spice of life but ringing the changes too often, as you're rather inclined to do, will only result in muddle, confusion and much wated time, not progress. Be more diplomatic in your handling of other people, try to get some continuity into your daily affairs and don't expect the impossible from any relationship or you will be disappointed.

GEMINI/THREE/ONE

Provided you stick to what you know best and don't give in to the temptation to diversify your interests you shouldn't go too far wrong. Self-control, hard work and fidelity are the order of the day, if a relatively trouble-free existence is what you're after. If not, 'then live now — pay later' would be more appropriate.

GEMINI/THREE/TWO

Which is it to be — a good steady job, a fulfilling relationship and personal security or constant change, dramatic upheavals and a lonely existence? The choice is yours, because you have within you, all the ingredients to create either. Your confused emotional state is at the bottom of it all and unless you pull yourself together and stop being so moody and difficult no one will be prepared to put up with you for very long.

GEMINI/THREE/THREE

It will probably be more down to luck than sound judgement that you get on in this life. Admittedly you are versatile, intelligent and expansive but you lack discipline, staying power and reliability. Initially you are always full of enthusiasm until something else comes along to take your fancy and then off you go at yet another tangent. You are also far too outspoken and need to learn the wisdom of silence.

GEMINI/THREE/FOUR

Your career advancement will ultimately be dictated by your own attitude. If you remain keen and interested then progress is possible but once you allow your mind to wander your performance will do the same. In private you seem to make the same mistake time and again. Try to learn more from experience and don't imagine that just because things are going well no further effort is required.

GEMINI/THREE/FIVE

You are a born gambler, a dreadful fidget and about as predictable as a nuclear reactor which has reached melt-down. At work your efforts are erratic while in private your thoughts are generally of an erotic nature. Your approach lacks subtlety, your performance lacks finesse and it seems to be quantity rather than quality which is your main consideration.

GEMINI/THREE/SIX

You have an eye for colour, a flair for design and a fertile imagination. You need to express yourself artistically and should bear this in mind when making career decisions. You're also a born homemaker with a style of your own. People are drawn to you because you are sympathetic, understanding and prepared to listen to their troubles but on no account should you ever take the law into your own hands and interfere in the domestic affairs of others.

GEMINI/THREE/SEVEN

Like an absent-minded professor you'd forget your head if it wasn't screwed on tightly. You're intelligent and well-educated yet you lack the basic ability to get yourself organized and this is reflected both at home and in your work. Smarten yourself up, show more interest in your appearance and get some order into your life. A new image could make all the difference between success and failure.

GEMINI/THREE/EIGHT

You are one of those people who will be either a resounding success or a spectacular failure because you're far too intractable. What you need is to find a middle, less hazardous path to take which would involve fewer risks. You find people difficult to handle in an amicable fashion and this is your main stumbling block. You're much too aggressive, far too ruthless and totally without scruples. You must try to be more sociable!

GEMINI/THREE/NINE

What you must learn is not to be quite so touchy. While you're not actually an out-and-out rebel you certainly border on insubordination. You dislike being told what to do, resent any form of interference in your affairs and simply cannot take criticism of any kind. Try to put your fighting spirit to better use, don't be quite so quick to take offence and be generally more diplomatic all round.

GEMINI/FOUR/ONE

An intense determination to succeed is what drives you relentlessly on but the goals you hope to achieve must be reached on your own terms. You will accept neither help nor advice because you're so fiercely independent. Don't be quite so ready to turn down offers of assistance and a word or two in the right ear can't do any harm.

GEMINI/FOUR/TWO

Organization, imagination and creativity are your three strong points but its your basic insecurity which lets you down every time. Without more confidence you'll never be able to project yourself. Unfortunately shyness prevents you from making new friends and your unpredictable moods often mar established relationships.

GEMINI/FOUR/THREE

Sometimes you can be a little too clever for your own good. Your quick wits keep you one jump ahead of everyone else but all too often you forget to look before you leap. Your know-all attitude could seriously damage the brilliant career prospects which lie ahead of you. On the personal front you're neither given to jealousy nor possessiveness but you seldom take relationships seriously enough and are generally much too restless and erratic in your behaviour patterns.

GEMINI/FOUR/FOUR

What you lack is will-power and self-control. All too often your plans misfire because you don't pay enough attention to detail. You're also inconsistent, and this shows up most at work. You must learn to pace yourself better and at home your attention and interest also seem to go in fits and starts which can be irritating for your partner and potentially damaging to your relationship.

GEMINI/FOUR/FIVE

By day you're a model citizen and a hard-working employee but by night its anyone's guess what you get up to. Your track record and general standard of behaviour is exemplary and faultless yet you have one great weakness which you do your best to hide. The opposite sex is a source of constant attraction to you, the urge to gamble is strong and the high life is something you'd like to take up full time if only you could afford to.

GEMINI/FOUR/SIX

Although you would far rather stay at home it's not always possible to do as you please. Domesticity suits you but unless you can come up with some home-based way of earning a living, you'll have to go out to earn a crust like everyone else. Remember to take your creativity and artistic flair into consideration when making career applications or decisions.

GEMINI/FOUR/SEVEN

Your main problem is that your right hand seldom knows what your left hand is doing. Try to be more open about yourself and your movements, extend the hand of friendship more often and, above all, be more trusting. Your suspicions are likely to be unfounded, your fears imaginary and your jealousy misplaced.

GEMINI/FOUR/EIGHT

Can't you ever see the funny side of life? You're so serious about everything, particularly money, that you never take time off to relax and enjoy yourself. Devote more time to your private life because it needs it. The wheels of industry won't grind to a halt if you go missing for a couple of days, your relationship should improve and you'll return to the foray feeling refreshed and invigorated.

GEMINI/FOUR/NINE

Your prospects look promising because incorporated in your character are some very useful components such as originality and quick wits. Unfortunately you also crave affection and tend to make a lot of silly mistakes in your personal life. Try to distinguish between physical attraction and compatability — there is a subtle difference! Don't try quite so hard to please and don't go baring your soul to all and sundry on first acquaintance.

GEMINI/FIVE/ONE

A career in sales would be right up your street because you're very persuasive. You go down particularly well at social gatherings, quickly assuming the role of 'life-and-soul-of-the-party', yet your relationships tend to be tempestuous and short-lived affairs. Develop wider interests and learn new skills because your looks won't last forever.

GEMINI/FIVE/TWO

Not only are you restless and changeable, you're also fickle and undisciplined. You crave emotional and financial security yet you adopt a lifestyle and attitude which will deny you both. The sooner you stop wishing for the moon and blaming your shortcomings on everyone else the sooner you'll be able to get yourself organized.

GEMINI/FIVE/THREE

A certain amount of interest shows intelligence and asking the odd carefully chosen question will give you a clear picture, but to go blatantly tramping around in other people's private affairs is unforgivable. Friendship involves an exchange of ideas, relationships shared intimacy but you want to own people and that's where you go wrong. Learn to keep your distance and don't interfere in matters that don't concern you.

GEMINI/FIVE/FOUR

Not only are you careless, you're also rather weak-willed, preferring to take the easy way out whenever possible. At work and at home you act like an ostrich pretending that problems don't exist, rather than facing up to them in an adult, responsible manner. You're not stupid but you sometimes act as if you are.

GEMINI/FIVE/FIVE

You are sensual, superficial and quick-tempered. Like a fractious child you need constant amusement. Variety is a spice you can't get enough of and your energy is inexhaustible, as is your sexual appetite. You are virtually impossible to tie down, and it's no good offering you advice because you just wouldn't listen. You will have to learn the hard way or not at all.

GEMINI/FIVE/SIX

When it comes to throwing an impromptu party or entertaining in a lavish style you're the one to do it. People fascinate you and your wide circle of friends includes men and women from all walks of life. You seem to know instinctively how to put others at their ease, to keep the conversation flowing and the pot boiling. It's a pity you don't treat your work with the same enthusiasm.

GEMINI/FIVE/SEVEN

What you need is stimulation, variety and a challenge worthy of your steel and you won't find that unless you go and look for it. It's no use sitting around idly bemoaning your lot, use that imagination of yours, stir yourself and stop procrastinating. If your job doesn't suit you, then change it when a suitable opportunity arises.

GEMINI/FIVE/EIGHT

Actions speak louder than words. There's a vast difference between talking about what you're going to do and actually putting your plans into action. You need to take a tougher line with yourself, show a bit more determination and make a positive effort. Your boss is probably fed up with hearing your lame excuses and your partner equally sick of empty promises.

GEMINI/FIVE/NINE

You have a visionary quality about you but unfortunately you're always looking so far afield that you fail to notice what's going on under your nose. You are so busy scanning the papers for vacancies in exotic, foreign countries that a heaven-sent career opportunity in your own area completely escapes your notice. In your private life too you tend to live in the future rather than the here and now.

GEMINI/SIX/ONE

On the credit side you have charm, intelligence and talent but unfortunately your books won't be easy to balance because you're extravagant, superficial and lazy. You need to make a greater effort all round; try to be less wasteful with your time and much more careful with your money. Remember that you don't go to work to play, you are there to earn a living and if you don't pull your weight your employers will soon find someone else who will.

GEMINI/SIX/TWO

Deep down you are shy and insecure but trying to make up for your shortcomings by pretending to be something you're not simply won't work. Relax, be yourself; you may not win an Oscar for your performance but you won't have to playact any more either.

GEMINI/SIX/THREE

It is always such a pity to see so much talent going to waste when, with just a little time, effort and application, you could carve a brilliant career for yourself. You have a fine brain which you won't use, gifts you squander and abilities you don't appreciate. Only your wit and conversational skills are ever given a proper airing.

GEMINI/SIX/FOUR

You spend far too much time nursing other people and not nearly enough on yourself. You work your fingers to the bone but never in a way that will ultimately benefit your own career or personal life, always on behalf of others. The agony aunts of newspaper fame are paid for their advice — you are not. Weed out the time-wasters, don't be such a soft touch and learn to say 'no' firmly, irrevocably but in the nicest possible manner.

GEMINI/SIX/FIVE

Pathos, comedy, tragedy, farce — you could handle them all without batting an eyelid because play-acting is your forte. You could be an outstanding performer and a resounding success. Unfortunately the character you choose to play in real life is not you, but just an act you put on to make yourself appear more interesting. Sadly it attracts all the wrong people.

GEMINI/SIX/SIX

How you'd love to join the ranks of the idle rich with nothing to do and all day long to do it in. But unless you've a private income or are planning to rob a bank the chances of this happening are negligible. Try to look on the bright side and count your blessings. You've got a lot going for you if only you'd be serious for a minute.

GEMINI/SIX/SEVEN

Anyone attempting to compile your autobiography would never be able to give a true representation of your character because you don't really know who you are yourself. There would certainly be plenty of amusing incidents to recount, a fair sprinkling of spice in your personal life and a few noteworthy points to include concerning your career but when it comes to judging whether you were happy or not it would be impossible to tell. You keep your thoughts to yourself, your ambitions a secret and your true feelings well hidden.

GEMINI/SIX/EIGHT

You really are very wicked pretending to be someone you're not because this gives you an unfair advantage but then you were never known for your scruples. Although you are well aware of what's right and what's wrong you will alter the definition to suit your purposes and bend the rules to fit in with your plans. On the surface you appear charming, agreeable and rather amusing but this is a ploy. Underneath you're as cunning as a fox and as dangerous as a rattlesnake.

GEMINI/SIX/NINE

Confidence and self-assurance are admirable qualities which can help you get on in life both at home and at work but you have taken these both a step too far. You're self-centred, conceited and arrogant. You often bore everyone with your opinions and never tire of admiring yourself in the mirror. Once you start considering everyone else the balance can be redressed but until then people will usually continue to avoid you.

GEMINI/SEVEN/ONE

With hard work and dedication success should be within your grasp particularly if the career you opt for provides you with the opportunity to travel and be generally mobile. Your relationships could also be rewarding if you bear in mind that it takes two to argue but only one to cry off and end things abruptly. Unfortunately most of your potential is wasted because you're disorganized, fanciful and unrealistic.

GEMINI/SEVEN/TWO

Most of your problems at work are of your own making. You need to stand up more for your rights and stop being so submissive. It is hardly surprising that you often become saddled with all the rotten jobs and are at the bottom of the pecking order. Your private life would also look up if you weren't so jealous and possessive. Deep down you may well be feeling afraid and insecure but you won't sustain any relationship if you persistently strangle it at birth.

GEMINI/SEVEN/THREE

It's unbelievable how anyone quite so intelligent can make such silly mistakes. You're versatile, clever and observant. In fact you ought to be an asset to any employer yet you persistently open your mouth and put your foot right in it. You are outspoken and totally lacking in tact or discretion. However, on the personal front it is what you don't say that matters. You're far too easy-come-easy-go about your relationships.

GEMINI/SEVEN/FOUR

There must be a method somewhere in your madness otherwise you would surely have come unstuck by now. You never seem to have any set routine to follow, a target to aim at or deadlines to meet. You're really quite an enigma. You can turn your hand to most things, never flap in a crisis, seldom get ruffled and rarely blow your top. But just think what you could achieve if you really put your mind to it. Your potential is enormous.

GEMINI/SEVEN/FIVE

It is very hard to say what goes on in that head of yours because you give so little away. Sometimes you seem to be in a world of your own and at other times are busily engaged in some absorbing task. However it is plain to see that your partner doesn't get much of a look in and it's quite obvious that you work best on your own. If you choose to remain in such enforced isolation you could eventually become very lonely.

GEMINI/SEVEN/SIX

You have a wonderful imagination so why not put it to good use both at work and at play. Businesses thrive on good ideas and while not all yours are strictly viable propositions the odd one or two have great potential. What is more your relationship would benefit from a break in routine. You could probably dream up fantasies far quicker than you and your partner could enact them.

GEMINI/SEVEN/SEVEN

If you spent more time doing and less time thinking, you'd begin to get somewhere. When given a choice you are indecisive, when given an opportunity you'll daydream and when given the sack you'll know why. This applies equally to your private affairs. Your intentions are good but you rarely get around to converting your plans into realities.

GEMINI/SEVEN/EIGHT

Energy can be expended both positively and negatively. You can use your time and effort constructively when hopefully you'll benefit from the results but you can so easily dissipate both on foolish schemes and ill planned ventures. You score heavily in terms of tenacity and application but fall down every time when it comes to ground work and preparation.

GEMINI/SEVEN/NINE

A fool and his money are soon parted, you have only to look at the red figures on your bank statement to realize how true this old adage is. You buy things on impulse, invite people over to dinner too often and spoil your partner wickedly. And where does it get you — into debt. Don't be so reckless with your money, stop and see how many friends ask you back for a meal and be more generous with compliments and attention rather than surprise presents and treats for your loved ones.

GEMINI/EIGHT/ONE

What you need to watch out for is the danger of becoming a workaholic. Your performance does you credit, your punctuality and time-keeping are faultless and your dedication to duty is only too apparent as you wend your way home each evening with a sheaf of files and papers to read through. Unfortunately your private affairs are seldom shown the same consideration because you're rather inclined to take people for granted. Sexually you're unimaginative and emotionally unfeeling.

GEMINI/EIGHT/TWO

Poorly controlled emotions will let you down time and again if you don't make an effort to stop them clouding your judgement. At work shyness and lack of confidence are the culprits. In private jealousy, suspicion and possessiveness are the root causes of all your personal problems and in general terms insecurity of both the emotional and financial variety lies at the bottom of everything.

GEMINI/EIGHT/THREE

A set of stabilizers is what you need to stop you bouncing around all over the place and to keep you on an even keel. You lack discipline and this is a vital ingredient for someone as ambitious as you. Without some form of order or routine in your life the results you'll achieve will only be mediocre at best. However, when your energy is channelled in a constructive direction and your attention properly focused you will be well on the way to realizing your full potential.

GEMINI/EIGHT/FOUR

You're in real danger of becoming a bore, if you're not one already. You're like an automaton which has been programmed to perform a single task — work. You are thorough, precise and totally efficient. You never make a mistake because you double check everything, never live beyond your means because you calculate to the last penny and you never talk about anything but your job because that's all you're interested in.

GEMINI/EIGHT/FIVE

No one could fault the work you turn out because you know exactly what you are doing and you do it well. But the wisdom of many of your other actions could certainly be questioned as only a fool would combine business with pleasure in the way you do. There's a time and place for everything and frequent amorous involvements with colleagues and workmates may well be enjoyable but will ultimately be damaging to your career.

GEMINI/EIGHT/SIX

Talent will always out and in your case it would be a good idea to seek a position where your undeniable artistic skills and flair for design could be commercially marketed because a dull, routine job would soon get you down. You need room to express yourself and at home you'll soon run out of space. You are good and you know it; however, your danger lies in letting arrogance get out of hand.

GEMINI/EIGHT/SEVEN

Laziness, lack of motivation and inconsistency are your three great stumbling blocks, without which you could be well on your way to success both at work and in private. Commit yourself to a course of action and stick with it even when the going gets difficult. You need a bomb behind you to get you started, a sheepdog at your heels to keep you on course and a good accountant to keep track of your winnings as they could be considerable.

GEMINI/EIGHT/EIGHT

You could be one of two things. Either a resounding success or a complete and utter failure. Mediocrity is one label you will never bear because you have no shades of grey. You're an all or nothing person. You are ambitious, tenacious and hell-bent on making it to the top and the only thing which will stop you is your own inability to spot minor flaws before they do any great overall damage.

GEMINI/EIGHT/NINE

Don't be tempted to run before you've learned how to walk. This advice applies equally to your work and your personal affairs. You're impulsive by nature, not the most patient of people and rather inclined to give up at the first sign of trouble. Get more discipline into your life, be more consistent and take matters one step at a time. Don't be in such a hurry and allow things more time in which to develop.

GEMINI/NINE/ONE

Rigid self-control and a fiercely independent nature are your two greatest assets. The former because you don't suffer fools gladly but have the sense not to put them right and the latter because you don't need any help or encouragement to achieve your goals. However, you're such a forceful, dominant character that although aggression and tenacity often pay dividends at work, a gentler touch would be more preferable in your private affairs.

GEMINI/NINE/TWO

You need to be a bit quicker off the mark if you're ever going to take full advantage of opportunities that come your way. Playing safe is all well and good but the odd calculated risk could be even better. Your motivation seems to have deserted you and the sooner it's found again the better. Be more decisive, don't let people wipe their feet on you and remember that fear of failure is tantamount to an admission of defeat.

GEMINI/NINE/THREE

It's about time you stopped being quite so witty and amusing and settled down to some good, old-fashioned hard work or the last laugh will undoubtedly be on you. How often does the life-and-soul-of-the-party become a captain of industry or have a demanding, responsible job to hold down? You have tremendous potential which you squander in the pursuit of pleasure and fun.

GEMINI/NINE/FOUR

You'll only ever go wrong if you act impulsively or from emotion and that's out of character because you pride yourself on your discipline. However, too much icy self-control could mar a potentially rewarding relationship. Learn to relax more in private, let your guard drop and don't be so afraid of allowing your true feelings to show.

GEMINI/NINE/FIVE

You're restless, impulsive and far too fond of playing with fire. Your mind is never on your work, you seem unable to concentrate and you take too many risks. You've got adventure on the brain, the gypsy in your soul and an insatiable appetite for the opposite sex. Luck fortunately favours you so whatever difficulties you get into you usually manage to bounce back again smelling distinctly of roses.

GEMINI/NINE/SIX

Why won't you learn that you don't need a sledge hammer to crack a nut. Tact and discretion have never been your strong points and you should make every effort to acquire a little of both without delay. You must learn not to be so critical of others, to think before you speak and not to go in giving your two pennyworth when it's not required.

GEMINI/NINE/SEVEN

What you lack is initiative and application. You're much too fond of sitting around waiting for opportunity to beat a path to your door. You need to get out and about more and to create your own openings if none already exists. With a wider circle of friends and interests you stand a better chance of improving your personal life and with a more determined attitude hiccups in your career should be easier to deal with.

GEMINI/NINE/EIGHT

The only point of view you can ever see is your own, you only concern yourself with others' problems when they have a knock-on effect on you and the only tears you ever shed are the crocodile variety. It's evident from your behaviour that you fail to realize the importance of any kind of relationship and the sooner you see the light the more fulfilling life could be. A simple show of kindness won't cost anything but the rewards could be incalculable.

GEMINI/NINE/NINE

There's very little you cannot accomplish if you remain calm and in full control of yourself and your hasty temper. Once you allow your passions to run high and the adrenalin to start pumping round your system you might just as well call it a day because you are bound to say things you'll later regret. At work you must learn to take orders more willingly and accept criticism with as much good grace as you can muster.

CANCER/ONE/ONE

At work even though you have butterflies in your stomach and your legs feel like jelly, the display of confidence and self-assurance you present to the world would fool anyone into thinking you were a force to be reckoned with. Truly you are, because who knows better than you the art of putting on a brave face and projecting the right sort of image?

CANCER/ONE/TWO

What you need are an ego-booster and a thicker skin, otherwise you'll be doomed to spending the rest of your life in hiding or being battered about from pillar to post by other people. You suffer from basic insecurity which makes you not only very vulnerable but also easy prey to the manipulators of this world. Don't get out of your depth and only take on commitments which you really feel you can handle.

CANCER/ONE/THREE

You're reasonably versatile and adaptable but people in glass houses should never dish out criticism and sarcasm they can't take themselves. Try to remember how easily you get hurt, stop trying to impress and be something you're not and remember to treat other people in a way you'd like to be treated yourself. That way everyone can be happy.

CANCER/ONE/FOUR

Work, for you, represents nothing more than a means to an end and the sooner it's over and done with the sooner you can return to base. However you should try not to put all your eggs quite so much in one basket. Friendships need to be kept ticking over, outside interests will provide you with stimulation and stop you growing stale and the occasional night off would allow your partner room to breathe because although togetherness is wonderful, possessiveness can become stifling.

CANCER/ONE/FIVE

You are sensitive and easily hurt, yet you will often insist on engaging in sexual high jinks which can only lead you in one direction — down the road to ruin, grief and disenchantment. You give the impression of being so worldly wise yet in many ways you're very naive. You need not only to take a long, hard look at yourself but also to get yourself better organized and into some semblance of a routine.

CANCER/ONE/SIX

You show neither the inclination nor the desire to earn a living, see the world or do anything other than potter about between your own four walls. While this may be intensely satisfying it won't get you very far. Be more decisive, broaden your horizons and get generally more into the swim of things otherwise life will pass you by.

CANCER/ONE/SEVEN

Your danger lies in becoming so self-sufficient and withdrawn that you'll completely lose the ability to relate to the outside world. People are your best therapy. Try to find work in a busy environment where there's lots to do and plenty going on, and make a greater effort to establish some sort of private life.

CANCER/ONE/EIGHT

You need to be more honest and less suspicious because you're not the only person around who may be feeling vulnerable and insecure. No relationship can flourish without simple trust, understanding and sincerity but you never give people time to prove their worth or demonstrate their loyalty. Ease up and don't be so hard on yourself or those around you who could care given the right encouragement.

CANCER/ONE/NINE

You hate to feel insecure in any way yet your impatience drives you to make impulsive moves which threaten the very security you cling to. Rows and arguments upset your delicate sensitivity yet you speak out of turn, rub people up the wrong way and quarrels occur. You crave affection yet you treat those who try to give it to you with mistrust and suspicion. Think before you act, guard your tongue and don't judge everyone by yourself.

CANCER/TWO/ONE

Confidence isn't your strong suit and you'll need to muster all you can to cope successfully with the demands and pressures of a competitive working environment. Your powers of leadership are built upon your innate ability to organize and delegate but unfortunately your authority won't stand up to cross-questioning. In private you can be charming and affectionate and so long as you're prepared to compromise, hopefully most of your domestic troubles will only be little ones.

CANCER/TWO/TWO

You need to buck up your ideas at work and make a more positive effort to pull your weight. Shyness and laziness are not synonymous. Your private affairs too, could do with a thorough overhaul — stop throwing dramatic, emotional scenes and wallowing in self-pity. Be more optimistic and find the bright side to look on for a change.

CANCER/TWO/THREE

As a child you probably drove your mother mad with your constant stream of questions and incessant ploys to gain her undivided attention. Nothing's really changed and it is about time you grew up. Take your work more seriously and learn to co-operate with those around you. Adopt a more mature attitude, honour your commitments and show your partner greater love and respect.

CANCER/TWO/FOUR

Without order, routine and discipline your life would be a shambles. At work you're efficient, industrious and generally far too busy to allow your imagination to run riot. On the home front, common sense is your greatest asset and should be in evidence at all times. Jealousy could prove to be a problem although not an insuperable one whereas moodiness could be the bane of your partner's life unless you make an all out, concerted effort to stamp it out.

CANCER/TWO/FIVE

You're moody, sensitive and easily hurt yet you will insist upon putting your head on a sexual chopping block. You could easily indulge in casual affairs, steamy nights of passion and then tearfully complain that your life is meaningless and no one understands you. Keep away from the oven if you can't stand the heat, you have neither the stamina nor the stability to cope with it.

CANCER/TWO/SIX

Caring for others and ministering to their needs seems to be your self-appointed role in life but is this because your concern is genuine or are you hiding from something? Everyone likes to feel useful and wanted but your self-sacrifice bears all the hallmarks of willing martyrdom. Don't keep making excuses for yourself and trying to live your life second-hand through other people.

CANCER/TWO/SEVEN

You spend far too much time on your own in study or meditation and this has to stop or soon you'll lose all touch with reality and won't be able to distinguish fact from fiction. Get out and about, make contact with groups whose interests are similar to your own and generally be more sociable.

CANCER/TWO/EIGHT

You wouldn't dream of sulking, pouting and behaving petulantly in front of colleagues and customers so why treat your partner in this way? Stop expecting reassurance and encouragement, which you don't deserve, and try to be more understanding and demonstrative.

CANCER/TWO/NINE

Sentiment and romance are all very well in their place but they won't help you very much with your career. Stop behaving like one of the leading characters in a soap-opera, come down to earth and be more realistic. Remember that emotionally charged scenes are unnecessary and unproductive especially in public. Try not to be quite so sensitive and dramatic about everything you do.

CANCER/THREE/ONE

You don't work well on a full stomach, it dulls your wits, so steer clear of executive lunches and avoid discussing anything of a sensitive or political nature over drinks. These tactics may well soften up the opposition but they can also put you off your natural guard. In private, however, the more openness and honesty the better.

CANCER/THREE/TWO

You have many admirable qualities which unfortunately you're not forceful enough to project in a useful direction. Socially you're popular, and from a business point of view you're astute and well-organized but you won't push yourself forward because you lack confidence and ambition. At work you need to set yourself a series of targets to aim for, while in private it's time you came out of your shell.

CANCER/THREE/THREE

You have a natural flair for handling people of all ages from every walk of life. Your face is friendly, your interest seems genuine and your manner is both likeable and inoffensive. However, in private you have the ability to attract partners but never keep them for long.

CANCER/THREE/FOUR

You dislike change and resist it every inch of the way. You need to move with the times, keep abreast of new developments and march with progress instead of fighting against it all the time. Unless you're prepared to accept computers, high-technology and satellite communications as part of the scene you won't get anywhere.

CANCER/THREE/FIVE

You are far too versatile and talented for a dull, routine existence but you still need to toe the line a little more because given an inch you will insist upon taking a mile. As far as your relationships are concerned you undoubtedly go too far by taking the most enormous liberties.

CANCER/THREE/SIX

You are almost too good to be true — efficient, intelligent and successful. You're a hard act to follow and set an example which is virtually impossible to copy. But are you happy? Potential partners could find an angel a little out of their league while saints tend to be celibate. Stop being such a goody-goody, come down from your pedestal and live life properly.

CANCER/THREE/SEVEN

Try to choose a career which will allow you sufficient time to develop your ideas at your own pace, not at the dictates of tight budgets and impossible deadlines. In private avoid the type of person who will try to push you into commitments you're not ready for or make demands on you which you are unwilling to meet. You would be better off missing the boat than getting on the wrong one.

CANCER/THREE/EIGHT

Money isn't everything but in your case it is the root cause of all your problems. You are far too mercenary and inclined to weigh up everything in financial terms. But you can't buy health, friendship or happiness and these are three commodities which are sadly lacking in your life. You're always tired and tense because you work too hard, never seem to have any real friends because you use people and as for happiness how can you ever achieve that when your private life is so hit and miss? It's high time you stopped pricing up the goods and started to learn the value of people.

CANCER/THREE/NINE

Good manners will cost you nothing but impatience, intolerance and rudeness could cost you dear in terms of career and friendship. At home you try hard to please but there's still room for improvement. Your hasty temper could be better controlled while tact and understanding are still on the wanted list.

CANCER/FOUR/ONE

Workaholics seldom live to a ripe old age because they push themselves too hard and make demands on their strength. Relax more and enjoy what you've achieved before pushing on to greater things. You need to pay more attention to your partner or you'll have no one around to look after you if you do crack up.

CANCER/FOUR/TWO

Life is a game played without rules or referees and while the meek may rest assured of a place in heaven they don't fare too well here on earth. Ruthlessness would be out of character for you but a greater show of confidence and determination would improve your prospects enormously at work, while at home you can stay just as sweet as you are.

CANCER/FOUR/THREE

The ability to delegate wisely is a skill you could do with at work. In private don't think its a sign of weakness to accept help when your plate is full to overflowing. You may like to think you can handle anything, and you probably can, but don't insist upon proving it all the time. No one gets medals for being stubborn and pig-headed.

CANCER/FOUR/FOUR

While you may never reach the heights of fame and success, through sheer hard work, there should be simple rewards waiting for you at the end of the day. You've never really asked for anything more than a modest bank balance, a comfortable home and someone to share it with. You have opted for the middle path all along so don't complain, when looking back over the years, you realize that you could have achieved so much more.

CANCER/FOUR/FIVE

Stop cutting corners, taking chances and pushing your luck. Adventure and excitement are luxuries you can't afford. Unless you become more realistic you'll go through life learning lessons the hard way and have nothing much to show for your time but a few painful cuts and bruises.

CANCER/FOUR/SIX

You are a good listener, which is why people confide in you, and if you don't turn into the local gossip you should keep your friends. But remember that when you become involved in other people's business you put yourself in a precarious position so make sure any advice you give is sound and unbiased, any criticism you make is fair and the time your 'counselling service' takes up is not at the expense of your own family.

CANCER/FOUR/SEVEN

Socially you have much to offer. When you do become engaged in conversation what you have to say is witty, interesting and usually topical. At the odd times you're seen out and about you appear to be enjoying yourself and on the rare occasions that you entertain you do so lavishly and well. Stop behaving so mysteriously and denying others the pleasure of your stimulating company.

CANCER/FOUR/EIGHT

Few things escape your notice and those that do you usually spot, and correct if necessary. However if you should happen to suffer a broken marriage, disastrous short-lived relationships or personal unhappiness no one will be at all surprised. In private you're demanding, offhand and temperamental. Unless you stop being the big 'I am' you'll soon find another word gets added to that title — *alone.*

CANCER/FOUR/NINE

Throwing your weight around comes quite naturally to you but if you're hoping to hold down a position of command these tactics won't earn respect. Never ask anyone to do a job you couldn't do yourself if necessary and remember that the quickest way to undermine your own authority is to dish out to others what you can't take yourself. In private you need to be more thoughtful.

CANCER/FIVE/ONE

Originality is the strongest link in your chain of talents. Many other people are capable, hard-working and independent but your ability to create new concepts or fresh variations of old themes puts you one jump ahead of the rest of the pack. Now all you need to find is the confidence to promote your ideas and the staying power to see them through.

CANCER/FIVE/TWO

Whoever programmed you forgot to include stability but gave you an extra helping of sensuality and emotion instead. You will have to work very hard to put this to rights because your basic insecurity will be difficult to overcome particularly as it is counterbalanced by strong sexual desires and moodiness. You need a strong anchor in your personal life to cling on to when the going gets rough.

CANCER/FIVE/THREE

It would be a good idea if you put a brick in both pockets to help keep your feet more firmly on the ground. As it is you're rather inclined to go off at a tangent without completing, or indeed giving a further thought for, the matter already in hand.

CANCER/FIVE/FOUR

You need to stop dithering and be more positive otherwise opportunities won't just come and go — they'll stop altogether. Your personal affairs could also do with some reorganization. Try to go more for quality and rather less for quantity. You may be of a nervous disposition but you risk setting everyone else's nerves on edge too.

CANCER/FIVE/FIVE

You have got a one track mind brought on by a double helping of the earthy number Five. Hot blood courses through your veins, and strong sensual urges prompt you into action. There's no real cure for rampant sexuality and unfortunately you're not well equipped emotionally to handle such strong desires. What you need is rigid self-control and more commonsense.

CANCER/FIVE/SIX

People are important to you for many reasons. You find company stimulating, entertaining a pleasure and are always willing to lend a helping hand. You're also a good listener and can be relied upon to give sound advice. Where work is concerned you would do well in public relations, counselling, nursing or just generally being of service. However, in private you really need to choose a sociable partner who's neither possessive nor jealous as you have many friends and a whole host of interests outside the home.

CANCER/FIVE/SEVEN

Travel broadens the mind and you're a person who likes to do both by visiting new places and gaining as much first hand experience as possible. It's a pity however that you usually have to do so on your own. If you didn't appear quite so studious and standoffish your social life would improve dramatically. Get yourself some new, more modern clothes, read up on confidence and how to acquire it then take a deep breath, put your best foot forward and project yourself.

CANCER/FIVE/EIGHT

You think you can handle anything and frequently bite off more than you can comfortably chew. You need to listen more, that way hopefully you'll learn something useful, get a few accomplishments under your belt and before you even think of picking up your trumpet again remember to depress the soft pedal hard when dealing with members of the opposite sex. Steamroller tactics are for road-menders not would-be lovers.

CANCER/FIVE/NINE

When your imagination is put to positive use it can be both beneficial and constructive but when used in a negative frame of mind it can destroy most things, particularly relationships. At work let it help you build your career, especially if you're involved in a creative field, but in private keep it under tight control or it will soon join forces with jealousy and fan the smouldering embers of suspicion into a major conflagration.

CANCER/SIX/ONE

Until you learn to distinguish between fact and fiction there'll be no fairy tale endings for you — only a series of distressing and traumatic glimpses of reality. The sooner you come to terms with the fact that hopes are only realized through effort, application and hard work the sooner you'll get on in life. Dreams are for those who can afford the luxury and you're not one of them — yet.

CANCER/SIX/TWO

Home is not only where you prefer to be it's probably also the safest place for you until you manage to get your act together. You need to be tougher, more realistic and develop a thicker skin and at the same time try to appear confident, decisive and unemotional. Remodelling your personality isn't easy but its easier than giving in without even a token struggle.

CANCER/SIX/THREE

Frustration appears on the menu for you most days but just because its been dished up doesn't mean you have to accept it. A large helping of humble pie would make a pleasant change. In private you're so fond of talking about yourself that you never stop to listen. You may well be brilliant, versatile and quick-witted but unless you work harder to prove your worth you'll never get anyone else to believe in you.

CANCER/SIX/FOUR

Given a modest budget, an old property to renovate and free rein you could achieve miracles and still have something left over in the bank. But given a high-powered job, unlimited funds and a tight schedule you'd run a mile. You're not cut out to be a captain of industry but if you can manage to organize what resources you do have in a calm and efficient manner then a fair degree of success is within your grasp.

CANCER/SIX/FIVE

You are rather inclined to bottle problems up instead of getting them out into the open where something can be done about them. Secretly you want to be successful yet publicly you go the wrong way about it. You need to get yourself better organized and learn to control your fiery temper before it gets you into trouble. You're sensual, demonstrative and demanding and you tend to frighten people off with your sheer animal magnetism. Don't be quite so obvious nor in quite such a hurry to make a conquest.

CANCER/SIX/SIX

Charm, tact and imagination are yours to command. All you need is the confidence, drive and ambition to put them to good use. You have artistic flair, undeniable talent and the ability to express yourself boldly but without a suitable outlet your potential will neither be recognized nor realised. Stop being so faint hearted and sell yourself, you've so much to offer.

CANCER/SIX/SEVEN

To strike when the iron is hot is sound advice but you always forget to plug yours in and consequently miss opportunities which come your way from time to time. Like a boy scout you should be prepared for all contingencies and that way you won't keep losing out. You're much too fond of day-dreaming, fantasizing and blaming others for your own mistakes.

CANCER/SIX/EIGHT

The desire for financial security often prompts you to act in a ruthless, unscrupulous manner and while this attitude should keep the wolf from your door it certainly won't encourage other callers. You may know all about influencing people but when it comes to winning friends you're off course.

CANCER/SIX/NINE

Some people try far too hard to please and you're one of them. At work you get so side-tracked by trivia and trying to create just the right impression that you completely lose sight of your objective, while at home you naturally assume the role of door mat and then wonder why you're never shown any respect. You need to aim for a point of balance where you're neither too soft nor too forceful.

CANCER/SEVEN/ONE

At work try not to set your sights any higher than you feel you can comfortably reach otherwise you'll only be building disappointment into your plans. In your case it's far better to be a big fish in a relatively small pool than a minnow who's out of his depth and struggling hard for survival. In private although you may dream of partnering someone rich, famous and highly desirable don't for one minute imagine that this could be possible.

CANCER/SEVEN/TWO

Life can be very hard on those who can't, for one reason or another, cope with its demands and unless you toughen up considerably you could be one of those who'll feel the pinch. You need to come much further out of your shell and learn to be a better mixer. You could also do with more confidence and a greater understanding of human nature. If you continue to be unrealistic, unworldly and generally rather naive you'll never get anywhere.

CANCER/SEVEN/THREE

If you were going swimming you'd probably test the temperature of the water with a toe first before plunging in so why don't you ever think to employ this simple test where other matters are concerned? At work you'll boldly push yourself forward without first finding out what you're getting yourself into and in private you'll make all sorts of promises and commitments without ever stopping to consider the consequences.

CANCER/SEVEN/FOUR

System, routine and superb organization are the three things which keep your feet planted firmly on the ground and your life in order. Unfortunately much of your private frustration stems from your inability to get others to slot neatly in with your plans. Stop being so rigid and bossy and try being more flexible and understanding instead.

CANCER/SEVEN/FIVE

Nobody knows better than you how to keep a secret and it's a good job you do because if some of your private comings and goings were ever to become public knowledge you'd have a full scale scandal on your hands. Try to get your drives and desires under better control and your insecurity into better perspective. Why not take up some demanding form of sport and channel your surplus energy into a less hazardous direction for a change.

CANCER/SEVEN/SIX

Home comforts are very important to you but unless you acquire some business acumen life's little luxuries will continue to elude you. Few artificially talented individuals manage to make a satisfactory living from their gifts so unless you happen to be a genius you'd do better trying to earn your keep in some other field. The meek seldom get singled out for promotion while the selfless always end up at the back of the queue. Is that really where you want to be?

CANCER/SEVEN/SEVEN

Escapism seems to have become a way of life for you and its one that you need to change. You can't keep running away from every little problem and difficulty, much as you would like to, because there will come a time when there's nowhere left to hide. The thought of responsibility frightens you, harsh words reduce you to tears and any overtures of friendship are treated with mistrust. He who hesitates misses many opportunities but he who continually refuses to make an effort is a waste of everyone's time and energy.

CANCER/SEVEN/EIGHT

What you need is to learn a few social graces, acquire some tact and stop treating other human beings as if they were alien invaders. You can handle business matters but now all you need to find out is how to get along with the populus both *en masse* and individually. A few private lessons at a charm school might be a help.

CANCER/SEVEN/NINE

You need to climb down a peg or two before someone else takes you down forcibly. You're also rather inclined to pretend that problems don't exist instead of trying to do something about them. You can't bury your head in the sand forever, neither can you go through life on an ego trip. Realism and humility are both urgently needed.

CANCER/EIGHT/ONE

Unless you're prepared to be more adventurous and take a few calculated risks particularly at work, you'll never meet with the degree of success you'd like or indeed deserve. Too often you play safe and all too often opportunity passes you by in favour of a foresighted colleague who's willing to move with the times. Your 'get up and go' needs to be revived before it lays down and dies altogether.

CANCER/EIGHT/TWO

In private you need to make a greater effort to become more independent and self-sufficient. You look too much to your partner for reassurance and encouragement and not enough to your own resources. There's no magic formula for personal happiness but if there were, it certainly wouldn't include moodiness, jealousy or suspicion. Unless you stop being quite so sensitive there won't be any significant change in the pattern of your relationships although there is ample room for improvement.

CANCER/EIGHT/THREE

Ambition alone won't be enough to take you to the top in your chosen career. You will also need patience, staying power and tolerance, none of which you seem to possess. You find it virtually impossible to take orders, criticism puts your back up and you simply have to have the last word on any subject. In order to catch up lost ground your attitude will have to change. In private a greater show of affection wouldn't come amiss. You may know how you feel but when did you last pass this vital information on to your partner?

CANCER/EIGHT/FOUR

If only you favoured your partner with the same love and devotion as you do your work then your life could be considerably more enjoyable. No wonder you're always in the dog house at home when you never stop talking shop. Try to spend more time with your family, learn to relax and do something your partner would like for a change. Your business won't crumble overnight but relationships have been known to.

CANCER/EIGHT/FIVE

On the surface you appear steady, calm and industrious, which you are, but deep down there's another 'you' who is only allowed out to play when work is over and done for the day. Behind that mask of respectability is an earthy, sensual creature well versed in the art of love-making. Unfortunately the other you is also insanely jealous and madly possessive. You need to acquire some trust otherwise your unfounded suspicions and clinging ways will destroy all that you hold dear.

CANCER/EIGHT/SIX

Although you may feel you've found the formula for a happy home life and a moderately successful career you can't afford to sit back and rest on your laurels. Your greatest danger lies in becoming complacent. Once you start to feel too smug and secure the rot will creep in unnoticed. When you've realized one set of ambitions set yourself more targets to aim for.

CANCER/EIGHT/SEVEN

The sooner you put into practice a little of what you preach the sooner you'll have something to show for yourself. You're full of wisdom and good advice but you lack the initiative to apply it to your own affairs. In theory you make a lot of sense but in actual fact you're lazy and unambitious. It's about time you found a direction for yourself and made an all out effort to do something positive.

CANCER/EIGHT/EIGHT

Your career triumphs could prove to be hollow victories if you have no one to share them with. Take steps to become a more likeable person. Emotionally you play things too cool. You need to be more demonstrative and let your icy self-control thaw out.

CANCER/EIGHT/NINE

You always have to argue the toss with everyone, often speak without prior thought and react violently to any form of interference in what you consider to be your own affairs. You need to keep a tighter rein on your temper and adopt a more tolerant attitude towards those around you. Spur of the moment actions could also cause problems and you should guard against impulse spending particularly where the household budget is concerned.

CANCER/NINE/ONE

You are single-minded, active and confident yet somehow you lack the ability to spot flaws in your own plans or stumbling blocks lying directly in your path. Try to be more critical of yourself. When you make errors try to summon up enough good grace to admit you were wrong instead of denying all knowledge or responsibility.

CANCER/NINE/TWO

You'll never reach the top in your chosen career if you continually over-react to competition and you'll certainly be unable to sustain a serious relationship while acting like a prima donna. Self-control, staying power and adaptability are all lacking from your make-up and you should take earnest steps to acquire a little of all three without delay.

CANCER/NINE/THREE

You waste a great deal of time and effort chasing your own tail instead of settling down and getting on with your life in some semblance of order. Versatility can be both a blessing and a curse and in your case it's probably the latter. There are so many things you can turn your hand to so unless you discipline yourself rigidly and select an area in which to specialize you'll never realize your full potential.

CANCER/NINE/FOUR

You need to set your sights higher, turn your confidence up a notch or two and your ambition on to full power. Where's your spirit of adventure? You are so set in your ways and programmed to play safe that even if the chance of a lifetime came along you probably wouldn't notice. Why not come out of your rut for a while, there's so much going on and you could be missing out on the fun.

CANCER/NINE/FIVE

You live far too much on nervous energy and don't take proper care of yourself. Stop burning the candle at both ends and have a few early nights for a change. Nobody's going to steal your job because you always make sure you're indispensable. And as far as the opposite sex is concerned you could appear even more attractive once those dark circles and bags have gone from under your eyes.

CANCER/NINE/SIX

Try to stop being quite so short-sighted both at home and work. Look further ahead than you usually do and project yourself more. Being over-cautious can be just as great a fault as being over-confident. Attempt to strike a happy medium between the two and whenever possible resist the temptation to be pernickety and petty-minded especially within your relationships.

CANCER/NINE/SEVEN

Without a better grasp of financial affairs you'll find your earnings come in one hand and out in the other. What you need is a foolproof method of saving, a good accountant or both. At home you're capable of great depths of feeling but no one would ever guess because you always appear aloof and unapproachable.

CANCER/NINE/EIGHT

You may well be extremely good at your job but that doesn't mean you have to go on and on about it all the time. Less pride and more humility would be a positive improvement. The same goes for your private life. Actions speak louder than words so keep quiet about yourself and put some effort into your relationship before your partner knows the script off by heart.

CANCER/NINE/NINE

Why do you always have to be different? Playing the role of rebellious non-conformist may be a source of personal amusement but it certainly won't count in your favour when careers are being reviewed or serious private commitments are being considered by your partner. Try to keep your opinions to yourself and make a greater all-round effort not to be quite such a square peg who deliberately turns up in round holes.

LEO/ONE/ONE

If only you'd stop being so conceited, not quite so patronizing and a little more tolerant you'd be a much nicer person. Your arrogance needs to go. Unless you treat your partner more as an equal, instead of some minion, your relationship could come to an abrupt halt when the time comes for a few home truths to be told. Come down from your lofty heights and start acting more like a human being and less like a minor demi-god.

LEO/ONE/TWO

Even though you seem able to cope with most people and situations you still need to work hard to keep your confidence up to full-strength. You prefer to play a supporting role both at home and at work but there will be occasions when the spotlight falls on you alone and at such moments you can't afford to appear shy or self-conscious. Make the effort to push yourself a little harder because with a gentle shove in the right direction you could ultimately go far.

LEO/ONE/THREE

The sooner you stop behaving like an adolescent and become more adult in your ways the sooner your relationships will stabilize and your career will prosper. You have a shrewd brain, boundless energy and plenty of ambition but you queer your own pitch every time by refusing to take orders or ignoring basically sound, well-meant advice. Try to accept limitations with better grace, restrictions with more tenacity and delays with greater patience.

LEO/ONE/FOUR

Ambition is one thing you're certainly not short of but it's your natural caution which could be a major stumbling block. Every time an opportunity for advancement occurs you're never quick enough off the mark to take full advantage of the situation. For this reason playing safe could be your undoing rather than your salvation. Learn to be more decisive and stop looking gift horses in the mouth.

LEO/ONE/FIVE

You are a difficult person to help or advise because you seem to have a built-in self-destruct mechanism. You're restless, intolerant and over-confident. You change jobs annually, direction monthly and partners weekly. Short of chaining you to a desk or handcuffing you to someone it's anyone's guess when you'll ever settle down.

LEO/ONE/SIX

One thing you'll never have to worry about is keeping up with the Joneses because you're already a fully paid up member of the clan. Your career record to date reads like the ultimate in success stories while your home is a model of elegance and good taste. Unfortunately you allow this to go to your head and instead of enjoying what you have you play the game of one-upmanship and must have more. The only job satisfaction you get is knowing that you earn more than your colleagues while your house is a showpiece rather than a home where people can relax and feel at ease.

LEO/ONE/SEVEN

You're one of those people who needs to spend some time on their own each day just to get your thoughts in order and your breath back. You have a strong, magnetic personality but other people seem to need you more than you need them. It's vital that you have this breathing space as without it you soon become muddled and confused.

LEO/ONE/EIGHT

At work you could do with far more patience while in private a better understanding of human nature is a must. Your career is of paramount importance but you do need to give things more time to develop. Worrying and fretting will only give you ulcers, advancement is a much slower process than you imagine.

You have all the right ingredients for a successful recipe but you will keep opening the oven door to see how things are cooking and, as any good chef will tell you, this is all wrong.

LEO/ONE/NINE

Not until you stop being intolerant, impulsive and impatient will you ever get along in harmony with others either at work or in the home. It's a lesson everyone has to learn and one you seem to be having difficulty in grasping. Don't be in quite such a hurry to get things done as this can lead to mistakes. Accidents usually happen when people are careless and relationships founder when one partner doesn't know how to compromise.

LEO/TWO/ONE

Time and again its only the application of some last-minute self-control which prevents you going over the top. Your life is like a soap-opera; the more drama and excitement you can cram into it the better. You are popular, entertaining and larger than life which is all part of the act but should you ever allow the character you're playing to take control then anything could happen.

LEO/TWO/TWO

At work you seldom buckle down with the job in hand, preferring instead to preen yourself, curry favour with the boss and delegate responsibility whenever possible, while at home you are possessive, jealous and domineering not to mention changeable and demanding. Put your ego aside for five minutes, stop being so selfish and self-centred and start putting other people first.

LEO/TWO/THREE

You won't be young and lovely forever and although you've probably never considered your old age you'd be well advised to do so because it comes to us all in time. Stop trying to be Peter Pan. Be more realistic, come to terms with your life and don't fritter your talent away. Try to put at least something away for a rainy day and make a greater effort to develop some character.

LEO/TWO/FOUR

There's a Scrooge-like quality about you because although you have a ready smile, which after all costs you nothing, you give very little else away either materially or emotionally. You seem to have no time to listen or indeed to help others because to you time is money. You'll take everything on offer yet your own generosity is virtually non-existent. It's about time you stopped putting a price on everything and learned about human values instead.

LEO/TWO/FIVE

Life could very well be the death of you unless you stop allowing your spirit of adventure to have free rein. You can never sit still for five minutes, always have to find out what's around the next corner and fondly imagine that the grass is greener everywhere else but where you happen to be. As for your private affairs they defy description. Find yourself an anchor and cling tightly to it no matter which way the wind blows.

LEO/TWO/SIX

Your career, which you tend to regard as an optional extra rather than the be-all and end-all of your existence, should be relatively trouble free. However, it's in the home that you're going to have your work cut out to keep everything happy, harmonious and on an even keel. There's no place for either jealousy or suspicion, little room for possessiveness but ample scope for improvement.

LEO/TWO/SEVEN

You are very good at keeping things to yourself but there are times when it's better to voice your opinions in the hope of finding a solution to your problems. Suffering in silence is the hallmark of the martyr and everyone knows what usually befalls them. At work you should stick up for yourself. In private, unless you learn to communicate the bad as well as the good, you will have very little to build a relationship on.

LEO/TWO/EIGHT

Ambition is what fuels all your dreams but unfortunately you tend to envisage everything on a vast overall scale and don't spend nearly enough time looking for minor flaws or imperfections. As far as your private life is concerned a greater effort is called for. You could start by listening to what your partner is trying to tell you for a change.

LEO/TWO/NINE

Patience is a virtue found rarely in a woman, seldom in a man and almost never in a Leo/Two/Nine. You're the sort of person who wishes their entire life away instead of enjoying what you currently have. Stop living years ahead and start getting to grips with the here and now. The only way to ensure future success is to work hard and leave idle speculation to those who can afford the time.

LEO/THREE/ONE

There's no need for you to climb the ladder by treading on other people's toes or going behind their backs. Your own ability isn't questioned, it's just your methods that are in doubt. Progress may be slower along the conventional way but should you ever slip there'll be someone around to pick you up.

LEO/THREE/TWO

You have the ability to blend in with a crowd but whenever the attention turns your way you tend to go to pieces. It is not easy to convince yourself that you're as good if not better than the next person but it's even more difficult to get others to believe in something you don't. Try to create a better opinion of yourself and don't let unkind remarks leave such big dents in your self-esteem.

LEO/THREE/THREE

You have to have a job with an impressive title, and of course a salary to match, a home full of luxurious furniture and labour saving devices which testify to your success and, on the surface at least, a relationship which appears perfect. Your values are all purely social or material which is a pity because there are so many other aspects of life you will probably never explore.

LEO/THREE/FOUR

You have champagne tastes and probably a beer income but although frustration is something you have to learn to deal with, a call from the bailiffs seems highly unlikely. Try not to let envy mar your friendships, greed lead you to make unwise career decisions or jealousy blight your partnerships.

LEO/THREE/FIVE

Deep down you're an honest, genuine person but as you're so easily led you often get into the wrong sort of company without noticing it. At work you leave yourself wide open to unscrupulous manipulators while in private your sensuality often lures you out of your depth into uncomfortably hot water.

LEO/THREE/SIX

Domesticity suits you and if at all possible you should try to find an occupation which can be carried out in the comfort of your own home. Socializing is something you enjoy and your circle of friends and acquaintances is wide and varied. But try not to let your guest lists get out of hand otherwise you'll find yourself feeding the whole neighbourhood and with little or no thanks for your culinary efforts.

LEO/THREE/SEVEN

In theory you have a keen grasp of financial affairs, plenty of business acumen and a textbook knowledge of human relationships. But when it comes to putting your plans into action the results are never the same as you expect. What you lack is first-hand experience and this can only be acquired through the frustrating process of trial and error.

LEO/THREE/EIGHT

You are the kind of person who will leave a mark on life come hell or high water but whether it's a bright gold star or a dirty smudge is another matter. This is true both at work and at play. You need to concentrate your efforts in a direction which carries fewer risks, learn to mask your materialism better and be more consistent in your private affairs.

LEO/THREE/NINE

You are not content simply to do well, you have to be sure that even the milkman or a chance acquaintance knows it. That's why you like to fill your home with flashy status symbols, your garage with expensive cars and your arms with a partner who makes you the envy of all your friends. But how long can you maintain such a lifestyle and still sleep easy in your bed?

LEO/FOUR/ONE

You have sufficient drive and energy to carry you onwards and ever upwards in your chosen career. But on the home front, you're so head-strong and determined that you leave your partner very little room for personal manoeuvres. It's unwise to force your ideas on someone else without so much as a by your leave. Be more considerate and less impatient in your private life.

LEO/FOUR/TWO

Efficiency is your strong point. You're well-organized, good with money and always plan ahead. Unfortunately you have such a thin skin and are so self-conscious that you find it extremely difficult to assert yourself. You're always making apologies, bending to someone else's will and fall too easily into a subsidiary, background role. It's quite possible to be forceful without getting nasty.

LEO/FOUR/THREE

You were obviously well to the front of the queue when they were handing out brains, confidence and energy. With all that going for you it is a pity you didn't bother to pick up any tact or patience because you're much too edgy, quick-tempered and outspoken for your own good. Try not to get so wound up when irritating delays hinder your progress, exercise far more self-control in potentially volatile situations and remember that silence is golden.

LEO/FOUR/FOUR

Your problem is that you allow spontaneous outbursts to occur during working hours and yet find it difficult to let yourself go in private. Try to practise more self-control when handling difficult clients, fractious colleagues or tricky situations in the course of your job, and try also to show your feelings more towards your partner. The odd bit of praise here and there wouldn't go amiss.

LEO/FOUR/FIVE

You are a born gambler so until you learn to curb this instinct very little in your life is likely to change. You're already ready to try a long shot, quite prepared to take the most alarming risks and even when the odds are stacked against you, you will still chance your luck. Why don't you learn something from your mistakes and turn over a new leaf? You're clever, talented and original but hell-bent, it seems, on throwing everything away for the sake of a little excitement.

LEO/FOUR/SIX

At work you tend to get bogged down with petty details and in so doing lose sight of the overall plan much to the irritation of your colleagues. At home you fret over inconsequential items much to the annoyance and chagrin of your partner. Learn to relax and stop being such a fusspot.

LEO/FOUR/SEVEN

You can't allow your personal beliefs to stand in the way of your career. You may well find office politics distasteful but until you wise up and learn to play the game like everyone else your progress is likely to mirror your attitude. You'll never change the world so it is you who needs to adopt a different stance in order to come to terms with yourself and your environment.

LEO/FOUR/EIGHT

Try not to hurt those closest to you with unkind and unwarranted remarks. Explain your emotional difficulties and enlist their help and support instead of alienating them with silence or bad temper. You need to work hard in this particular area to get your frustrations into perspective and two heads are always better than one when there's a problem to be solved.

LEO/FOUR/NINE

Why not take a leaf out of your own book and start to practise what you preach a little more often? You're quite prepared to do charitable works in your free time, yet you're impatient, intolerant and not in the least bit charitable towards those around you. It is about time you stopped worrying so much about things on a global scale and took a more localized, closer look at yourself.

LEO/FIVE/ONE

You work hard and you play even harder and it's about time you slowed the pace from your normal flat out gallop to a brisk walk. Why not take up meditation to help focus your attention away from pleasures of the flesh or squash, to help you work all the tension and stress out of your body?

LEO/FIVE/TWO

Until you can cope better with your emotional insecurity you'd be well advised to steer clear of all but the most uncomplicated of personal relationships. You are far too sensitive and unsure of your own feelings to be able to play fast and loose with all and sundry without getting hurt. Find out how to walk unaided long before you decide to run anywhere.

LEO/FIVE/THREE

Stimulation is something you need both at work and at home. Without it you soon become dull and lack-lustre. Unfortunately life isn't necessarily all fun and games and you're going to have to develop more staying power if you don't want to find yourself continually at a lose end. Be more thorough at your work and try to set yourself higher standards while in private give relationships more time to develop instead of discarding them once the original sparkle has dimmed.

LEO/FIVE/FOUR

Change is something you actively resist and yet deep down you can't help feeling restless and unsettled. You like a job which has some form of routine and a home which is neat, tidy and well-ordered. So why do you secretly yearn to travel, show such curiosity in new technology and an interest in what other people are up to. It is simply because your combination of sign and numbers is at variance. It's only when you decide to indulge your fantasies that trouble could start.

LEO/FIVE/FIVE

You're daring, reckless and adventurous; sensual, restless and insatiably curious. Self-control and caution are two vital characteristics which only you can develop. Think before you act and stop trying to prove you're superhuman because you're not.

LEO/FIVE/SIX

It doesn't take much more than a little flattery or sweet-tongued cajolery to get you jumping through hoops. Don't allow your head to be so easily turned by blandishments and instead stop and ask yourself what's really going on in the background. You can't possibly be liked by everyone, even though you'd like to be.

LEO/FIVE/SEVEN

With you, although the spirit is willing, it's your flesh which is the weakness. In your mind you can picture yourself reaching the dizzy heights of success in your career, being the winner of every popularity poll and attracting the love and admiration of members of the opposite sex. Until you decide to show some initiative you can't expect the same rewards as your more dynamic friends.

LEO/FIVE/EIGHT

Everything about you suggests authority, power and tenacity from your immaculate appearance to your tremendous self-assurance; your knowing smile to your ability to remain calm under pressure. At work you're a professional through and through and in private you have such charm and animal magnetism that you make the game of love seem like child's play. However there's one vitally important attribute which you need to add to your list of accomplishments without delay — the ability to relax.

LEO/FIVE/NINE

Deep down you resent interference in any guise and this attitude could eventually negate what progress you've already managed to achieve. Keep your temper under control, your opinions to yourself and your cool intact. Begin as you mean to go along because any backsliding on your part will only result in unnecessary friction.

LEO/SIX/ONE

You have tremendous poise and charm coupled with a well-balanced outlook on life. Although you prefer to do things on your own, especially work, this doesn't mean you won't compromise and co-operate with others should the need arise. Originality and creativity are your strong points as well as single-mindedness and confidence. However no one's perfect, yet you still strive to be, sometimes to the distraction of those around you.

LEO/SIX/TWO

Smile and the world smiles with you — unfortunately you often forget. Normally you're gentle and submissive but when the wind is in the wrong direction you're like a bear with a sore head and this anti-social behaviour has to stop before all your friends desert you and your partner decides that enough is enough.

LEO/SIX/THREE

If there's one thing you like its a good audience to listen to all your amusing tales and funny stories. You love to be the centre of attention, the life and soul of the party and hate to feel that you're being in any way upstaged. Unfortunately, like all other frustrated thespians, you don't always realize you're play-acting.

LEO/SIX/FOUR

Try not to be quite so cautious and precise. Bend more with the wind, inject a little spontaneity into your life and when a mood seems to be taking you, go with it for a change. Take your partner unawares with an impulsive little gift and give your colleagues food for thought by turning up in something different.

LEO/SIX/FIVE

You're one of those people who given an inch will take a mile. You're never content to simply get your nose round the door — you have to get your feet under the table as well. Pushiness and over-confidence can be as bad as being shy and retiring. What you need is to strike a point of balance between the two. Don't be in such a hurry to make conquests and allow your career to develop at a steadier pace.

LEO/SIX/SIX

No-one will thank you for poking your nose into their business. You'd be more usefully employed attending to your own family and career leaving other people to look after themselves. Maintain a sense of proportion in all things and don't be so quick to criticize or interfere in matters which are not your concern. Take people for what they are and stop trying to run their lives for them.

LEO/SIX/SEVEN

If only you could resist the temptation to pick up on other people's shortcomings you'd gain far more respect from colleagues and a wider circle of friends. Laziness is also something you're going to have to overcome as you are rather inclined to sit about doing nothing instead of getting on with matters which, although not urgent, certainly require your full attention.

LEO/SIX/EIGHT

You believe yourself to be a perfectly reasonable human being, yet others would disagree. They feel that there's a catch to your generosity, no warmth behind your smile and nothing more than personal greed prompting your actions. And they could be right. You're very ambitious and this could be what makes you lose sight of other people and their needs.

LEO/SIX/NINE

You dislike supervision, resent criticism and simply cannot abide inefficiency. Rules, regulations and restrictions of any kind get you down while your hasty temper often lands you in hot water. Try taking a leaf out of your leisure-time book and don't get quite so wound up about everything.

LEO/SEVEN/ONE

Have you ever stopped to consider that your independent nature could be a distinct disadvantage at times? By declaring that you prefer to do everything your own way it is tantamount to a flat refusal of all offers of help or assistance. Admittedly any success you do achieve will be yours alone but conversely some of your mistakes could possibly have had happier endings if some timely advice had been sought. Learn to be more flexible in your working life while in private you could find sharing is a rewarding experience.

LEO/SEVEN/TWO

You lack confidence which makes you feel anxious and insecure. You also have a jealous nature and this negative emotion eats away at you like a worm in an apple. To add insult to bodily injury your diet is all wrong, you seldom take exercise and rely too heavily on stimulants such as tobacco and alcohol to give you a lift.

LEO/SEVEN/THREE

You have got enough self-confidence for half a dozen people, a brilliant mind and tremendously versatility. However you fritter all your talent away on whimsical, unprofitable schemes. In private you're also conspicuous by your absence when the going starts to get heavy or in danger of becoming serious.

LEO/SEVEN/FOUR

Thank goodness for your commonsense because it stops you getting too fanciful and saves you from making too many errors. Listen to its voice at all times particularly when making important decisions or attempting to bring about changes in your life. With caution and care you shouldn't encounter too many problems.

LEO/SEVEN/FIVE

You may not gamble on horse racing or play cards for high stakes but the risks you take are just as silly and the penalties could be much higher than the loss of some of your hard-earned money. What stamina you do have should be put into making your career a success and any excess energy should be expended on making one partner happy, not trying to impress two or three.

LEO/SEVEN/SIX

Your strong sense of the dramatic is apparent in everything you say or do. Your gestures are flamboyant and carefully calculated to achieve the best possible effect, your dress sense is bold and undeniably individual while your home is striking and unusual to say the least. You know better than anyone else how to make an entrance, create a scene or arouse interest but where you fall short is in sustaining both effort and interest.

LEO/SEVEN/SEVEN

A double helping of the number Seven means that you're going to have to work twice as hard as everyone else to stay in touch with reality. You have an aura of both dignity and authority about you which you should cultivate and develop further. A presence which commands respect and attention is indeed an asset so make it felt especially at work and grasp every opportunity for advancement that comes your way with both hands. In private you're very much a loner but although you seem to prefer your own company, too much of it could be bad for you.

LEO/SEVEN/EIGHT

You could be heading for all sorts of problems simply because you just don't know when to down tools and relax. You must make time to take adequate exercise and rest in order to keep your body ticking over efficiently and in private it's amends you need to make, and fast, to keep your relationship from foundering on the rocks.

LEO/SEVEN/NINE

If you rest too long on your laurels someone else will surge ahead and steal the victor's crown from under your very nose. Fewer words and more action are the order of the day both at work and at home. Don't be so easily satisfied, keep your momentum going and, who knows, in a few years time you could have even more to be feeling pleased, but hopefully not complacent, about.

LEO/EIGHT/ONE

You tend to think that confidence is all that's needed to guarantee success and unless you do your homework with more care you're going to find your theory doesn't always turn out the right way. Belief in 'self' is one thing but an over-inflated opinion of your capabilities can be a recipe for disaster. Try to pay more care and attention to your plans at the drawing board stage and that way, hopefully, their construction won't be quite such a hit and miss process in the future.

LEO/EIGHT/TWO

People with sensitive natures and skins as thin as yours really shouldn't try to become first division players because they're not tough enough to take the inevitable kicks and bruises. Yet you will insist upon entering a field which is highly competitive, riddled with pitfalls and a magnet to all the tough, ruthless characters of this world. It is no wonder your nerves are continually on edge. Try, in future, to keep your ambition in proportion to your abilities and in private seek a partner who understands just how vital give and take is to any relationship.

LEO/EIGHT/THREE

Native wit and cunning can give you the advantage over people of slower intellect but they should never be the sum total of your stock in trade. It is time you started being more orthodox in your business affairs and more honest in private. Fast talking may have got you out of many a tight corner in the past but should you ever become tongue-tied what will save you then?

LEO/EIGHT/FOUR

Yours is an ideal combination of sign and numbers for business success and in that area you should have little to worry about although that ruthless streak does need constant monitoring. It is in the home that you're ill-equipped to make a real go of things and where an effort is really called for. Try not to be so hard on your loved ones, show a little more appreciation for your partner's contribution and in the privacy of your own room don't be so straight-laced and undemonstrative.

LEO/EIGHT/FIVE

You exploit your undoubted physical attraction at work whenever possible to gain an inch of headway over your colleagues. Your leisure hours are spent in one long round of pleasure seeking and dissipation. Just because you've got it there's no need to flaunt it quite so openly. You have other talents that are long overdue for an airing and which could bring you greater rewards. Sexual athletes have neither security nor a pension scheme — astute business men and women invariably have both.

LEO/EIGHT/SIX

Deep down you really do care about other people but you just don't have the time to listen or help as much as you would like. In fact many of your favourite interests and pastimes have had to be shelved for the same reason. Why not resolve all your problems in one go by refusing to let the rat race spoil the quality of your life.

LEO/EIGHT/SEVEN

You take far too long to reach a decision of any kind and while you're carefully weighing up all the pros and cons someone else usually manages to steal a march on you. Don't let those at work score bonus points because of your own hesitancy and be more on the ball in your private life. Learn to strike while the iron is hot.

LEO/EIGHT/EIGHT

You want more than anything to be the ultimate in success stories but unless you learn to wield power wisely and handle others with tact, all your plans could evaporate into thin air. Make every effort to pace yourself better and don't go taking the co-operation and good will of others for granted. Run a few random spot checks occasionally and adjust your calculations according to your findings.

LEO/EIGHT/NINE

If only you would adopt a policy of non-aggression at work your opportunities would be greater and your chances of promotion enhanced. The trouble is you harbour grudges and instead of letting bygones be bygones you insist upon continuing feuds which were far better forgotten. A peaceful co-existence is what you must strive to achieve, not only in your place of work but also at home where you take great delight in throwing your weight around. Relationships should be based upon love and understanding not intolerance and hostility.

LEO/NINE/ONE

You have the determination and staying-power to achieve great things but don't make the mistake of crossing that thin dividing line where your authority gets used as a lever and your strong personality dictates all issues. At work be a wise master not a tyrannical boss and at home be a caring, all-round companion not merely a demanding, inconsiderate lover.

LEO/NINE/TWO

You'd like to feel that your job was safe and your private life guaranteed but your sensitive nature prevents you from projecting yourself and your fear of rejection, at times, reaches alarming proportions. Unfortunately nothing is a certainty until it's been accomplished and you're just going to have to be more positive if you ever hope to achieve even a small percentage of your dreams.

LEO/NINE/THREE

You may well be ambitious, goal orientated and decisive but how long does it last? Life isn't a game of musical chairs and the sooner you stop wasting everyone's time and decide to settle down the better. Put your talents to profitable use for a change by making that irrevocable decision to go in one particular direction in the company of a specific partner.

LEO/NINE/FOUR

You're so carefully programmed and efficient that for you to make a mistake must mean the end of the world. You seem to have no time for relaxation or enjoyment because you live solely for work. Try not to take everything so seriously, don't get so uptight when your precious routine is running five minutes behind schedule and, above all, try to get on better with those around you. It's far more fun to share a joke than to find yourself the butt of one.

LEO/NINE/FIVE

You crave attention, thrive on flattery, whether or not it's sincere, and would do almost anything to be noticed. Secretly you're afraid of failure although your definition of success isn't quite the same as everyone else's. You have a massive ego, enormous conceit and an overwhelming desire never to grow old.

LEO/NINE/SIX

The trouble is you really do believe that you're indispensable but no-one is. If you were to analyse your daily workload you'd soon discover that a high proportion of the tasks you perform are either totally unnecessary or relatively unimportant. Stop making a rod for your own back, don't fret and fuss so much over trivial little details and learn to delegate when really important work starts to pile up.

LEO/NINE/SEVEN

Physically you are out of condition which isn't helped by having a sedentary occupation. An intelligent person like you should realize that any piece of sophisticated equipment which is left idle for too long may start to deteriorate. What you need is some exercise. Nothing too strenuous at first but as your body gradually begins to recover from its long spell of inactivity you may notice changes taking place elsewhere too. Your concentration ought to improve, your output of ideas should increase and your partner, hopefully, will have rather more to smile about.

LEO/NINE/EIGHT

In order to avoid possible confusion, or indeed complications, it might be a good idea to let your right hand know what your left hand's up to rather more often. Unfortunately you're so devious its a wonder you can keep track of all the cunning plots and schemes you're involved in at any one time. Strictly speaking there are no reliable short-cuts to success yet still you cut corners and sail dangerously close to the wind in the hope of getting there ahead of everyone else.

LEO/NINE/NINE

You ought to be nicknamed the steamroller because that's precisely what you are. Once your fire has been kindled by ambition, you have plenty of fuel in the form of energy and determination to keep it blazing indefinitely. What's more, just like the vehicle in question, you drive off down the road to success, perhaps not at excessive speeds, but certainly flattening out anything or anyone that stands in your way. But how many of those dirty, smoke-belching iron monsters still take to the highways? Don't risk becoming a relic of the past!

VIRGO/ONE/ONE

There's no doubt about it, you're the human equivalent of a computer. You have a memory like an elephant, and the ability to process vast amounts of data without a sign of fatigue. However just like your mechanical double, you don't appear to have a heart. You find it very difficult to form any sort of one-to-one relationship, let alone an intimate one and your own sexuality frightens you.

VIRGO/ONE/TWO

You're so well-organized that you can lay your hands instantly on whatever you require. Unfortunately where you come unstuck is trying to catalogue people. They don't fit readily into convenient pigeon-holes to be picked up and put down again like a half-read book. The longer you continue to try, the more confused and muddled you'll become. Don't judge books by their covers, get well past the first few chapters before you form any opinions and don't read the last page first to see what happens.

VIRGO/ONE/THREE

You are one of those infuriating people who has a mind like blotting paper which can absorb facts and information with no apparent effort. However, despite all your knowledge and sound theoretical back-up, when it comes to putting it to practical use you go wrong every time because you're a show-off and a know-all.

VIRGO/ONE/FOUR

Unless you become more competitive you'll never reap the rewards you so richly deserve. No one else will push you forward for possible promotion neither will they go out of their way to provide you with a partner, unless of course you enlist the services of a dating agency. You have undoubted ability and much to offer both in the public and private sectors but your presentation and marketing leaves much to be desired.

VIRGO/ONE/FIVE

In a crisis, although you remain calm, you brain refuses to react quickly and make crucial, snap decisions. In an intimate situation you haven't the foggiest idea how to deal with passion or emotion. You need to become a better judge of character and acquaint yourself with the inner workings of the mind. You're not a robot built to perform a handful of functions so stop behaving like one.

VIRGO/ONE/SIX

It's undeniably true that when it comes to setting up a new filing system, breaking down a colum of figures or solving a difficult strategic problem you're the one for the task. However, you will insist upon applying logic, routine and a rather clinical approach to matters of the heart and that's where you tend to go wrong. Throw away your text books and let your instincts guide you more.

VIRGO/ONE/SEVEN

You're well-equipped to become a chess grand master or to set the questions for *Mastermind* but because of your own particular brand of snobbery you've set yourself so far apart from everyday society that you're going to find jobs hard to come by and a suitable partner virtually impossible to find. Don't be so difficult and pedantic all the time; you may know all the answers but your attitude is wrong.

VIRGO/ONE/EIGHT

Ambition coupled with greed makes you over hasty and when moving at speed you're more likely to make silly mistakes which could cost you dear. Spend more time over the planning stages of any venture or enterprise you become involved in and don't be in such a rush to see a profit that you skimp on the foundations. Whether at work or at play caution should be the initial watchword and don't go giving the 'full steam ahead' order until you're absolutely sure its safe to proceed.

VIRGO/ONE/NINE

Deep down you crave affection more than even success yet you have a funny way of showing it. Your body language says 'keep off' although secretly you wish people would show a greater interest in not only what you're doing but also in who you really are. Unfortunately it's not always possible to turn over a new leaf and wipe the slate clean at one and the same time. People have long memories so it's going to be quite a challenge for you to make them forget.

VIRGO/TWO/ONE

You're hard-working, well-organized and tenacious and with just a little more versatility and a slightly less rigid outlook you should be well on your way to the top. Your private life won't be so easy to improve because what's called for here is a major re-think rather than cosmetic surgery. Try not to get so uptight about every trifling little problem and keep telling yourself that conjugality should be a pleasure.

VIRGO/TWO/TWO

Overcoming the insecurity of a lifetime won't be an easy task to perform but provided you don't plan your comeback onto life's stage in too theatrical a manner you should be able to do it. Re-build your ego one step at a time in easy stages, don't let doubt hinder your progress and seek the support and encouragement of family and friends whenever you seem to be faltering.

VIRGO/TWO/THREE

With your flair for languages and other talents you could go far in the world of communications or the media. But no matter what career you choose to follow always ensure it leaves plenty of room for personal interpretation because you don't work well under supervision and, although you're well-organized, routine doesn't suit your volatile temperament. In private you're a very difficult person to pin down for long. Marriage is one trap you'd like to avoid getting into for as long as possible so you play hard to get in order to avoid capture.

VIRGO/TWO/FOUR

Pressure is the last thing you should be under because you can't take it. Your brain just won't think straight and consequently everything and everyone suffers as a result. Try to avoid stressful situations whenever possible and perhaps in your spare time yoga classes or hypnotherapy might help you overcome, and eventually eliminate, anxiety attacks altogether.

VIRGO/TWO/FIVE

You have a mind which yearns to travel but a body which prefers to stay in one place. When you go away foreign food upsets your stomach, a hot climate makes you irritable and your skin burns easily so what should have been a pleasure trip turns out to have been a pennance. You also feel irresistibly compelled to seek the company of the opposite sex yet when you've achieved this desire other more animal urges rear their ugly head to upset your normal composure. Personal hygiene is a fetish, therefore any form of physical contact you find both exciting and repellant at once.

VIRGO/TWO/SIX

Try not to be such an old woman all the time. You may be of a nervous disposition but you'll end up getting on everyone else's nerves too. Be more positive in your outlook, try to look on the bright side whenever possible. In fact, cheer up after all it may never happen so why go round looking as if it already had?

VIRGO/TWO/SEVEN

Sometimes to accept things at face value is the best policy. You're far too analytical, wanting to know the in's and out's of everything. At work you always have to probe and dig until you've discovered the reasoning behind management decisions while in private you're in real danger of ruining relationships by wanting explanations for feelings which are virtually impossible even to adequately describe.

VIRGO/TWO/EIGHT

There doesn't seem to be much room in your life for love or romance because your desire for fame and fortune overrides everything else. You are hell-bent on success and quite prepare to go for gold whatever the cost. Try to get your ambitions into better perspective and find a place for human relationships in your busy schedule. People are important although you may not realize their true worth until you need help and none is immediately forthcoming.

VIRGO/TWO/NINE

You'll drop everything to join a fun run to raise money for cancer research, will work long hours for no personal reward in order to aid orphans in a war-torn country and never think twice about helping out the old pensioner round the corner but the ones who love and need you most, your own family, never get a look in. Put your own house in order before you go any further as there are pressing amends to be made and in future leave 'do-gooding' to those who can afford the time.

VIRGO/THREE/ONE

You're one of those rare individuals who are able to discipline themselves sufficiently to work alone and unaided without ever being tempted to take a day off when things are slack. What's more you function just as efficiently as part of a team where your leadership qualities often prove indispensable. However, there are times when soft pedal tactics would be preferable to an outright show of force and aggression so you'd be well advised, if in any doubt, to adopt this approach when dealing with difficult workmates or an irate partner with an axe to grind.

VIRGO/THREE/TWO

No one but your poor, long-suffering partner would ever believe you were capable of hysterical outbursts or long periods of moody silence because outward appearances can be very deceptive. At work, in company or when simply returning a book to the library you seem like a perfectly reasonable, well-balanced human being. You've got a lively sense of humour, good manners and a pleasing appearance but behind closed doors it's another story. Jealousy clouds your vision like an ugly, green fog, possessiveness drives you to ridiculous lengths while insecurity does nothing to pacify your turbulent emotional state.

VIRGO/THREE/THREE

Your work can be very slapdash at times, probably because you're in too much of a hurry to get on with something else and there's no room for either negligence or carelessness in a competitive environment. You also seem to have difficulty in treating serious situations with the gravity they warrant. Don't be so frivolous and learn to keep a straight face in future when one is obviously in order.

VIRGO/THREE/FOUR

Although you're responsible, conservative and highly efficient your lively sense of humour prevents you from becoming too dull and dreary. You're very good at digging your heels in and refusing to budge an inch. You have set ideas, opinions and ways but remember, times change, and what may have sounded ridiculous or unacceptable ten years ago could now be regarded as perfectly normal. Try to keep a more open mind particularly when dealing with people you know little or nothing about.

VIRGO/THREE/FIVE

You're too clever by half and because you find so many things come easily to you, you don't really value or fully appreciate how lucky you are. But one of these days your devil-may-care attitude could land you in serious trouble which could defeat even your skill and ingenuity to escape from. And in private, love represents nothing more to you than a diverting adult pastime to be enjoyed at your leisure. But take care, the charmed life you lead may come to an abrupt end when some of your pigeons start coming home to roost.

VIRGO/THREE/SIX

Without your flair for organization you could find yourself in a real muddle but even with it you'll have to take care not to leave your partner out in the cold too often. A relationship which gives both parties room to breathe can be very successful but one which allows too much personal freedom can prove disastrous. Remember to check diaries from time-to-time to ensure that you spend at least one or two evenings a week together.

VIRGO/THREE/SEVEN

You're always full of brilliant and unusual ideas, pondering over some new pet theory or trying to commit your thoughts to paper. You have a remarkable brain but like many of your fellow intellectuals, a sadly neglected body. Make time for walking or swimming, take up a sport and rethink your routine. You'll find your concentration improves, inspiration will come more readily and your partner will stop nagging.

VIRGO/THREE/EIGHT

At work try not to be so aggressive in your approach, at home don't over-reach yourself financially by trying to improve your standard of living too fast and in private try to be more considerate. You may know exactly what you want but are you sure your partner shares your desires. It could be quite a revelation if you ever bothered to enquire.

VIRGO/THREE/NINE

Try to keep your temper under control and only blow your top in situations which merit a display of fireworks not just when you're feeling grumpy and out of sorts. Don't go boring everyone with long monologues about how clever and wonderful you are and, at home in particular, be prepared to take second place occasionally instead of automatically expecting everyone else to fit in with your plans.

VIRGO/FOUR/ONE

Even as a child you probably found it difficult to share because you have such an independent nature preferring, by and large, to do things on your own and for yourself whenever possible. But you're never too old to learn even such a rudimentary piece of social behaviour as this and if you would only show a little more willing you'd be half way there. At work resist the temptation to be responsible for everything from the holiday rota upwards.

VIRGO/FOUR/TWO

There's no need to wear your heart on your sleeve but a vow of celibacy is taking things too far the other way. Confidence is what you need to acquire and you could start by forgetting the past and adopting a more optimistic outlook on life. Greater self-assurance would make you feel more in charge of personal affairs and could even boost your career prospects.

VIRGO/FOUR/THREE

You're superbly well-organized, never forget a thing and are usually at least one jump ahead of any problems which could possibly arise. You're punctual, practical and precise. In fact what you could do with are a few vices as you're too virtuous and self-controlled to be true. Life isn't as neat and tidy as you try to make it. Don't deny yourself some of its greatest pleasures by adopting such a rigid attitude.

VIRGO/FOUR/FOUR

Each day you punish yourself with a rigid, unbending routine which must be strictly adhered to. You take an almost masochistic delight in denying yourself any show of feelings or emotion and never, ever allow time off for good behaviour. What you're trying to prove is uncertain but what you're doing is plain for all to see. It's time you came out of solitary confinement and went on a rehabilitation course.

VIRGO/FOUR/FIVE

You work hard, never live beyond your means and do everything you can to set a good example. But in private, when you let your hair down, it's a case of anything goes so long as the neighbours don't get to know about it. Stop pretending to be an angel because you're not, don't feel ashamed just because you have strong drives and desires and don't set such store by other people's opinions.

VIRGO/FOUR/SIX

When it comes to organization, precision and efficiency you're the winner. You can hold down a demanding job without any apparent effort and run a household better than Mrs Beaton. You never forget anyone's birthday, never over-spend by even a penny and never, ever appear flustered or bemused. But passion in the raw is something you find virtually impossible to come to grips with and your reluctance to participate could cause unnecessary complications in your private life.

VIRGO/FOUR/SEVEN

Your natural caution should prevent you from making any unwise investments or disastrous mistakes at work but when coupled with your natural insularity you're not going to find it easy to make new friends or indeed promote existing friendships. In private you don't express your feelings often enough for your partner to even guess at, let alone accurately gauge, their strength. By being more demonstrative and forthcoming you could open up new horizons for both of you.

VIRGO/FOUR/EIGHT

You're logical enough never to allow emotion to cloud your judgement and sufficiently determined to make it right to the top. However a lack of patience is your one weak point. As a child you probably couldn't wait five minutes for anything but as an adult let's hope you don't get too fractious if you have to wait.

VIRGO/FOUR/NINE

Check you've got all your facts straight before you go sounding off on any subject and double check your work to avoid the possibility of any errors slipping through unnoticed. On the home front the same advice applies. Don't automatically assume you know best, don't presume your partners wishes will coincide with your own and don't continue to argue your innocence when your guilt has been conclusively proven.

VIRGO/FIVE/ONE

You command respect, never give up when the going gets tough and somehow manage to get things done which your predecessors have failed to achieve. In private you're ardent and demonstrative but although not particularly jealous by nature you can be utterly ruthless should you ever catch your partner being indiscreet. What's more you wouldn't hesitate to finish the relationship without further thought.

VIRGO/FIVE/TWO

Why do you feel so ashamed and embarassed when your feelings show? At work you're efficient, conscientious and co-operative yet you try to remain as anonymous as possible, preferring to keep conversations with workmates to safe topics like the weather or the latest cricket scores and never voicing an opinion for fear of ridicule or contradiction. You're chronically shy and self-conscious and the sooner you make a positive effort to overcome this distinct handicap the better.

VIRGO/FIVE/THREE

If only you had a better opinion of yourself you wouldn't feel the need to impress others in the way you do, and if only you'd think before you speak you wouldn't fall so readily into the habit of prevaricating. Take more pride in who you are and stop pretending to be someone else because even if you don't get unmasked it can't be all that entertaining playing charades by yourself.

VIRGO/FIVE/FOUR

While no one's actually accusing you of being stubborn and pig-headed you might find that a more open, less narrow-minded attitude could be to your advantage. Try not to dismiss everything new that comes along and at least have the decency to listen to what people have to say before deciding to reject their schemes.

VIRGO/FIVE/FIVE

You give all the outward appearances of being rather dull and middle of the road which only goes to prove what a dark horse you really are. In company you positively sparkle, while in private you're certainly not backward at coming forward. Let's hope you never become confused and forget who and where you are.

VIRGO/FIVE/SIX

You're so anti-everything, except hard work, that it's a wonder you can find anything to do for kicks. Your sole pleasure in life seems to be telling other people where they're going wrong and how they can put their mistakes right and you advocate some pretty tough measures. It's about time you stopped being self-appointed guardian of public morality.

VIRGO/FIVE/SEVEN

Discretion should be your middle name as your private life, although lively and action packed, never seems to attract the attention of gossips or scandalmongers. As well as your diplomatic skills you have a fine, enquiring mind, a lively turn of phrase and a striking, unusual style of dress which, although hardly fashionable, suits you well. Unfortunately money sense is one important asset you lack.

VIRGO/FIVE/EIGHT

If only you could manage your private life with even half the skill and talent you display for business your personal relationships wouldn't prove quite so troublesome. You are jealous, and it shows. You are possessive, and that shows too, as well as being moody, undemonstrative and about as changeable as the weather. Try to appear more confident and self-assured in intimate situations.

VIRGO/FIVE/NINE

There are times when your rational, analytical mind can come in very useful. At work it could prove to be invaluable, but there are also occasions when it's not a good idea to probe too deeply into what makes things tick and your private life is one such area. Relationships shouldn't be put under a magnifying glass too often, love-making doesn't require a running commentary and you may never get the real truth even under vigorous cross questioning.

VIRGO/SIX/ONE

You have everything going for you providing you keep your intolerance under control. Few people can enjoy a combination of power, and friendliness at the same time. At home you take your responsibilities seriously and are willing to roll your sleeves up and get on with things that need to be done. The fact you are prepared to compromise stands you in good stead in your personal relationships, provided you are the one to instigate the compromise.

VIRGO/SIX/TWO

Your life tends to centre around the home where a consistent relationship based on understanding holds sway. You are a natural parent and can deal with most crises without fuss and with good humour. However, there is also a tendency to be too houseproud and too involved in gossip — these could cause problems. Your strong intuition is your best guide in most situations so let it be your initial yardstick.

VIRGO/SIX/THREE

You can fit into most social and business situations and at worst you are competent at what you do. Given the right choice of partner or career you can show brilliance and versatility combined with a friendliness which will always be your vital backstop. But, don't get drawn into criticizing those around you or broadcasting your own abilities. If you can curb your need to outshine others you should go far in your chosen course.

VIRGO/SIX/FOUR

That steady and clear sighted image you project runs the risk of being undone by either quixotic gestures or an irritating and unnecessary attention to detail. You have very little to prove to other people as far as your working abilities are concerned. But at a personal level your moods tend to swing between melancholy and excessive cheerfulness. Take confidence in the fact that others look towards you as guide and mentor and avoid letting your own personal doubts show through.

VIRGO/SIX/FIVE

Members of the opposite sex find it hard to resist you. There's an air of the swash-buckler or siren combined with wit and good humour which makes you attractive to all. This is backed up by resourcefulness and competency which makes you an ideal catch. But don't let your advantages be damaged by that tendency towards conceit, sarcasm and intolerance. Having learned that you possess such magnetism avoid turning it to selfish purposes.

VIRGO/SIX/SIX

At home or at work, whether pursuing pleasures or dealing with problems you're always the same — bright, cheerful and in total control. You cope coolly and calmly when the unexpected occurs almost as if some sixth sense had tipped you off in advance and in a crisis, when everyone else is in a state of near panic, you are superb. You make a considerate boss, a co-operative colleague and a near perfect partner. When it comes to rising to an occasion you seem to rise higher than anyone else.

VIRGO/SIX/SEVEN

Although you enjoy the merry-go-round of the social whirl there are the odd occasions when you prefer your own company to that of anyone else. This could cause difficulties within a relationship unless you take the time and trouble to outline your needs carefully to your partner from the word go. Once everyone knows where they stand, problems shouldn't occur but as you're rather inclined to be forgetful a reminder pad could come in very handy.

VIRGO/SIX/EIGHT

There is a world of difference between being knowledgeable and being a know-all. Unfortunately much of the time you fail to recognize the distinction because you can't resist an opportunity to show off your talents. Try not to be quite so pompous and pedantic and let someone else get a few words in edgeways once in a while. You'd do well to remember that expertise is usually sought by those who need it, not given free.

VIRGO/SIX/NINE

You tend to judge people harshly, often attempt to force your views upon loved ones and colleagues and seem to think you're the only one who should be at liberty to form their own opinions. This attitude will only provoke bad-feeling, if not actual arguments. Don't be so impatient with people of slower intellect than your own; faces often mirror thoughts and yours frequently shows signs of irritation.

VIRGO/SEVEN/ONE

At work you give the impression of being dynamic and aggressive but, as anyone who has ever carried out a close inspection of your output would agree, your results are erratic. The amount of effort you make seems to be either all or nothing and what you need to learn is how to pace yourself better to give a more balanced performance. In private your attention also tends to wander as you're an incorrigible day-dreamer and unless you keep a closer watch on your personal affairs you could be in for problems.

VIRGO/SEVEN/TWO

Colleagues and loved ones alike never know where they stand with you because you never seem to be in the same frame of mind for two consecutive days at a time. Don't let your changeable emotional state colour your relationships with others and try to keep a cheerful smile on your face even when, deep down, the last thing you're feeling is euphoric.

VIRGO/SEVEN/THREE

You're shrewd, observant and hard-working but much too easily angered by what you consider to be the crass, inane actions and views of those around you. Admittedly being in a subordinate position doesn't fit in at all well with the highflying image you have of yourself but if you ever hope to rise any higher on the ladder of success you'd be silly to go speaking your mind too often. Learn to hold your tongue, try not to be so impatient to get on in the world and don't allow that hasty temper of yours to lessen your chances of advancement.

VIRGO/SEVEN/FOUR

You're rather inclined to take life far too seriously, a point which the furrows on your brown only serve to emphasize. Why don't you ease up on yourself by taking the odd breather every now and again. Spend more time relaxing in the company of family and friends and don't go burning the midnight oil too often trying to catch up with paperwork. A few early nights would work wonders for your flagging concentration not to mention your relationships.

VIRGO/SEVEN/FIVE

You're much too restless and too easily bored to ever make a good job of anything yet you have the potential to achieve great things if only your mind wouldn't keep wandering off at a tangent all the time. Try to organize your days better, resist the temptation to drop everything just to make some easy money and concentrate more on the task already in hand. What's more your roving eye could cause unnecessary conflict in your personal life.

VIRGO/SEVEN/SIX

You have a positive flair for both organization and design but unfortunately this is coupled with an almost manic desire for perfection. Whether at home or in your place of work you drive those around you almost to the point of idstraction with your love of order and attention to even the most trivial of details. You're also inclined to poke your nose into matters which don't concern you. High standards are commendable but constant nervous activity can be intensely irritating.

VIRGO/SEVEN/SEVEN

You find the paranormal particularly interesting but unless you learn to keep a more open mind and let intuition be your guide frustration is likely to be your only reward. The same applies to everyday relationships. No two people are alike and not everyone is instantly fathomable. Make more allowances for the human factor and don't be so quick to pin labels on people just for the sake of your own convenience.

VIRGO/SEVEN/EIGHT

Fate has a habit of cutting you down to size every now and again and you certainly need it. But with your natural bouyancy you're seldom back at square one for long. You have tremendous self-confidence, a relentless application to work and an almost superhuman determination to succeed at all costs. However, where you go wrong is in your dealings with other people. You're far too hard on your loved ones, much too bossy with colleagues and utterly ruthless with competitors.

VIRGO/SEVEN/NINE

You're not one of the most tolerant people and you usually make little or no attempt to hide the fact. You're quick to criticize and swift to anger but never the first to apologize or to try to make amends for unwarranted harshness. Try to be more understanding of both the needs and feelings of others, especially those closest to you and make every attempt to get your hasty temper under greater control.

VIRGO/EIGHT/ONE

You're certainly not a born team member because you lack that vital willingness to co-operate, but as a solo performer you're pretty formidable. However, as a potential partner you do little to encourage members of the opposite sex in your direction. Try to acquire a few social graces if you possibly can. You won't become the life and soul of the party overnight but at least you might get invited to a few for a change.

VIRGO/EIGHT/TWO

You run the very real risk of letting life pass you by unless you do something soon to conquer your shyness and sensitivity. You're so quiet and self-conscious that you deliberately hide yourself away in order to escape attention and that's no way to carry on. Get a few hints on style and fashion and launch yourself gently into society with a new image. It's not easy to break the habits of a lifetime but in your case the effort could be worthwhile.

VIRGO/EIGHT/THREE

In most areas of life you manage to acquit yourself with honour because you're worth your weight in gold to any employer and make a loyal, reliable friend to members of your own sex. But as far as your personal relationships are concerned you tend to run a mile once they start getting serious. Inhibitions can be difficult to overcome and although shyness can be endearing, frigidity is a real turn off.

VIRGO/EIGHT/FOUR

There's very little that can actually manage to ruffle your feathers because your concentration is good, your nerves shatterproof and your calmness in a crisis legendary. However, you're rather good at upsetting others both intentionally and unintentionally. You're obstinate, demanding and, at times, utterly ruthless. Although this sort of behaviour may be quite acceptable on an army parade ground it won't go down well with workmates or at social gatherings.

VIRGO/EIGHT/FIVE

That secret fear of failure, which is never far from your mind, is likely to be the root cause of your erratic behaviour. You're afraid to relax for any length of time in case a golden opportunity passes you by and although undeniably attracted to members of the opposite sex the thought of total commitment and all that it implies makes you a difficult catch to land. You like to test the water with one toe but rarely allow it to come any higher than your waist before deciding to back off.

VIRGO/EIGHT/SIX

Everyone needs a safety valve, a way of getting pent up feelings and emotions off their chest but unfortunately yours is nowhere to be seen. You never shout, lose your temper or indeed make any attempt to stand up for yourself when others are treating you unfairly. Do you really want to be the dogsbody at work or the doormat at home – you are worth far more than that?

VIRGO/EIGHT/SEVEN

You live to work and your private life is a closely guarded secret which you refuse to share. Try not to be so insular and standoffish all the time. Despite popular opinion you do have a heart, it's just that you are so afraid of getting it bruised or broken that you prefer to keep the world at arm's length.

VIRGO/EIGHT/EIGHT

Nobody deserves to be a resounding business success more than you because you pursue your career with single-mindedness and devotion to the exclusion of all else. Financially you may be a mogul but emotionally you're a mouse. One to one relationships have never been your *forte* so you decided to ignore them altogether. Don't be so defeatist in your attitude.

VIRGO/EIGHT/NINE

Your partner would probably prefer realities to dreams and your boss results to projected figures. You need to come down to earth before you are brought down with a bang. Be more realistic and let tomorrow take care of itself. The present is what really matters, not what may or may not materialize ten years from now.

VIRGO/NINE/ONE

Your concentration tends to go in fits and starts and you need to make a greater effort to keep your thoughts from wandering. You also need to pay closer attention to your private life as it won't fly forever on automatic pilot. At home you're often conspicuous by your absence as your working life makes heavy demands on your leisure time. This is unavoidable if you want to get on but when you do get five minutes to relax with your partner do all you can to make them moments to treasure.

VIRGO/NINE/TWO

The sooner you realize that relationships can't be run along the same lines as businesses or households the better yours will prosper. You've got one of those neat, tidy minds which likes everything to be scheduled and pre-determined and unfortunately personal matters aren't always that orderly. Try to adopt a more flexible attitude when other people's personalities and feelings are involved because you can't expect life to revolve solely around your wishes all the time.

VIRGO/NINE/THREE

Try not to let minor irritations anger you so easily. If only you would stay calm you wouldn't rub quite so many people up the wrong way. People like you who live on their nerves often irritate others which only causes unnecessary friction, that could so easily be avoided if you had more patience.

VIRGO/NINE/FOUR

You've got everything it takes to make a first-class executive or administrator. You love to see things running in an orderly, efficient manner; never lose patience of interest when teething troubles develop in a scheme and like to see a job through to its conclusion. However, when it comes to handling people you could do with a few lessons in tact and diplomacy. You seem unable to see things from someone else's point of view and unwilling to make any attempt to do so. Don't be so stubborn and intractable.

VIRGO/NINE/FIVE

It's unlikely that your life will ever run smoothly because you're too fond of taking risks. You're as highly-strung as a thoroughbred racehorse and about as predictable. Although you'd secretly like to settle down in peace and quiet you're just not programmed for that sort of existence. Routine drives you to distraction, monogamy becomes monotonous and the grass always seems to be of a greener hue anywhere else but where you happen to be.

VIRGO/NINE/SIX

You try so hard, particularly at home, to make everyone happy and to make your surroundings as near perfect as they can possibly be. You go out of your way to please even when you're feeling tired and will work far into the night, if necessary, to complete tasks that could well wait until tomorrow. That is where you go wrong all the time — trying too hard. No one will thank you for working your fingers to the bone and dancing constant attendance on your family will only encourage them to be lazy.

VIRGO/NINE/SEVEN

At work you don't seem to have the patience with either people or problems, while at home you're always so uptight that you never relax long enough to let your true feelings come to the surface. You don't seem to cope very well with either stress or tension, much of which you generate through your own actions, and the greater the pressure the more nervous and restless you become. Try to find a safe outlet for all your pent up frustration and try to be more tolerant of other people.

VIRGO/NINE/EIGHT

You've never made a secret of your intentions neither have you ever pretended to be anything more than socially ambitious. You may not have letters after your name or a whole string of paper qualifications but you have the native wit and cunning to take you where you want to go. You are strong, determined and utterly ruthless. However, as you well know, everything has its price and the loss of personal happiness might be what you have to pay for your dreams.

VIRGO/NINE/NINE

You get far too excited, take everything personally and, on the rare occasions that an opponent gets the better of you, are a sore loser. What's more you often go out of your way to provoke arguments just for fun. Constant aggression and firework displays can be very wearing for all concerned and not the best way to create a happy atmosphere. Don't go round spoiling for trouble all the time it could damage both your career and your relationships.

LIBRA/ONE/ONE

Although quite prepared to co-operate and well able to act as a responsible team member you shine when working alone. Even in private, although you have no problem forming relationships, your independence and love of freedom makes you wary of entering into serious commitments. You like to play the field and have every intention of doing so for as long as possible. Don't leave it too long however before you make a final selection.

LIBRA/ONE/TWO

You have a deep-seated need to feel loved and secure but unfortunately you make all the wrong moves to achieve your desires. Flattery instantly turns your head, you mistake harmless flirtation for the real thing and pin too many hopes much too fast on someone you've only just met. Don't leave yourself so wide open to hurt, don't be in such a hurry to settle down with the first person who so much as glances in your direction and keep away from situations you can't handle.

LIBRA/ONE/THREE

Your thoughts are always going off at a tangent, you are much too easily side-tracked and you can only concentrate for short periods without a break. The most likely object of distraction, in your particular case, is a member of the opposite sex. You are always ready to turn on the charm in order to create a favourable impression usually at the expense of your work. Try to conduct personal affairs outside office hours and put your other, rather less obvious talents, to more profitable use.

LIBRA/ONE/FOUR

You seem able to cope with the demands of a busy working life because you tackle everything in such a practical, no nonsense way. You soon get yourself into a routine and then it's just a case of dealing with matters efficiently and in the right order. The problem is that you adopt the same tactics at home and instead of being flexible you will insist upon doing everything in a rigid, unbending way. Personal needs and desires are not that easy to predict as much depends upon the prevailing mood so don't draw up a timetable and then expect your partner to adhere to it.

LIBRA/ONE/FIVE

You never seem to be content unless you have at least two or three members of the opposite sex all vying for your attention at any one time. You burn the candle at both ends and in the middle too. However, there are some reputations which, once earned, are hard to live down and you'll need a very large cupboard with a security lock to hide all your skeletons.

LIBRA/ONE/SIX

You know instinctively how to put others at their ease and are always willing to listen to all their troubles. However being the leading neighbourhood socialite can be demanding and doesn't allow much time for your partner to get a look in. Try not to get such a full engagement diary that you can't spend a few evenings together during the week. You're an incorrigible flirt and don't always realize when you're over-stepping the mark.

LIBRA/ONE/SEVEN

In the company of your intellectual cronies you have no problems whatsoever in holding your own and indeed, at times, ruling the roost. Its when you find yourself having to mix with ordinary men and women who never have, and never will, lean in the same direction as you that you run into trouble. Unfortunately your awkwardness is often mistaken for a snub and unless you make a greater effort to overcome this stumbling block you could find yourself branded as a highbrow or a snob.

LIBRA/ONE/EIGHT

You have much to feel proud about but there's no need to shout about your accomplishments quite so loudly. Try to take a back seat more often, even though you do prefer to drive; give your colleagues a chance to get their thoughts in order and your partner an opportunity to speak. You try to eclipse and outdo everyone and its about time you showed some consideration.

LIBRA/ONE/NINE

At work you're respected and popular because you're team-spirited and co-operative but watch out you don't get too big for your boots as there are others around who don't belong to your fan club. In private, although socially much in demand, you crave the deep affection and fulfilment that only a close personal relationships can bring. Unfortunately the adolescent way you go about establishing such a bond often results in you making a fool of yourself.

LIBRA/TWO/ONE

It takes quite a lot to persuade you of your own worth but a discerning employer should be able to see that hidden behind all that natural modesty is a talented individual who needs nothing more than the right opportunity, plus a little encouragement, to bring out the best. And in private, with a strong, understanding partner to turn to when your confidence is waning, you shouldn't experience more than the normal quota of emotional ups and downs.

LIBRA/TWO/TWO

Emotional security is what you desire more than anything else and its only your own deep-seated insecurity which stands in your way and prevents you from finding it. You lack the confidence to elbow your way into a conversation, the decisiveness to grasp what few opportunities chance to come along and the drive to propel yourself anywhere in particular. Anxiety is a problem you have got to overcome one way or another and if you can't do it by yourself you may have to enlist professional assistance.

LIBRA/TWO/THREE

Your confidence and courage always fail you at precisely the wrong moment, but if you would only stand your ground this problem could be quickly and successfully resolved. Not only do you have a desire to be important, you're also very concerned about what people think of you. You're rather two-faced in this respect because although you can't bear to be thought badly of you're always ready to gossip or criticize someone else behind their back. You should get on with your own business and leave others to mind their own.

LIBRA/TWO/FOUR

You're one of those rare people who have a well-balanced outlook on life. Your home and career are of equal importance with one neither outshining nor overshadowing the other. You get on well with people, small children and dumb animals because there's nothing about you which they could possibly dislike. That comfortable feeling of being one half of a pair gives you just that extra confidence you need.

LIBRA/TWO/FIVE

At work you never seem to settle because you think people may be laughing at you or talking behind your back in the rest room. And at home the problem is even worse; you're suspicious, disbelieving and quick-tempered. Anyone emotionally involved with you will need the patience of a saint to last the course.

LIBRA/TWO/SIX

You don't particularly enjoy going out to work prefering, whenever possible, to get on in your garden or with one of your creative hobbies. You're either one of the happiest, most contented people around or you're so insecure that you're afraid to leave your safe refuge for too long.

LIBRA/TWO/SEVEN

'When in doubt, do nothing' should be emblazoned on your coat of arms because it certainly sums up the way you operate. You're a thinker, not a doer, which is why your career advancement is slow and your relationships far from sparkling. Not until you get up out of your armchair and do something positive will your life progress.

LIBRA/TWO/EIGHT

Personal security is vital to you and you set great store by your house and possessions. In fact you're an avid collector with an eye for a bargain and a nose for items that will appreciate in value. Your major problem area is likely to be in establishing and maintaining a balanced relationship. You can often be a difficult person to get along with because you're moody, changeable and easily wound-up.

LIBRA/TWO/NINE

At work or at home you prefer someone else to make decisions; that way there's somebody to blame if things go wrong. You need to stand on your own two feet instead of someone else's and learn to take the rough with the smooth. You don't even play safe on a fair basis so its about time you brushed up on the rules.

LIBRA/THREE/ONE

You'll need to keep a close watch on your bank balance, especially if you carry a credit card, as you're prone to the odd little extravagance or impulse purchase. You could end up with an ulcer brought on by financial stress. Cut down all round and try to live within your means for a while.

LIBRA/THREE/TWO

You want to stay eternally young and the only way you can gauge how attractive you are is by the number of members of the opposite sex you can lure into your arms and, occasionlly, into your bed. You're vain, conceited and always ready to believe insincere flattery or induldge in superficial flirtation. Whatever it is you're looking for, happiness certainly won't be waiting for you at the end of your journey, only old-age and loneliness.

LIBRA/THREE/THREE

You seem to have a never-ending capacity for pleasure in all its forms and a wide assortment of people to share it with. You like fun, games and parties; theatres, restaurants and race meetings. If it feels good you'll do it time and again, but remember, although you're calling the tune can you afford to pay the piper quite so often.

LIBRA/THREE/FOUR

Thanks to your innate commonsense where money is concerned you seldom experience any great problems on that score. But you seem to have rather more difficulty controlling your food intake. Your health does need careful monitoring as you're rather inclined to overdo it every now and again.

LIBRA/THREE/FIVE

While there is no real harm or malice in you, you do have some faults and failings which need urgent attention. Whatever the odds you can't resist having a wager; when an attractive member of the opposite sex happens to cross your path you immediately take off in hot pursuit and at work you're always on the lookout for some amusing diversion to break the monotony for a while. This hedonistic lifestyle is superficial and offers nothing permanent nor any promises for the future.

LIBRA/THREE/SIX

You're a born host but until you learn to be a more careful housekeeper your culinary extravangazas are likely to cost twice as much as necessary because you're so incredibly wasteful and uneconomical. Even in conversation you always use three or four words where one would do and frequently repeat yourself without even realizing.

LIBRA/THREE/SEVEN

Eating and drinking are your favourite occupations although you prefer consumables to be of the instant or take-away variety as traditional cooking is too much of a chore. Sexually your spirit is willing but the flesh never quite seems to get its act together in sufficient time to make a good impression. Fantasy more often than not is the name of your game.

LIBRA/THREE/EIGHT

You're a climber who won't hesitate to use every available foothold, even if it means going out on a dangerous limb or clinging on by your fingernails to negotiate tricky obstacles. You tend to move in the right circles among people who make useful contacts rather than mixing with those whose company you'd actually prefer. Everything you do has a reason; whatever you say has been carefully rehearsed and even your choice of partner can't be left to chance.

LIBRA/THREE/NINE

What you could do with is a secretary, a housekeeper and a wet-nurse to help organize your busy life because you try to pack far too much into every twenty-four hour period with the result that some jobs are done better than others and some never get touched at all. The trouble is you try so hard to please everyone that you end up pleasing no one in particular. Try not to take on commitments you know you've not got time to handle; don't make promises you're not in a position to keep and learn to say 'no' politely.

LIBRA/FOUR/ONE

Yours ideas are original but never cranky; you think fast but never at such high speeds that mistakes slip by unnoticed and once your mind is made up on any matter nothing will divert you from your chosen course. You make a first-class worker, a conscientious, caring partner and a devoted parent.

LIBRA/FOUR/TWO

You do your level best to keep your home as happy as possible and the atmosphere at work harmonious. However, this often means that you play second fiddle to someone else and although the resultant tune is far from discordant it would be nice to see you playing a solo every now and again. You seem to have developed your own formula for a stress-free existence and once you find a way to control your changeable moods and tendency to melancholy you could rise to even greater heights all round.

LIBRA/FOUR/THREE

Although you'd like nothing better than a little peace and quiet, it seems to be the last thing you're likely to achieve if you continue to follow your present course, because whenever you speak out of turn it causes shock waves in all directions. It won't take much to get you balanced except a little time and patience, always assuming of course you're willing to co-operate.

LIBRA/FOUR/FOUR

If you ever feel that life is unbearably dull and boring you've only really got yourself to blame. You're much too conservative to ever consider doing anything frivolous or unusual; you've played safe for so long that you wouldn't know how to take a risk if you tried and because you've got yourself into such a strict, unbending routine are you really surprised that nothing unexpected or exciting ever occurs? Both at home and at work the rut you've dug is very deep and will take a superhuman effort to rise above.

LIBRA/FOUR/FIVE

The sooner you realize that Victorian morals no longer hold water the quicker you'll unload all that guilt you've been carrying round with you for years. Because you have such strong sexual drives and unusual desires you act as if there was something dreadfully wrong with you. Don't listen to all those narrow minded bigots who try to tell other people what's right and what's wrong. Provided you and your partner are consenting adults, go ahead and enjoy yourselves.

LIBRA/FOUR/SIX

Just because you've managed to get your life together with apparent ease and with few major problems there's no need to become smug and complacent. Roll up your sleeves and see if you can lend those less fortunate than yourself a helping hand. It's not a good idea to rest on your laurels as you never know what's round the next corner and when charity has ceased to be necessary in your home there are always plenty of others that could do with some.

LIBRA/FOUR/SEVEN

It's when the unexpected happens that your nerves get frayed and your feathers become ruffled. You even prefer to seek your livelihood in a safe, time-honoured profession and when selecting a partner you go more for practicality and commonsense than good looks every time. But unless you become more versatile and adaptable you'll find life progressively more difficult the older and more set in your ways you become.

LIBRA/FOUR/EIGHT

You'd like to feel you were successful both on a business level and in your private affairs but although financial rewards are usually yours for the taking little of a personal nature is ever going to be offered up to you on a plate. You're going to have to work overtime to gain even a rudimentary understanding of the opposite sex. Try to be more demonstrative, less demanding and above all totally honest if you ever hope to enter into a stable, permanent relationship.

LIBRA/FOUR/NINE

Just as your career looks set to take off you have to go and upset your immediate superiors with a thoughtless word, while in private you think you can get away with murder. There are times when the description 'walking disaster area' fits you very aptly — take greater care in future.

LIBRA/FIVE/ONE

You would particularly like to make a name for yourself in your chosen field with one of your pioneering schemes; you'd also love to travel the world at your leisure visiting some of those far away places with strange sounding names; and you'd like to feel your relationship was strong enough to stand the test of time. All things are possible, and once you've managed to conquer your natural impatience to see results there's no real reason why you shouldn't gradually be able to turn your dreams into realities.

LIBRA/FIVE/TWO

Jealousy and envy are two deadly sins which you need to cast out. Restlessness won't get you anywhere except on everyone's nerves and will only add to your feelings of frustration. Possessiveness, sensitivity and a tendency to sarcasm will also take an effort to erase but you'll be glad to hear that you can hang on to your excessive sensuality as this appears to be your best way of unwinding after a hard day.

LIBRA/FIVE/THREE

You are one of those people who goes through life making all the mistakes in the book yet still manages to keep one step ahead. At work you're always in hot water because basically you're insubordinate, don't like being told what to do and choose to answer back at all the wrong moments. In private you're not nearly serious enough, treating your partner like a chattel and your actual relationship as something of a joke.

LIBRA/FIVE/FOUR

Ambitions are for the adventurous, plans and schemes are for designers but playing safe is for you. It's not that you lack imagination or indeed courage, as anyone who's ever witnessed you standing up for yourself must surely agree, it's just that you like a quiet life which conforms wherever possible to the generally accepted pattern of behaviour. This doesn't mean that you're either dull or boring — it's just the need to make changes and adjustments never arises.

LIBRA/FIVE/FIVE

If all your good points were put to one side and your shortcomings to the other and the two piles were weighed against one another it's just possible that a point of balance could be reached but it wouldn't take much to upset the applecart either way. It's entirely up to you whether you put your talent and creativity to profitable use or whether you decide to fritter your time away in the pursuit of sensual gratification.

LIBRA/FIVE/SIX

Whether its the first thing in the morning or last thing at night you're always cheerful because you have such an easy-going, sunny personality. At work you're co-operative, dependable and always willing to lend workmates a helping hand. When socializing you're utterly charming and great company; while, in the privacy of your own home, you're sensual, passionate and sexually adventurous. But woe betide anyone who ever gets on the wrong side of either you or yours.

LIBRA/FIVE/SEVEN

You must select a career with care because anything too dull or repetitious would soon get on your highbrow nerves. Additionally its in your nature to laze about whenever you get the chance and when it comes to handling money you have no sense whatsoever. It's hardly surprising that you don't get on well at work as you're a difficult person to place and don't always give an employer full value for money in terms of output.

LIBRA/FIVE/EIGHT

Impatience and frustration go hand in hand when you're about. At work you're continually champing at the bit and angling for swift advancement, while at home you never sit down for any length of time because you're frightened of missing something. Too much tension isn't good for you, particularly when you manufacture most of it yourself, and unless you calm down you might be sowing the seeds for all sorts of nervous ailments.

LIBRA/FIVE/NINE

Providing nobody upsets you and life is running reasonably well you couldn't hope to meet a more charming individual than yourself. You whistle while you work, laugh and joke with everyone and make your partner feel like royalty. Unfortunately it doesn't take very much to shatter the prevailing atmosphere of peace and goodwill. All that's needed is some minor criticism, interference or frustration to bring thunderclouds onto the horizon and a menacing frown to your brow.

LIBRA/SIX/ONE

It's about time you started helping yourself rather more often, particularly at work, because in a competitive environment you're going to need either an influential sponsor or a 'me first' attitude. At home you can afford to stay just as sweet as you are with one small proviso, try not to wrap your partner in cotton wool because you can suffocate people with kindness.

LIBRA/SIX/TWO

You can rarely see when you're being cheated or when your rights are being flagrantly infringed. Check out your contract of employment, find out exactly what all the small print means and make sure that in future no one oversteps the mark. And in private the sooner you stop worshipping from afar and get to grips with your passion the more stable your relationship will become.

LIBRA/SIX/THREE

You're creative, artistic and imaginative, shrewd, original and incredibly lucky. However you'll need to be decisive and very positive to reap all the rewards you could earn from life and you can't afford to be lazy or complacent about anything. And in private, although you're undeniably witty and charming, don't trade too much on your physical attributes.

LIBRA/SIX/FOUR

Someone ought to buy you a referee's whistle for your birthday because the atmosphere where you work probably wouldn't be so harmonious without you there to keep the peace. At home you're the one who always has to come up with a solution to family problems or who has to pacify everyone from the cat upwards. You're capable, practical and utterly unflappable. However, don't become such a tower of strength that no one ever stops to consider your feelings and needs.

LIBRA/SIX/FIVE

You have a fine mind and a colourful imagination. Both need not only constant stimulation but also a continual supply of new interests and ideas to weight up and consider. Sexually your needs are much the same — plenty of variety and lots of scope. Unfortunately not everyone sees eye to eye with your free and easy lifestyle and occasionally it may be necessary to appear to conform.

LIBRA/SIX/SIX

They don't come much more helpful or good-natured than you. You're kind caring and utterly selfless. Your own needs and wishes are purely incidentals and never cross your mind until you've ensured that everyone else is happy and settled. You make a loyal friend, a dedicated partner and a responsible parent. People are important to you and you're at your best when fussing round.

LIBRA/SIX/SEVEN

You're very good at understanding the needs of others. You're also generous with your time and money and like to feel your door is ever open to those in trouble. So why do you get so embarassed when others try to repay your kindness in some small way or when friends attempt to return your hospitality? Try not to snub other peoples' efforts on your behalf; after all fair exchange is not robbery.

LIBRA/SIX/EIGHT

Money rules your life and every move you make is an act of devotion to the god Mammon. If you continue in this cold, uncaring course you'll probably have to learn all your lessons the hard way. Should you ever need help who do you know who would volunteer; if you ever fall sick who would willingly minister to your needs; and if you run into trouble who would stand and fight by your side?

LIBRA/SIX/NINE

Start redeeming your boss's faith in you by making the extra effort to get jobs finished on time. Also what about all those empty promises you made to your partner? Couldn't you go out of your way to fulfil just a few of them at least? Actions speak louder than words and although your intentions are good its time you showed more willing and got stuck into something for a change.

LIBRA/SEVEN/ONE

It's sad but unfortunately true that you lack the determination and drive required to unlock more than a very small portion of your true potential. You're talented, original and creative but what good is that if you don't know how to sell either yourself or your ideas? Try to be more forceful where business matters are concerned and firmer in your personal life. If you attempt to stretch yourself just a little further each day you can't fail to make some progress in the right direction; albeit slowly.

LIBRA/SEVEN/TWO

You have the sensitivity to experience great extremes of emotion with agony at one end of the scale rising to ecstasy at the other. You set great store by personal relationships but tend to expect far more from them than any one human being is capable of providing. Wishing for the moon is not only a foolish thing to do because it's such a waste of time but also because your impossible desire will only lead to disillusionment. Try to be more realistic in future.

LIBRA/SEVEN/THREE

You're always in such a hurry to leap that you seldom bother to look before you do, and that's why you invariably end up in a mess. You're very good at allowing your imagination to take the place of proper research and thus when confronted with new situations the reality bears little or no resemblance to your pre-formed opinion. At work you need to pay greater attention to detail while in private keep both feet firmly on the floor.

LIBRA/SEVEN/FOUR

You follow the same old routine week in week out, not because you're dull or unimaginative but simply because you lack the drive and impetus to effect any changes. You've probably been in the same job most of your life and seldom say more than a handful of words during the course of any evening to your partner. Perhaps you should occasionally try to break the monotony.

LIBRA/SEVEN/FIVE

The problem is that you're thin skinned and easily hurt so in order to protect yourself from possible emotional injury you behave in a defensive manner. If you'd ever stopped to consider how offensive some of your own remarks and actions can be to others you'd probably die of embarassment but as it is, you hide behind your shield of sarcasm and never give it a moment's thought.

LIBRA/SEVEN/SIX

You're shy, sensitive and peace-loving; not very good at looking pain and suffering in the face but very good at sweeping anything unpleasant or distasteful into a dark corner of your mind where it can be forgotten. It's time you took off those rose-tinted glasses and faced up to the fact that society isn't perfect and that there are some aspects of it you're just going to have to learn to live with because they're here to stay.

LIBRA/SEVEN/SEVEN

You are a soulful, creative individual who just wants to be left alone to study the mysteries of the universe. Peace and quiet are more important to you than physical love although a true marriage of minds is something you're always dreaming of. Hang on to a corner of reality and don't let go because you're in danger of drifting out of touch, which once lost is virtually impossible to regain.

LIBRA/SEVEN/EIGHT

A balanced emotional outlook is what you need more than anything else otherwise your judgement will be better on some days than others and your relationship will be subject to a great many ups and downs. You have a brilliant, calculating mind which can add up columns of figures in a matter of seconds and dream up revolutionary new ideas overnight. Don't let your feelings cloud any further issues and try not to let moodiness affect your work or your attitude towards others.

LIBRA/SEVEN/NINE

You'd do almost anything for even a small show of affection and you leave yourself wide open to be taken for a ride by every Jezabel or conman in town. Don't be in such a hurry to buy drinks for strangers; don't make your loneliness quite so pathetically obvious and try to widen your circle of friends by joining evening classes or a choral society rather than hanging round all the pubs and clubs in the neighbourhood.

LIBRA/EIGHT/ONE

You're a very independent individual and can manage to get things done all by yourself with neither help nor encouragement. You're respectable, responsible and as honest as the day is long. Socializing is not a pastime you enjoy as you're far too self-controlled to ever let yourself go and much too prudish to find many jokes funny. This straightlaced attitude also acts as a dampener at home.

LIBRA/EIGHT/TWO

For someone who disapproves so strongly of most innocent forms of enjoyment you seem to take a keen, if rather furtive, interest in members of the opposite sex, other people's relationships and the act of procreation itself. You'd like nothing more than to be madly loved — passionately and to the point of distraction. But until you change your tune and stop being so cold and inhibited nothing of the sort is ever likely to happen.

LIBRA/EIGHT/THREE

By day you're the sober, upright employee; hard-working, efficient and totally dedicated to duty. By night and at weekends a definite switch takes place. You swap your straight face for a warm, sunny smile, your self-control for a lively sense of humour and your air of respectability for an old towelling bathrobe and a pair of slippers. Being a model of respectability is not easy for any length of time, so when you return home you want nothing more than to relax and be your other self.

LIBRA/EIGHT/FOUR

No problem is too great for you to cope with and no emergency could possibly throw you into a state of panic. You do your work in a steady, orderly manner and your private life, even the intimate moments, are conducted in much the same way. Painting by numbers is a pleasant hobby but love-making in the same manner is ridiculous. There are some things which should be spontaneous.

LIBRA/EIGHT/FIVE

Life would be a lot easier if you'd stop trying to live it in a way you believe other people would approve and followed your own inclinations instead. You dress soberly and conservatively purely to create the right impression; you voice views and opinions which are not only middle of the road but also unlikely to provoke violent reactions. It's time you broke the mould and did your own thing for a change. Don't worry what others think.

LIBRA/EIGHT/SIX

It would be a tremendous shame if you let all your creativity and artistic flair go to waste. There's no law against expressing yourself in vivid colours or poetic phrases and if your dabblings and scribblings embarrass you in front of others the answer is quite simple — keep them somewhere they won't be seen. In many ways you're a model of respectability and a pillar of society. Just because you enjoy 'putting brush' to canvas, there's no need to become a full blown Bohemian.

LIBRA/EIGHT/SEVEN

Unless you force yourself to get out and about more often you could find the solitary lifestyle you choose to lead begins to have some nasty side effects. Apart from going to your job each day you rarely set foot outside the front door and even at work you tend to keep yourself to yourself and your mind on the task in hand. You need a hobby or an interest which will turn your thoughts in an outward direction instead of inwards upon yourself.

LIBRA/EIGHT/EIGHT

There are many parallels which can be drawn between your attitude and that of a Victorian mill-owner. You're self-made, hard-working and, for these reasons, successful. You like everyone to know how well you're doing and surround yourself with expensive symbols of your status. However you wouldn't like it to become too widely known how badly you treat subordinates, how offhand and uncaring you are at home or how unscrupulous you can be when you want to get your own way.

LIBRA/EIGHT/NINE

You always get angry when you can't see a joke, even when it's been explained to you. And when you discover you're the butt of one, you react even more violently than Rumplestiltskin when his name was discovered. It's unlikely you'll ever become the office wit or the life and soul of the part, but try to stop being so grumpy all the time.

LIBRA/NINE/ONE

Once you've set your heart on something, whether it's a house, a job or a member of the opposite sex, you'll neither relax nor be satisfied until it's yours. Even when your plans lead you into a collision course with disaster you still won't call it a day; you'll carry on to the bitter end. You're tough, determined and more obstinate than any mule. You put tremendous effort into everything you do and expect to see the same dedication from your partner and colleagues.

LIBRA/NINE/TWO

Your heart rules your head; you mix business with pleasure; and anyone who doesn't instantly agree with everything you say gets black-balled. Try not to let personalities divorce you from the truth and don't base all your assumptions on pure gut feeling, do some background checking before forming any opinions.

LIBRA/NINE/THREE

They don't come much more forceful or dynamic than you. At work you know exactly where you're going and which route to take — usually the most direct. You're positive, professional and streets ahead of colleagues and competitors. You're a very physical person who prefers actions to words every time especially when it comes to showing feelings. However, patience and tact were never your strong points and you still have to learn how to wait and when it's wise to keep a still tongue.

LIBRA/NINE/FOUR

With efficiency and precision, which you have, and good firm foundations, which no doubt you could supply, you've got exactly what it takes to build yourself a small empire, so long as you remember that Rome took more than a day. Impatience is the weakest link in your chain so take care you don't let it prove to be the one which lets you down.

LIBRA/NINE/FIVE

You're restless and impatient; tactless and irresponsible; lustful and promiscuous. You change jobs and partners with some regularity and yet never seem to be any better off for all that, either financially or emotionally. You're about as subtle as a sledgehammer yet it has to be said you're honest.

LIBRA/NINE/SIX

You always seem to be torn between two courses of action and until you make the decision to commit yourself to one or the other you'll never know any real peace of mind. Your dilemma is a working one — whether to opt for commerce or art. You have sufficient talent and flair to make quite a name for yourself in either.

LIBRA/NINE/SEVEN

Your passions run deep, your ideals are lofty and your thoughts are frequently of higher things. You're a persuasive orator, a true pioneer and undoubtedly a leader of the people. Yet a brilliant career, although quite likely, is not your prime concern, neither is a stable relationship, although that's on the cards too. You seek your rewards on a spiritual level even though your religious persuasions are bound to be unorthodox and your path to enlightenment not a conventional one.

LIBRA/NINE/EIGHT

No matter what your chosen career you have such drive and ambition that you're sure to be a success. You are tough, tenacious and adaptable which means you'll be able to weather the storms which will inevitably blow up from time to time. You're hard-working, conscientious and highly professional which should ensure your promotion. In personal life, although you find the initial stages of any relationship rather trying, once you've settled into some sort of routine you make a devoted, demonstrative partner.

LIBRA/NINE/NINE

You throw yourself enthusiastically into everything you do and sometimes you get so carried away that tact and discretion go completely out of the window. You must learn to keep things more to yourself, particularly information of a confidential nature, or you could find friends accusing you of betraying their trust and your partner won't be quite so ready to let you into secrets if your silence can't be guaranteed.

SCORPIO/ONE/ONE

Nothing is sacred when you're around and you'll steal someone's partner just as casually as you'd steal their job. You're ruthless, unscrupulous and only out for your own gain and self aggrandizement. However, it doesn't always pay to take chances quite so regularly and one of these days you could come unstuck. When you do it's a sheep you'll be hung for never an innocent lamb.

SCORPIO/ONE/TWO

At work you probably have to project yourself in a forceful manner in order to attract any attention at all but in one to one situations there's no need to rant and rave because your audience is small and usually captive. Try not to get so wound-up about your problems that you become a bore and try to extend more thought and understanding in the direction of your partner.

SCORPIO/ONE/THREE

Some rewards can only be earned the hard way and some goals may never be achieved however determined you are. Try to be more realistic in your desires, not quite so unscrupulous in your dealings and rather less cold-blooded in your personal affairs. Real love cannot be brought and success only tastes good when it's been honestly achieved.

SCORPIO/ONE/FOUR

No one would ever guess what lengths you'd go to to achieve your ends because nothing about your appearance or attitude gives so much as a clue to your burning desires and deep inner secrets. You're certainly a very dark horse indeed. Much of your success is entirely due to your carefully laid plans and faultless groundwork.

You never make an impulsive move nor allow growing impatience to make you careless.

SCORPIO/ONE/FIVE

You seem to run entirely on nervous energy which you generate yourself in a never-ending stream. Provided your health remains sound and your wits stay sharp you're sure to survive extremely well but should either even let you down, you could be in serious trouble. Take out some insurance now by cutting fewer corners in future and not relying so heavily on adrenaline alone to get you out of difficulties. It may cramp your style but it should pay dividends in the long term.

SCORPIO/ONE/SIX

You're not as hard as you'd like to think – in fact, quite the opposite. Secretly you're afraid that caring for others will make you vulnerable, and it could well be true, but there's no need to go out of your way to be cruel and nasty as a counter-measure. Soften up without going soft and try to show more compassion on occasions when its needed.

SCORPIO/ONE/SEVEN

You have one major advantage over all your competitors at work and rivals in love, namely the ability to keep your thoughts to yourself and your intentions a closely guarded secret until the right moment comes to reveal all. You make an exciting partner because as well as being passionate, earthy and demonstrative you're also full of unexpected little surprises. And you cut a dynamic professional figure whatever your chosen career because you're decisive, determined and ambitious.

SCORPIO/ONE/EIGHT

You don't spend nearly enough time at the drawing-board or at experimental stages, so when errors finally come to light they're twice as difficult to correct. Don't be in such a hurry to run when you haven't yet mastered the art of standing unaided and, in future, try not to let your big ideas get out of hand. With care and caution you could go far and with better preparation you could achieve miracles.

SCORPIO/ONE/NINE

You are a strong, forceful individual yet the easiest way to influence people is to win them as your friends not terrorize them into submission. Its much easier to make progress when you have the help and assistance of others and this is a commodity you should make a greater effort to enlist, because swimming with the tide is much less exhausting than continually battling against it.

SCORPIO/TWO/ONE

You're almost impossible to fathom because your face seldom betrays any sign of emotion and your choice of clothes says nothing more than 'respectable'. However, your innate ambition is no secret, your ability to command is plain for all to see and, upon first acquaintance, your power can definitely be sensed if not actually felt.

SCORPIO/TWO/TWO

Intrigue is the name of your game and because it requires no more equipment other than a devious mind you can play it anywhere and frequently do. At work it's generally known as 'office politics' and you're a past master, playing as you do one rival off against another and then capitalizing on their mistakes. You're fly enough not to run into trouble but should you ever discover your partner in a compromising situation your ensuing rage could reach nuclear proportions.

SCORPIO/TWO/THREE

You're a highly talented, extremely gifted individual with a first-class brain and a shrewd, penetrating intellect. You can quickly home-in to the root of any problems and can usually solve them with the same speed. At work you're a force to be reckoned with and in private your partner probably regards you as a blessing to be counted. You're loyal and generous to those you love and tremendously entertaining both in and out of bed.

SCORPIO/TWO/FOUR

You're one of those rare individuals who could take a secret to the grave if necessary but you can't bear to feel that you're not fully in the picture at work or that your partner is keeping something from you. Within your relationship you demand total honesty from your partner, because deep down you're eaten up with unreasoning jealousy.

SCORPIO/TWO/FIVE

You're a fiercely private individual with an independence of spirit which you value above all else. This makes establishing any form of rapport between yourself and colleagues at work virtually impossible and also makes it very difficult for your partner to gauge your reactions. Try not to be quite so uncommunicative in future.

SCORPIO/TWO/SIX

You find it virtually impossible to share anything with your partner on a fifty-fifty basis and if you had your way, which is most of the time, you'd own them lock, stock and barrel. When you give your heart it is an irrevocable step but it can have a stifling effect on the subject of your affections. You're possessive and intense; very overpowering and often demand more than is humanly possible to give.

SCORPIO/TWO/SEVEN

Everything you do is usually shrouded in secrecy because you like to keep yourself to yourself and your business as private and confidential as possible. You seem to spend most of your spare time either researching at the library or pouring over ancient volumes in your study at home. You are fascinated by the occult and are quite likely to dabble on its fringes.

SCORPIO/TWO/EIGHT

Once you've made up your mind on a particular objective you go for it by the most direct route regardless of who or what stands in your way. There are times when the devil himself would seem like a harmless kitten alongside you because your anger can be a fearsome spectacle. Try not to make your life such a reign of terror, there's more than one way of skinning a cat and although your methods are undeniably effective they can hardly be said to promote universal peace and goodwill.

SCORPIO/TWO/NINE

At work you seem to have discovered precisely the right formula not only to command respect but also to achieve results and guarantee your promotion. You're tremendously self-controlled and for this reason always have the whip-hand in difficult situations because you never allow emotion to cloud your judgement for even a second. However in private, much as you would like to call the tune for your partner, it's not always so easy.

SCORPIO/THREE/ONE

Although you prefer to keep most people at arm's length, you're certainly very persuasive and can usually get even the crustiest old stick in the mud seeing eye to eye with your progressive ideas. You rarely experience problems attracting members of the opposite sex because you could charm the birds from the trees. But while you are prepared to take all that's on offer you give little or nothing in return.

SCORPIO/THREE/TWO

When it comes to organization you're a genius. You always know exactly where everything is, how much it costs and where to get a replacement. At work your expertise is invaluable but you should never be tempted to apply it to your personal life. Feelings can't be categorized, people don't fit into convenient pigeonholes and a strict routine allows no room for spontaneity within a relationship.

SCORPIO/THREE/THREE

You have quick wits, a brilliant mind and usually far more than your fair share of good luck so why do you find it necessary to stoop to devious, underhand methods when you could so easily achieve progress by conventional means? Whatever the reason it doesn't alter the fact that your behaviour is unnecessarily harsh and unpleasant and the sooner your attitude shows change, the better for all concerned.

SCORPIO/THREE/FOUR

You tend to be cold, hard and joyless as if programmed solely to peform a specific task of work and nothing more. But there is more to life and you're missing out. Try not to be so rigid and unbending. Come out of that rut, look on the bright side and let yourself go. You may never become a top-flight socialite but anything is an improvement on being a hermit.

SCORPIO/THREE/FIVE

Whatever it is you're afraid of the sooner you come to terms with it the sooner you'll get some balance and continuity into your life. You fidget about like a cat on hot bricks. You rarely keep a job long enough to have any prospects worth considering and you hastily change partners whenever things threaten to become serious. Until you show a little maturity no great changes can be expected but don't leave it too long as you have tremendous potential.

SCORPIO/THREE/SIX

You want to succeed above all else and as far as you're concerned no price is too high to pay for the goods on offer. You're strong, ambitious and determined. You have great confidence in your own abilities, absolutely no scruples of any kind and the devotion of a religious fanatic to the task in hand. The feelings and opinions of other people are of absolutely no concern to you and of no particular interest either.

SCORPIO/THREE/SEVEN

You have a will of iron, nerves of steel and an overpowering desire to succeed which defies all description. What's more you'll know neither peace nor rest until your dreams have all been converted into tangible realities and your hopes into hard cash. You refuse to accept 'no' as an answer. Fair means or foul — it's all the same to you provided you get what you want at the end of the day.

SCORPIO/THREE/EIGHT

You have to be noticed and you'll go to almost any lengths to gain the attention you desire. Unfortunately you don't care who gets hurt in the process so long as you get star billing. Even your private life has to be public property and provided your partner is rich, famous and preferably both, love doesn't even enter into it. You're a sensation seeker and a social climber.

SCORPIO/THREE/NINE

You instinctively know how to motivate other people. You're a strong, ambitious individual and so shrewd and calculating that you've usually worked out every move to win the game long before the first pawn has left its square. You undoubtedly deserve to succeed because strategically you're brilliant but in private it would perhaps be better to let matters take a more natural course.

SCORPIO/FOUR/ONE

Provided you project your pioneering spirit in a useful direction and don't go throwing it away on some lost cause or cranky project, then your financial and business success is virtually guaranteed. Your ideas are original and you have the enviable ability to produce outstanding results when working alone and unaided.

SCORPIO/FOUR/TWO

You must realize that there are certain aspects of life which will never change however distasteful you may find them; that you're not going to be able to win the love and affection of everyone you chance to meet; and that you'll never get anywhere by burying your head in the sand like an ostrich. Try to be more tolerant and don't be in such a hurry to throw in the towel every time something goes wrong.

SCORPIO/FOUR/THREE

You seem unable, or unwilling, to concentrate on one thing at a time and your insistence upon having a finger in several pies at once only results in mediocrity at best and disaster at worst. Your thoughts are too scattered and your efforts insufficient to ever make much of a name for yourself although the potential to achieve great things is undoubtedly there.

SCORPIO/FOUR/FOUR

You're superbly well organized, tremendously efficient and one hundred per cent loyal and trustworty. Unfortunately you get mixed up with all the wrong people and either get persuaded to fight on behalf of causes which were lost before they begun or for organizations that are divided among themselves. With realistic goals and sound backing you could go far.

SCORPIO/FOUR/FIVE

You expect to be a resounding success at work without having to go through the boring business of working your way up from the bottom and you seem to think that stable relationships just happen after the first intimate encounter. Your ideas need straightening out and perhaps once this has been achieved you'll find it easier to fit in with other people.

SCORPIO/FOUR/SIX

You're an active reformer who cares deeply about everyone however lowly their station or humble their origins. Unfortunately most of your efforts prove to be futile. You'd be better employed tending to the needs of your own family and maybe even more satisfied with your own relationship if you worked just a little harder at it.

SCORPIO/FOUR/SEVEN

Politics and religion are both subjects you rarely discuss but this doesn't mean you're ignorant about either – in fact, quite the reverse. You have strong feelings, heartfelt convictions and firm beliefs but you prefer to keep them very much to yourself. You're wise enough to see that voicing revolutionary opinions will only lead to arguments.

SCORPIO/FOUR/EIGHT

You wouldn't dream of trying to preach to the converted so why do you insist upon taking coals to Newcastle? It just won't work however professional your approach. And in private you'll only get out of a relationship what you're prepared to put in, which in your case is very little. Be more realistic, it could make quite a difference all round.

SCORPIO/FOUR/NINE

Your temper is always an uncertain commodity at the best of times but when passions are running high and the adrenalin starts pumping it can so easily get out of control. Try to keep your opinions to yourself, or at least until you've mastered the art of public debate. Before you start getting hot under the collar remember that everyone is entitled to an opinion and that it doesn't necessarily have to be wrong.

SCORPIO/FIVE/ONE

Great achievement is within your grasp provided you pace yourself carefully and resist the temptation to push yourself beyond the limits of endurance. You have the kind of determination which could take you right to the top and the powers of leadership to inspire others to take up your cause or follow in your footsteps. However, a quiet social life might be the price you have to pay for success as without adequate rest and relaxation you'll soon lose your edge and perhaps with it, your command of situations.

SCORPIO/FIVE/TWO

Although your spirit is willing your flesh is not, so unless you take care of not only your body, but your mind as well, you could find stressful situations getting the better of you and your slender reserves of strength quickly becoming depleted. Don't push yourself any harder than you know you can safely handle and don't ever allow your colourful imagination to run riot, particularly in emotive situations.

SCORPIO/FIVE/THREE

When it comes to intelligence, versatility and quick wits you're in a class of your own as you frequently demonstrate by running mental rings around all and sundry. However, you have a massive ego. And you'd better watch out because pride not only comes before a fall it very often precipitates one.

SCORPIO/FIVE/FOUR

The sad fact is that despite your vast knowledge and wide range of personal observations you can be about as dull as ditch-water. You could put a dampener on any proceedings and could even make tales of heroism and bravery sound boring and mundane. The sooner you learn to make more of yourself the sooner more attention will come your way.

SCORPIO/FIVE/FIVE

Your wits are razor sharp, your intellect brilliant and your repartee punctuates a conversation like parries from a verbal rapier. But this exhausting choice of lifestyle can only be safely supported for short periods at a time and unless you allow yourself adequate opportunity to relax and unwind you could be stirring up all kinds of trouble for yourself later on.

SCORPIO/FIVE/SIX

You have much to offer and tremendous potential which would benefit from intellectual stimulation and the opportunity for creative expression. But unless you select a partner with care and take pains to choose one who is mentally your equal you could be heading for grief and disillusionment. Once the first heady taste of romance has lost its enchantment and your conversation revolves around nothing more uplifting than the weather you won't have much left to either enjoy or look forward to.

SCORPIO/FIVE/SEVEN

There's something intensely magnetic and compelling about you from your sombre dramatic clothes to your expressionless, penetrating eyes. You can appear powerful, mysterious and strangely menacing at one and the same time. Although people are drawn to your side either in the hope of winning your friendship or enlisting your support you always manage to remain aloof and detached no matter how close they try to get.

SCORPIO/FIVE/EIGHT

Some people are prepared to wait for their rewards in heaven — however you're not that patient. You want yours here and now. You're mercenary and materialistic. You have a flair for business, a talent for making money and a positive genius for showing a quick return. You're a showman, an entrepreneur, a financial wizard. Unfortunately you lack understanding and finesse when it comes to personal relationships.

SCORPIO/FIVE/NINE

At work you can never resist the temptation to make a workmate or colleague appear small and stupid any more than you can stop yourself from picking on your partner's shortcomings and blowing them up out of all proportion. It's unkind and unpleasant to gain cheap laughs at the expense of other people's feelings and you should do everything you can to curb your natural inclination towards spitefulness and cruelty.

SCORPIO/SIX/ONE

You fly in the face of convention, rail against the Establishment and stubbornly refuse to toe any line you chance to come up against. In private you're ardent and passionate although your performance is more akin to that of a rutting animal than a civilized human being. You're red-blooded, rebellious and rudely outspoken but a likeable rascal for all that.

SCORPIO/SIX/TWO

It's a wonder you ever manage to survive financially because as far as visible means of support go you don't appear to have any. You're an artisan, a Bohemian, a strolling player — in fact anything but a conventional nine to fiver. You're a talented artist, an aspiring poet and a persuasive orator; you lean to all things creative as a means of making a living and you revel in all things sensual and romantic as a way of passing the time.

SCORPIO/SIX/THREE

You need constant stimulation to prevent you from growing bored and once one source dries up you soon move on in search of another. Your private life runs on similar lines as you're always looking for not only something new and exciting to do but also for somebody weird and wonderful to do it with. Once the familiar ceases to feel different you know it's time for a change.

SCORPIO/SIX/FOUR

You are much too conservative and conventional to even consider earning a living as a freelance artist or classical musician. Your deep-rooted commonsense tells you that these enjoyable methods of self-expression are nothing more than hobbies from which a little pin-money can be made if you're good enough. But what you fail to realize is that you do have considerable talent which is going to waste simply because you lack the foresight, courage and imagination to put it to the test.

SCORPIO/SIX/FIVE

You thrive on excitement, stretch yourself to the limits and never know when you've had enough, and if that wasn't tiring enough your social life is even more hectic. There are only two courses of action open to you. You can carry on the way you're going and have a short life but a full one or you can take immediate remedial action in the form of a long holiday followed by a drastically pruned agenda when you return to harness.

SCORPIO/SIX/SIX

You're an out-and-out rebel from the peace sign in your parlour window to the piles of unpaid parking tickets and rate demands on your desk. You don't like being told what to do, neither do you like to be told what company to keep. What goes on in your bedroom is thankfully nobody's business but your own and certainly not a topic for polite conversation.

SCORPIO/SIX/SEVEN

You question everything, have to know all the in's and out's and even then probably won't be satisfied until you've added a few finishing touches of your own. Even in private you insist upon analysing every intimate detail of a relationship and this sort of attitude is likely to do more harm than good. Put away your magnifying glass, shut your eyes and go by feel for a change.

SCORPIO/SIX/EIGHT

You've never found it easy to conform because your views and opinions seem totally different from those of others. But the very fact that you do things in your own, fiercely individual way, could prove to be the ace up your sleeve. Who else would ever dream of half the things you do let alone have the courage of their convictions to put their schemes into action.

SCORPIO/SIX/NINE

You ask for just about everything you get. In fact the majority of your problems are self-inflicted. At work you hate being told what to do; you abhor rules and regulations of any kind and give those in authority over you a very hard time indeed. You'd be the archetypal shop steward if only you belonged to a union. In private you have about as much tact as a five year-old who's just spotted some sweets. Try not to make your desires quite so obvious.

SCORPIO/SEVEN/ONE

The reason for your personal success isn't solely your exceedingly retentive memory nor your ability to solve age-old problems by unique and unorthodox methods of your own devising. Probably the greatest single factor responsible for your enviable achievements is the way you can not only tune in to your subconscious mind at will but also trust it to be your guide. You should continue to rely on your finely tuned instincts.

SCORPIO/SEVEN/TWO

Anyone as fanciful and imaginative as you who considers dabbling in the occult would be well advised to enlist help and guidance. It's not only foolhardy but also down-right dangerous to meddle with things you know little or nothing about.

SCORPIO/SEVEN/THREE

You're a natural clairvoyant, a surprisingly accurate forecaster of future events, a good dowser — in fact, a born psychic. However, you're far too well balanced and easy going to ever get fanciful or carried away by your talents. Besides which your hobbies and interests take up so much of your spare time that you rarely give your ESP much of a thought.

SCORPIO/SEVEN/FOUR

On the surface you appear practical, conventional and very down to earth. You always live within your means, rarely go out on the town and although your friends are few in number their worth to you is inestimable. However there is a strange inexplicable side to your character which you never discuss. You have the uncanny knack of knowing what's happening to members of your family, even when they're far from home. It's a shame you feel it necessary to hide such a gift.

SCORPIO/SEVEN/FIVE

You seem to think you can bend all the rules, break all the established codes of conduct and still come up smelling of roses. But one of these days you're going to come unstuck. Leopards are not well known for changing their spots but a few manage to do so successfully — perhaps you might be one of them.

SCORPIO/SEVEN/SIX

Natural gifts come in many different forms and packages. Your particular blessings are an eye for colour and a flair for design. However, like all true artists whose work borders on genius you have the unpredictable temperament that goes with it. You have a colourful imagination, changes of moods and a way of seeing pictures in your mind long before you commit them to canvas or paper.

SCORPIO/SEVEN/SEVEN

If society were to break down all around you and civilization ceased to exist, its debatable whether you'd even notice until your library books needed returning and you discovered the library was no longer there. You're totally self-sufficient needing neither the company of other people to keep you amused nor their assistance to achieve your ends. You're in very real danger of losing touch with reality.

SCORPIO/SEVEN/EIGHT

You seem to be obsessed with making money and none too fussy how you do so. For a supposedly ambitious, sophisticated individual you have some extraordinarily naive and superstitious ideas in that head of yours. Try not to spend quite so much time brooding on your own, rely more on common sense than mystical mumbo-jumbo and never admit in public to the unorthodox beliefs you hold in private.

SCORPIO/SEVEN/NINE

Don't worry so much about the fate of mankind and the reason for life. You'd be much better occupied finding yourself a decent job and putting your own affairs in order. The devil makes work for idle hands and the sooner yours are fully occupied the much less likely you'll be to stray into trouble.

SCORPIO/EIGHT/ONE

You need neither help nor encouragement to get you going or to keep you on course. Even when things get difficult the thought of giving up and trying something else would never cross your mind for an instant. Unfortunately work is your only interest and you seem to have neither the time nor the inclination to form personal attachments.

SCORPIO/EIGHT/TWO

When all is said and done you're not really cut out to be a business tycoon. You're full of big ideas and lofty intentions but you lack the determination to see them through or the emotional stability to keep your balance. Your delusions are of grandeur and for that reason the only castles you'll ever build will be in the air.

SCORPIO/EIGHT/THREE

You'd go a lot further if you stopped treating life as one huge, enormous joke and buckled down to some hard work for a change. In private, go for a partner with plenty of sparkle. You need someone to keep you on your toes or you'll soon get bored and wander off. You also need someone of the same intellectual capacity as your own, otherwise, no-matter how effervescent they might be, it will be no kind of contest at all.

SCORPIO/EIGHT/FOUR

You never seem to miss a trick because you keep you ear to the ground and your eyes open. 'No' is one word you won't accept for an answer, 'impossible' only makes you all the more determined to succeed and 'rest' is something you don't know the meaning of. You're as hard as nails and about as comforting as a cold hot water bottle. You are bound to go far.

SCORPIO/EIGHT/FIVE

You're a bit of a 'cowboy', a fixer who, on the surface, appears to have done a good job, that is until a closer inspection is made. Try to be more professional in all your business undertakings if you don't want to get a bad reputation and try to cultivate a few more honourable intentions in private if you don't want your name blackened.

SCORPIO/EIGHT/SIX

Sentiment easily moves you to tears, and you'd sit up half the night tending an injured bird. But you have two very different sides to you nature one of which could do with some improvement. Try not to be so hard and cold when seated behind your desk. By being more understanding and less rigid you'd gain far more respect and greater co-operation from your colleagues.

SCORPIO/EIGHT/SEVEN

You find it virtually impossible to delegate responsibility, not because you don't trust others to do the job properly but because you're secretly afraid of losing control. Power is something you refuse to relinquish even for a short time. Unless you learn to share the reins occasionally you could be kissing goodbye not only to all your leisure time but eventually to your relationship too.

SCORPIO/EIGHT/EIGHT

You never seem to relax or get any pleasure from life other than amassing vast amounts of money. Your relationship is a mess and your health won't stand up to such punishing treatment indefinitely. It is high time you got your priorities right before fate decides to intervene and readjust them for you.

SCORPIO/EIGHT/NINE

If only you weren't quite so quarrelsome and hard to please you'd probably have many more friends and a much happier life. Its doubtful whether a school of etiquette would be prepared to accept an application for lessons from someone as difficult as you but it's worth a try.

SCORPIO/NINE/ONE

You have nerves of steel, a will of iron and tremendous self-discipline. Physically you're capable of almost super-human endurance simply because you take great care of your body and mentally your concentration is unbreakable because that's the way you've trained it. In private your heart is beyond reach. Many have tried to reach it but few have ever succeeded.

SCORPIO/NINE/TWO

Your constantly changing moods are the root cause of most of your problems because no sooner do you seem to have got on to an even emotional keel than you slip mooring and drift off into the main shipping lanes. Not until you learn to control yourself will you ever be able to take charge of your own destiny and not until you treat other people with the consideration they deserve will you ever receive any in return.

SCORPIO/NINE/THREE

You are one of those infuriating people who puts everyone else to shame. Not only can you turn your hand to most things in a highly professional manner, you can also work back-breaking shifts without showing any sign of fatigue and are so superbly organized that nothing ever seems to disrupt your private arrangements. But if you have a heart you never listen to it and if you're capable of deep feelings they usually erupt in the form of temper.

SCORPIO/NINE/FOUR

Although you have an almost inexhaustible supply of energy, a highly ambitious nature and enough confidence for three other people besides yourself, you never allow your self-assurance to run away with you and make you careless. Caution is one of your watchwords and although you like to see quick results whenever possible, if any part of your overall strategy is less than one hundred per cent perfect you won't proceed until it is.

SCORPIO/NINE/FIVE

You're a born gambler, perhaps not of the variety that haunt casinos and racetracks, but the sort who's never afraid to take their life in their hands for a little adventure and, who knows, perhaps even a substantial profit. Your personal life is conducted in much the same devil-may-care way and when one partner begins to pall you have little or no problem finding a replacement.

SCORPIO/NINE/SIX

Although you're active and courageous, you seldom stick your neck out any further than you know to be safe except in matters concerning your family of whom you're fiercely protective. You would fight to the death for any member of your brood because the survival of the family unit is far more important to you than anything else. You are loving, affectionate and faithful but about as deadly as a coiled snake if anyone dares to tread on your tail.

SCORPIO/NINE/SEVEN

You always prefer to hide your light under a bushel. Not because you're particularly modest or unassuming but simply because the less other people know about you the better you like it. It's probably just as well as some of the things you get up to, particularly in private, are enough to bring an instant curl to anyone's hair. You're powerful, strong-willed and active but that mask of secrecy can make you appear rather frightening and sinister.

SCORPIO/NINE/EIGHT

You rarely seem to be in full control of your temper and it doesn't take much to set it blazing. An ill-timed remark is quite sufficient to see you explode and when you do it can be an awesome sight. You can be hard, violent and ruthless and this sort of behaviour will neither win you friends nor help influence people. No one will put up with being brow-beaten into submission forever.

SCORPIO/NINE/NINE

By day you're a workaholic; confident, tough and really going places. By night you're all animal passion and earthy desires. You work hard by you play even harder. However, there's a nasty sadistic streak in you which needs better control and a good sprinkling of latent violence mixed in with your sexual preferences. You must do everything you can to keep your actions to accepted levels.

SAGITTARIUS/ONE/ONE

You can't bear to feel restrained or restricted in any way. At work you prefer change and variety to security every time and in private the door to freedom must always stand open or you feel as nervous as a trapped rat. Permanence is unlikely to feature anywhere in your life for very long but the vast store of experience you'll gain on your travels should be compensation enough for a nomad like you.

SAGITTARIUS/ONE/TWO

Your moods are so uncertain and changeable that it's very difficult for those around you to guage your response to even perfectly normal questions. Try to get more discipline into your thoughts and emotions and don't let your restlessness get out of proportion, otherwise, not only will you become a bag of nerves, you'll also drive everyone else to distraction with your constant fidgeting.

SAGITTARIUS/ONE/THREE

You're a very difficult person to help, too quick tempered for your own good and virtually impossible to pin down. Commitment and responsibility are two things you'll go to great lengths to avoid because you need to feel free to come and go as you please. The thought of settling down appals you and it's probably just as well because although you're charming and good company you're much too undisciplined and unreliable to be much of a catch in the marriage stakes.

SAGITTARIUS/ONE/FOUR

You like to dream of travelling the world, changing your job or living a glamorous, film-star life but all the time that little voice in your head tells you not to be so fanciful and stupid. However, there are times when you act out of impulse simply because your deep-seated restlessness has been allowed to surface. You'll forget appointments, ignore responsibilities and generally act in a selfish, uncaring manner. Fortunately these outbursts are usually few and far between.

SAGITTARIUS/ONE/FIVE

You have neither a thought nor a care for anyone in the world except yourself and so long as you happen to be enjoying life then everything must be fine and dandy. It's a wonder you ever manage to keep a job because they don't come much more idle and insubordinate than you. And it's an even greater wonder that you ever find time to sleep as you're always out catwalking in your spare time.

SAGITTARIUS/ONE/SIX

Anyone with a modicum of talent can draw a vase of flowers or paint a passable landscape but you have the depth of feeling to make your work come alive and such an adventurous imagination that you'll use colour combinations no one else would ever dream of. Even though you may seldom leave your own home town your range of subject material knows no limits. You're neither reliable nor disciplined when it comes to tedious tasks at work or routine duties around the home but as far as your true vocation is concerned you have the patience of a saint.

SAGITTARIUS/ONE/SEVEN

Travel is one of your greatest pleasures although you like to get as far away from the well-beaten tourist track as possible, preferably under your own steam. When it comes to earning a living you could hardly be described as a model employee as you lack discipline or interest in routine matters. And as a lover, although you make an exceptionally exciting one, you're very wary of getting trapped into marriage.

SAGITTARIUS/ONE/EIGHT

You're intelligent, energetic and ready to go anywhere for opportunities even if they are half-way round the world. But where you fall down is in your inability to cope with restrictions. Rules and regulations of any kind are like a red rag to a bull where you're concerned and unless you learn to come to terms with the necessity to be regimented and disciplined during the early stages of any career you may not get very far up the ladder.

SAGITTARIUS/ONE/NINE

Few things ever seem to capture your imagination or indeed hold your interest. The only thing which stimulates you at all is the far horizon and wondering what's over it. Don't be so quick to turn away from promising situations or people who care as history may not be so quick to repeat itself again.

SAGITTARIUS/TWO/ONE

Your style, charm and generosity are legendary. No-one knows better than you how to put on a lavish performance and no one loses interest quite so quickly either. Try not to let restlessness and lack of discipline mar your career chances. Don't let your tendency towards depression wreck your relationship and stay away from sticky buns and calorie-laden alcoholic drinks.

SAGITTARIUS/TWO/TWO

Work is a necessary evil as far as you're concerned and although you change jobs fairly frequently you've yet to find a niche to suit either your liking or your temperament. You lack grit and determination so consequently opportunity for promotion is unlikely to knock at your door. However, you do know how to relax and enjoy yourself. You're a superb cook and a born entertainer.

SAGITTARIUS/TWO/THREE

If you devoted half as much time and energy to carving a career for yourself as you do on having a good time you could be a resounding success three times over. As it is you waste your potential preferring to loaf about. A good dose of poverty would soon see you knuckling down but as things stand you manage to keep your nose financially above water.

SAGITTARIUS/TWO/FOUR

Provided life is running smoothly and those around you seem to be doing as they are told, then you're a happy, contented individual. But when problems occur or difficulties threaten to block your path you don't appear nearly so placid and serene. You're hopeless at coping with the unexpected because you're so indecisive, and unprepared when it comes to handling fractious people.

SAGITTARIUS/TWO/FIVE

At work you're far too jumpy and restless to ever complete a task properly let alone on time because your thoughts are always somewhere else. In private you can't be relied upon to keep your word for five minutes let alone till death you do part. Fidelity is not one of your strong points while loyalty and devotion rarely feature in your vocabulary.

SAGITTARIUS/TWO/SIX

It is on the home front that you manage to excel yourself time and again. Not because you're an exceptional lover or a particularly brilliant housekeeper but simply because you know not only how to relax and enjoy yourself but how to make those around you happy too. As a parent you're conscientious and responsible without ever wrapping your offspring in cotton wool. As a partner you're priceless because you have the gift of laughter and tremendous depth of feeling.

SAGITTARIUS/TWO/SEVEN

You need more order in your affairs. Get yourself a diary to keep track of appointments, change your appearance and make yourself look more presentable and get that neglected brain of yours ticking over before life passes you by once and for all. A complete overhaul is what you need.

SAGITTARIUS/TWO/EIGHT

You're going to need quite a substantial income to indulge all your big ideas. You want to see the world but only on a first class ticket, stay at all the best hotels and mix with the cream of society. Remember, moderation in all things, learn to walk before you decide to run and never get into debt just to impress others. Success won't be handed to you on a plate but it is within your grasp if you're prepared to work for it.

SAGITTARIUS/TWO/NINE

Nobody ever knows which way you're going to jump once your fuse has been lit and it doesn't take much to get you going. Even a chance remark will send you into orbit and criticism of any variety drives you nearly insane. You're volatile, unstable and very hard to handle. Try to keep calmer in future even though you're boiling up inside.

SAGITTARIUS/THREE/ONE

Although you'd do anything in your power to help loved ones through difficult patches in their lives, when it's all plain sailing you show little interest in their welfare. Try to be more caring even if it's not demanded of you because there's a vast difference between self-control and being undemonstrative and the gap seems to be widening daily.

SAGITTARIUS/THREE/TWO

Emotionally you are painfully insecure yet your behaviour does little or nothing to improve the situation. You are jealous without any real cause, possessive to the point of strangulation and totally lacking in trust. Until you learn to be more positive and less changeable very little improvement seems likely.

SAGITTARIUS/THREE/THREE

You are versatile, intelligent and on occasion some of your ideas can be quite brilliant yet time and again you'll ruin your chances at work by speaking out of turn or being none too careful in your choice of words. While in private you seem to be so totally besotted by yourself that it's hardly surprising your partner never gets so much as a look in.

SAGITTARIUS/THREE/FOUR

There is very little chance of you ever coming off the rails because you're far too sensible and level-headed. At work you make, not only a great effort, but also produce some outstanding results. At home you're placid, even-tempered and very demonstrative. If you have any faults at all, perhaps being too materialistic is your worst.

SAGITTARIUS/THREE/FIVE

If there's one person who goes through life doing it all wrong and breaking all the rules you have to be the prime candidate. You may well have the luck of the devil but you push it so far and so often that one of these days it's going to let you down — probably when you least expect it. Try to realize that others may not find your private life quite such a fascinating subject as you do.

SAGITTARIUS/THREE/SIX

You are original, open-minded and observant not to mention shrewd, intelligent and very astute. On a more intimate, personal level you are affectionate, generous and extremely demonstrative while in company your conversation is sparkling, your wit razor-sharp and your charm quite obvious for all to see. You are one of those rare individuals who can have the best of both worlds.

SAGITTARIUS/THREE/SEVEN

You are like the archetypal cartoon professor, maybe not quite mad but certainly absent minded; able to work out complex sums in seconds yet utterly hopeless at finding your own car keys or remembering to feed the goldfish. Organization is what you need and the sooner the better, or you'll continue to turn up for work wearing your slippers.

SAGITTARIUS/THREE/EIGHT

You want to be fabulously wealthy, socially sought after and the success story of the century. Unfortunately what you'd like and what you actually manage to achieve are two completely different matters. Being loud and flashy is not quite the same as being well bred and good mannered.

SAGITTARIUS/THREE/NINE

Generally speaking, others couldn't wish for better company than yours. Your conversation is interesting if a little spicy at times, your ideas are novel and imaginative and your wide knowledge of current affairs makes you a mine of information. Unfortunately there is another side to your character which is not nearly so charming or easy going and this tends to show when someone has rubbed you up the wrong way with either a word of criticism or some well-meant, but badly taken advice.

SAGITTARIUS/FOUR/ONE

You have the ability to anticipate and correct problems long before they do any damage to your grand overall schemes. It is in private that your plans don't go down quite so well. Try to be more spontaneous and demonstrative towards your partner even if it does mean putting the split-second timing of your unbendable routine out by a few minutes every now and again.

SAGITTARIUS/FOUR/TWO

You appear cool, conservative and very conventional from your smart city suit to your neat haircut and well-polished shoes. However, when time is your own not only do you manage to get mixed up with all the wrong kinds of people, either because of their political beliefs or private habits, you also have the unhappy knack of chosing the most unsuitable partners. You ought to know better being so easily hurt as you are.

SAGITTARIUS/FOUR/THREE

You're a rebel and you don't care where or to whom you voice your opinions. You challenge rules and regulations, bitterly resent restrictions of any form and, as far as you're concerned, figures of authority are there only to be baited.

SAGITTARIUS/FOUR/FOUR

You may be found shouting back at the television during party political broadcasts or threatening to lobby your MP about proposed education cuts but you won't actually get around to doing anything about it. You are an armchair activist and they are by far the safest sort. Your mind is your own, your spirit individual and reformative but your body much too set in its ways and fond of comfort to ever take to the road to protest.

SAGITTARIUS/FOUR/FIVE

You seem to think you can change partners as often as you would library books and that, provided they are returned undamaged and on time, is where your responsibility ends. You treat relationships in too casual a fashion putting yourself and your desires first along the line. Try to show more consideration for others in future and far more respect for their finer feelings.

SAGITTARIUS/FOUR/SIX

If ever there was a born committee member, a Madam Chairman or a Mr Secretary — it's you. You enjoy nothing more than organizing charity events, taking care of funds or sitting poised with pen in hand noting the minutes of one meeting or the agenda for another. The thought of making tea and sandwiches for five hundred people on a rainy summer's afternoon, or playing host to a troop of scouts never daunts you for a moment. Unless your partner shares your public spirit you could be heading for stormy weather.

SAGITTARIUS/FOUR/SEVEN

You are passionately interested in all things scientific, progressive and revolutionary, not to mention the paranormal. You believe ardently in freedom, particularly of thought, even though you usually keep your opinions to yourself. Your inclinations are more intellectual than political and while not actually a political 'don't know' you're more of a 'don't care' instead.

SAGITTARIUS/FOUR/EIGHT

You tend to take on far more than you can comfortably handle. Consequently when your resources begin to feel the strain you have nothing left in reserve to fall back on. In future try to cut your cloth according to your means leaving plenty of margin for error and never mix business with politics however tempting the idea may seem.

SAGITTARIUS/FOUR/NINE

Try to find more practical ways of helping those in need and don't be in such a hurry to take on the world. Concentrate more on your immediate neighbourhood where your actions might possibly have some effect and don't be tempted to move on to bigger and better things. Think small and look close — that's the best way to play it!

SAGITTARIUS/FIVE/ONE

You are head-strong, dynamic and determined to go it alone. However, your favourite pastime requires a minimum of two players and this is probably the only time you're prepared to concede a point and share. As a lover you're passionate, red-blooded and athletically demonstrative but as a steady partner you leave much to be desired.

SAGITTARIUS/FIVE/TWO

You need discipline, routine and regimentation to keep you on your toes. You have a naturally restless nature upon which anything new or exciting acts like an enormous magnet. You're easily led, tempted and distracted and you're going to need either a firm hand to guide you or some rigid self-control if you're ever to realize your full potential at work.

SAGITTARIUS/FIVE/THREE

On occasions you are both mentally brilliant and outstandingly versatile but you have neither the humility of the truly great, nor the common sense of the average person in the street to realize that modesty is more becoming and socially acceptable than a fanfare of self-blown trumpets. You've obviously realized how clever you are but how long will it take before the penny drops and you learn to keep quiet about it?

SAGITTARIUS/FIVE/FOUR

It is unlikely there's anyone around quite as resourceful as you. 'Waste not, want not' is your motto and by making do and mending you attempt to live by it. You are careful, cautious and systematic; practical, handy and abundantly capable. As a worker you are the answer to an employer's dream and as a partner you're worth your weight in gold — no matter what side of the sheets.

SAGITTARIUS/FIVE/FIVE

Permanency and security, just like a promising career, have no great allure for you. It's obviously quantity rather than quality you're after and it's through the pleasures of the flesh and the gratification of the senses that you intend to seek your satisfaction in life. Unfortunately youth and vitality won't always be your stock in trade.

SAGITTARIUS/FIVE/SIX

You're good-natured, popular and reliable at your work while on the home front you're domesticated, romantic, fun loving and full of surprises. You should almost be too good to be true but don't start preening your feathers yet as you do have a couple of faults that need some attention. You're not very good at keeping secrets, especially the kind people tell you in confidence. You're also inclined to be rather conceited, particularly about your appearance.

SAGITTARIUS/FIVE/SEVEN

Your spirit of adventure tends to manifest itself mentally rather than physically. It is your mind that will take you into new realms of fantasy and imagination not your body. Basically you're a thinker; except when it comes to doing what comes naturally when you're as red-blooded as the next — if not a shade redder. Your private life is usually a discreetly conducted affair and seldom, if ever, attracts any great interest or notoriety but it is by no means dull or mundane for all that.

SAGITTARIUS/FIVE/EIGHT

You are buoyant, versatile and virtually indestructible. Spiritually you seem to have no aspirations but mentally you're in tune with business and commerce and bodily you're into contact sports of the most intimate variety. You work hard and you expect to enjoy yourself.

SAGITTARIUS/FIVE/NINE

It's virtually impossible to ignore someone like you because everything you do is on a larger than life scale and instantly attracts attention. But for all your flambuoyance you do have a fine brain and some useful talents. Unfortunately you seem to spend more of your time arguing the toss than actually getting on with the task in hand. Although you're capable of achieving outstanding results they're usually very few and far between.

SAGITTARIUS/SIX/ONE

Mentally they don't come any more agile and adventurous than you but physically you are sluggish. By and large you seem to prefer to work alone in a situation which provides both stimulation and variety but off duty you like to have plenty of people around the place; the more the merrier. You're charming, sociable and gregarious although when deeper feelings are involved, fickle and rather selfish.

SAGITTARIUS/SIX/TWO

You'll never make a convincing solo performer because you lack the confidence to do your act without an emotional safety net. You like to think you can play fast and loose with all and sundry yet you're afraid to let go of your poor, long-suffering partner. You need to grow up fast because your behaviour is spoiling not only your own happiness but that of your partner too.

SAGITTARIUS/SIX/THREE

You're undoubtedly clever, versatile and talented but you lack the application to put your abilities to really profitable use. However, when it comes to entertaining, hitting the high spots or drumming up all the unsuspecting guests for an impromptu party — you're the tops. You have gourmet tastes in food and drink and a connoisseur's eye for beauty.

SAGITTARIUS/SIX/FOUR

Although you're highly efficient, well-organized and very down to earth there's certainly nothing dull or boring about you at all. You are a fascinating character with a whole host of amusing tales to tell, mostly about your travels abroad and a positive arsenal of conversational gambits at your disposal. You lead a busy life with a demanding career and a full social calendar. But on those rare occasions when you have a day entirely to yourself you can be as lazy as sin.

SAGITTARIUS/SIX/FIVE

Work is simply a necessary evil through which you fund your adventures while marriage seems superfluous and unnecessary. You are footloose and fancy free and until old age gets the better of you or some deadly tropical disease finally stops you in your tracks that's probably how your life will continue. New horizons, fresh company and total freedom — at the expense of comfort, security and roots.

SAGITTARIUS/SIX/SIX

The high life is your natural element and in bright, stimulating company you truly excel yourself. But where are you when there's washing-up to be done, tables to clear and ashtrays to empty? Or indeed when a little gentle physical exercise is in order after an evening of excess? Generally nowhere to be seen.

SAGITTARIUS/SIX/SEVEN

Try not to neglect your physical health, particularly as you're prone to over-eat. Preventative action is always much easier to take than remedial and no one with an ounce of commonsense wants to suffer any more discomfort than is really necessary. Your body could be as supple as your intellect if only you'd make more effort to keep it in trim and, with a more attractive physique, your personal life might also undergo a few changes for the better.

SAGITTARIUS/SIX/EIGHT

A high-powered, executive job with all its attendant dead-lines and pressures can put a tremendous strain on frayed nerves and a sagging constitution. Working breakfasts, business lunches and entertaining customers can overload the system even more so with excess calories and alcohol while long hours spent at a sedentary occupation, inadequate rest and no exercise can lead to all sorts of problems. Try to see sense before you do irreparable damage to your system.

SAGITTARIUS/SIX/NINE

Learn to be more moderate in your habits and intake, never choose sex as a subject for after dinner conversation and try to gauge how well you're going down in company by the expression on other people's faces. Better to say nothing than to bore everyone to tears and if in doubt as to someone's marital status, steer completely clear rather than stir up a hornet's nest.

SAGITTARIUS/SEVEN/ONE

You have a fine mind which is neither hampered by preconceived ideas nor warped by social brainwashing; you have a flair for the written word; and a distinct talent for all matters artistic. All you need is a fairly determined push in the right direction before any results can be achieved.

SAGITTARIUS/SEVEN/TWO

Artistically and creatively you seem to have been doubly blessed. You have considerable flair and talent in this direction. But when it comes to realism, commonsense and organization you appear to have none. It's a wonder you survive, let alone get anywhere in this life as you don't have the first clue about running a business any more than you do a live-in relationship. Despite your lack of acumen your work seems to flourish as if magically self-promoting and your private affairs somehow limp along.

SAGITTARIUS/SEVEN/THREE

Life is something you rarely have time to take seriously because you are always much too busy enjoying yourself. You seem to care little or nothing for your job or the security it offers yet you take a pride in anything you've either hand-crafted or produced yourself outside working hours. You treat your relationship with just a shade more care, but only because you know on which side your bread is buttered.

SAGITTARIUS/SEVEN/FOUR

You are a particularly difficult person to either analyse or define. You seem to care and not to care; to be neat and untidy; to be capable and totally incapable; all at once. At home or at work, in public or in private you're always the same — an enigma with all manner of variations.

SAGITTARIUS/SEVEN/FIVE

Financially you somehow manage to get along, more by luck than good judgement. In private you are never short of volunteers to fill your arms or warm your bed even though you decry marriage and all that it stands for. You are a rebel with no particular cause to follow but your own, and it's one that rarely lets you down.

SAGITTARIUS/SEVEN/SIX

From a creative viewpoint you're the tops; you have perception, imagination and flair. Unfortunately easy money tends to make you lazy while almost constant distraction does little or nothing for your concentration. You are vague, easygoing and totally disorganized but blissfully happy in your own small way because you seem to have got most of your problems well and truly solved.

SAGITTARIUS/SEVEN/SEVEN

You tend to lack the grit and determination of the truly career-minded although you have more than your fair share of useful talents. In private, a person of your Bohemian habits and beliefs, can be quite an eye opener to a partner coming from a strict, conservative background. But when all's said and done, love is love the world over it's just that you don't pussyfoot around or make any excuses for your behaviour.

SAGITTARIUS/SEVEN/EIGHT

You're moderately ambitious and with a little luck and rather more dedication to duty you could achieve a great deal. Unfortunately your private life looks neither promising nor easy to remedy because not only are you infuriatingly vague and casual, you're also prone to jealousy, suspicion and black, moody depressions.

SAGITTARIUS/SEVEN/NINE

You haven't got the first clue about planning ahead, putting something aside for emergencies or taking evasive action. You're impatient, outspoken and irresponsible; unrealistic, far too easy-going and totally disorganized. The sooner you get a grip on yourself the better and if you can only manage to install some semblance of a routine into your daily comings and goings it would certainly benefit.

SAGITTARIUS/EIGHT/ONE

You are hard-working, decisive and so self-controlled and superbly disciplined that you work just as well alone as you do when forming part of a team. You're steady, determined and tenacious so provided you keep your nose clean and your copybook in pristine condition there's no reason at all why you shouldn't rise to the top in your chosen career. Unfortunately you always tend to give your relationship fairly low priority when deciding how much of your leisure time to allocate to interests and so on.

SAGITTARIUS/EIGHT/TWO

Natural caution, coupled with inhibitions and hang-ups, suggests that you're unlikely to have a particularly fulfilling or stable personal life. You crave love and affection more desperately than most people yet you repel the very thing you're trying to attract by being moody, suspicious and extremely difficult. Your uncontrollable jealousy ruins nearly every relationship you become involved in, usually sooner than later, and even those that do get further than the teething stage generally succumb.

SAGITTARIUS/EIGHT/THREE

You are the joker in the pack, the loud-mouthed misfit, and it's not a particularly pleasing or flattering title to be given. Try not to be so adolescent, learn when to keep a still tongue in your head and don't keep blowing your own trumpet because even the most beautiful of melodies can become stale if repeated too often and the tune you play is neither catchy nor apparently popular.

SAGITTARIUS/EIGHT/FOUR

You are hard-working, patient and responsible but you have no sense of humour, absolutely no idea how to enjoy yourself and have probably never had an original idea or thought in your life. You're unlikely to ever reach the dizzy heights of success because you don't know how to project yourself and in private it's anyone's guess what you and your partner get up to when alone but it's unlikely to be strip scrabble.

SAGITTARIUS/EIGHT/FIVE

Relating to people has always been your greatest problem; you're chronically shy and very emotional. You'll agree to things which you'd prefer not to get involved in simply because you don't like to say 'no' and risk offending anyone and consequently you get lumbered with all sorts of irksome, unpleasant jobs in the process. However, it is in private that you suffer the greatest agonies especially when you try to speak and can't utter a sound or you find your hands have gone cold and clammy.

SAGITTARIUS/EIGHT/SIX

You're a first-class organizer and provider, but when it comes to bringing sunshine into your loved ones' lives you haven't the first clue how to go about it. Cleaning up, paying the bills and tending the garden just isn't enough any more than saying 'I love you' every now and again. You've got to show that you mean it by being more demonstrative, spontaneous and fun loving.

SAGITTARIUS/EIGHT/SEVEN

You always have been a bit of a loner but if you're truthful it's probably because you find it difficult to break the ice and make new friends. Try to get involved in a few group interests, maybe at your local evening school. Inhibitions must be overcome before any positive progress can be made and someone with your patience should be able to do just that, particularly as time has never been your prime consideration although companionship is.

SAGITTARIUS/EIGHT/EIGHT

At work your performance never varies from day to day or even from decade to decade. You are punctual, precise and practical. You're conservative, reliable and you have apparently few opinions and little imagination. Even at home you have no earth-shatteringly unusual hobbies or even any noteworthy vices.

SAGITTARIUS/EIGHT/NINE

The trouble with you is that you're impatient, suspicious and far too imaginative for your own good. Whether at home or at work you can never wait five minutes for attention and when it's not instantly forthcoming you over-react like a spoiled child. What's more you find it virtually impossible to either trust people you know or take strangers at face value. You seem to think everyone is out to cheat you or talking about you behind your back.

SAGITTARIUS/NINE/ONE

At work you love the challenge that goes with competition yet you prefer to enter the lists as a lone combatant rather than part of a team, however much of a winning side it may be. You are ambitious, determined and quite likely to succeed even when the going is tough and uphill. In private you also prefer to hunt alone but unfortunately once the victor's spoils have come your way the quarry tends to lose its appeal.

SAGITTARIUS/NINE/TWO

You allow yourself to be carried along by prevailing circumstances and fall all too easily victim to the heat of the moment only to discover that having once given your all, that was all you had to give. You try too hard to attract love and affection; what's more you go about it completely the wrong way. Try not to wear your heart on your sleeve in future and be more selective about the company you keep.

SAGITTARIUS/NINE/THREE

You are one of those people who could fall out of an aeroplane without a parachute and still land safely on both feet. There's no two ways about it — you have the luck of the devil. You cut corners, run risks, chance your arm and never seem to come unstuck. You have got the gift of the gab, the Midas touch and the most incredible cheek. You certainly live a charmed life but it still wouldn't hurt if you calmed down a little and tried to act sanely and sensibly at least some of the time.

SAGITTARIUS/NINE/FOUR

When it comes to making an all out effort and really going for what you want, you're superb. You plan your campaign with all the precision and strategy of a military commander and you never disclose your targets until you're one hundred percent certain of success. You make a wonderful ally but a formidable foe as anyone who has ever crossed swords with you will testify. Your partner rarely gets a look-in due entirely to your demanding career.

SAGITTARIUS/NINE/FIVE

You're restless, highly-strung and irrepressible. You change your mind every couple of days and it doesn't take much to persuade you to try something different or indeed to down tools altogether. At work you need plenty of free rein and room to breathe if you're going to produce good results. Responsibility and total commitment are the last things you want because there's a big world out there which you want to remain at liberty to explore.

SAGITTARIUS/NINE/SIX

You're homeloving, domesticated and reliable; imaginative, intelligent and open-minded. But when something comes along which threatens your precious personal freedom it's a whole new ballgame. You are tremendously high-spirited once you get the bit between your teeth as just below the surface of your calm exterior runs an aggressive, belligerent streak. You're the sort of rebel who never casts the first stone but one who won't give up until they've had the last word.

SAGITTARIUS/NINE/SEVEN

Although you're a reasonably physical person who enjoys a game of tennis or a round of golf almost as much as an early night with your partner, it's within your mind that the really top class athletics take place. You are intelligent, intellectual and highly imaginative. You love nothing better than plenty of stimulating data to digest or a good brain teaser to solve.

SAGITTARIUS/NINE/EIGHT

You seem to have neither feelings nor compassion just a destructive urge to make it big and you'll kick, fight, bite and struggle until you do. Not surprisingly you appear to have neither friends nor allies in your camp and if you do still have a partner somewhere in the background then they deserve sympathy. You're aggressive and irrepressible.

SAGITTARIUS/NINE/NINE

There's nothing like a good set of rules and regulations to get you hopping mad. You simply can't bear being told what you can and cannot do, especially by some petty little official in a uniform. You are intolerant, impatient and insubordinate. Try not to get so wound-up about petty annoyances and invasions of privacy that we all have to suffer from time to time during the course of our lives.

CAPRICORN/ONE/ONE

You are controlled, patient and single-minded. However, although you seem to have so many admirable qualities as far as work is concerned you don't seem to know how to relate to members of the opposite sex. Not only are you a loner by choice, you're also unemotional, rather than cold, and never particularly demonstrative.

CAPRICORN/ONE/TWO

You crave security more than anything else. Financially you need to feel you have sufficient capital behind you to meet every conceivable contingency while emotionally you desperately need to feel loved and wanted. Unfortunately it's here that you go wrong every time because your attitude is more one of suspicion that trust. Try to be more friendly; don't go looking for trouble where none exists and be prepared to take a chance on your judgement.

CAPRICORN/ONE/THREE

You are tough, materialistic and ambitious. No problem is ever big enough to put you off your stroke and, as far as you're concerned, no difficulty is impossible to overcome if you're sufficiently determined to do just that. Apart from a keen grasp of business affairs you also have a quick brain, original ideas and the ability to bend with the wind. You're versatile, clever and energetic. You also consider yourself much too fly to ever be talked into marriage.

CAPRICORN/ONE/FOUR

Stubbornness is by far your greatest fault. Once you've dug your heels in nothing on this earth will ever persuade you to alter your mind because you're pig-headed and immovable. Even on the rare occasions that you're proven to be wrong you'd still rather choke than admit it. At work you're slow, deliberate and infuriatingly methodical while in private its often rumoured you have no feelings because they've probably never been seen in public.

CAPRICORN/ONE/FIVE

Self-doubts can be overcome by bringing your resourcefulness and originality into play. Lurking in the background is an urge to branch out on a limb and do something which your natural caution might counter. You will almost certainly find that if you throw caution to the wind more often you will be more successful and develop better relationships with others. In this way you will achieve most of your ambitions.

CAPRICORN/ONE/SIX

While you are always ready to help others your motives may not be totally altruistic. There is a deliberate and calculating element in your character which means that few gestures come fully from the heart. But despite this you tend to get on well with people and are loyal to your close friends and colleagues. Try to be less selfish and realize that doing good deeds for their own sake is not a sign of weakness.

CAPRICORN/ONE/SEVEN

For you the only way to solve a problem is to be alone, and think the difficulty through. But be careful that this trait isn't maintained just for the sake of it. Other people need you and look upon you as a trusty friend or a responsible parent so avoid burying your head in the sand when things don't go according to plan. Your major plus point is your tenacity which, in the end, will automatically see you through day to day problems.

CAPRICORN/ONE/EIGHT

You are very much a cold fish both in business and home life, although you do your best to disguise this. As a rival or enemy you make a formidable adversary particularly as you can subjugate any emotion and replace it with ruthlessness, deliberation and icy self control. You are likely to achieve your material ambitions but the prospects for personal relationships do not look very encouraging.

CAPRICORN/ONE/NINE

While you like to instruct, care for or negotiate with people you never seem to want to get to know them. Because of this others regard you as aloof and distant and until you can pull the barriers down you will rarely achieve any close relationships. Try to let your humanitarianism overcome your caution and insecurity and rely upon your tenacity to act as a final back stop.

CAPRICORN/TWO/ONE

From a professional point of view you need neither guidance nor assistance to help you along because you're well qualified, hard-working and clockwork smooth in the way you operate. You're ambitious, materialistic and very, very serious about anything which could either promote or, perish the thought, damage your career in any way. However your life is rather one sided as you appear to live solely to work. Despite communication difficulties you should try harder to relate to others.

CAPRICORN/TWO/TWO

The greatest problem you're up against is your own deep-rooted insecurity. You've allowed it to get out of proportion and not only does it overshadow everything you do, it also eats away at what little confidence and self-esteem you have. Try to be more decisive in your handling of day to day matters while in private stop allowing self-doubt and shyness to mar relationships.

CAPRICORN/TWO/THREE

Your dedication to duty is legendary but the way you push yourself physically and mentally past the bounds of endurance is foolhardy to say the least. You need to work harder on your private life and to take the occasional breather from your job. Balance is what you should strive to achieve and the sooner you strike that happy medium the better you'll get along all round.

CAPRICORN/TWO/FOUR

While you wouldn't actually decline promotion you're equally prepared to continue doing the same thing, day in day out. On the home front there's very little of great note or interest that ever occurs as you're neither dynamic nor unpredictable. You're in a gigantic rut and that's where you're more than likely to stay.

CAPRICORN/TWO/FIVE

You have strong sexual drives but insufficient emotional stability to do anything concrete about them. You are afraid of rejection yet desperately crave love and understanding; you're also jealous, suspicious and highly strung which doesn't do anything to help your predicament. Try to be more patient when personal problems arise and don't be in such a hurry to call everything off when remedial action can still be taken.

242 The Wheel of Fortune

CAPRICORN/TWO/SIX

Emotionally you seem to have the greatest difficulty expressing yourself. This doesn't mean that you're totally unfeeling, in fact quite the reverse, you seem to feel things much more deeply than anyone else. Force yourself to get out and about more, to form new contacts and break new ground otherwise your private life will continue to be empty and your desires will remain nothing more than unfulfilled dreams.

CAPRICORN/TWO/SEVEN

A suitable career opportunity should be relatively easy to come by but the perfect partner may not. Don't be so moody and sarcastic; try not to show jealousy where none is warranted; nor suspicion or possessiveness. Trust is what you'll need to develop and that won't be easy to achieve for someone like you who has little to build upon in the first place.

CAPRICORN/TWO/EIGHT

You are one of the most difficult people on this earth to live with in any semblance of domestic bliss and harmony. You should stay away from members of the opposite sex until you've discovered how to treat them with the understanding and honesty they deserve. Get your act together first and your scrambled emotions in order before you make even a preliminary move or you're doomed to failure.

CAPRICORN/TWO/NINE

At work, although you're undoubtedly very professional and goal-conscious, you can't resist having the odd 'scrap' with colleagues. At home you treat your partner more like a punch-bag than a human being. Curb your impatience, try to be more tolerant of those around you and don't lose your temper quite so quickly in future. Life is too short to be spent fighting and quarreling.

CAPRICORN/THREE/ONE

Caution is your watchword but when combined with shrewdness and a touch of aggression the three seem to gel and produce a working formula for success. Unfortunately you spend so much time and effort steering your career in the right direction that you seldom if ever relax. Try to regard leisure time as being of great therapeutic value.

CAPRICORN/THREE/TWO

The truth of the matter is you're never content unless you feel you have something to complain about and without plenty of problems to overcome you'd feel cheated and miserable. Admit it — you thrive on crises and when there's none handy you'll create a few of your own just to keep the adrenalin flowing and to make life worth living.

CAPRICORN/THREE/THREE

You pick up new skills with ease and dexterity, only having to be shown how to do something once, or twice at the most, before you've mastered the technique. You also have a quicksilver mind which can stretch itself in several different directions at once and a charming personality. However, what you need is to carefully monitor your health.

CAPRICORN/THREE/FOUR

Carelessness is your main culprit although you're also much too impatient to do a job thoroughly and find it difficult to concentrate under pressure. Try to pay more attention to detail in future and get someone else to check out your work if you feel errors may have been made. Care and cuation should be your watchwords while slipping into a lower gear might just possibly slow you down and make you less prone to silly accidents.

CAPRICORN/THREE/FIVE

You're one of those fortunate people who seem to have a sense of proportion. Admittedly you work hard and make a conscientious employee but when work's over and done for the day you can switch off and worry no more about it until the next morning. Executive stress is one complaint you'll never suffer from because you'll only do so much and then no more. What's more you also know how to relax and let your hair down.

CAPRICORN/THREE/SIX

Although you thoroughly enjoy your work and the company of your colleagues you simply can't wait to hurry home at the end of the day because that's where you prefer to be. However, all too often you bring work back with you to finish after supper and this could put quite a strain on your relationship if it is allowed to become the norm. Workaholics seldom have the opportunity to enjoy the fruit of their labours and many are intensely lonely individuals at heart.

CAPRICORN/THREE/SEVEN

Sometimes it's not a bad idea to keep colleagues and workmates at a respectable distance. But you carry this principle to ridiculous lengths and won't even discuss the weather in case you give away some personal snippet of information about your private affairs. You're a loner, workaholic, and emotionally rather lazy hence your singularity.

CAPRICORN/THREE/EIGHT

Ambition drives you on and there are times when only automatic pilot keeps you going. You'll work day and night, till you drop if necessary, to make a name for yourself and you'll neither rest nor be satisfied until you've reached the very top of your profession or worked yourself into an early grave — whichever comes sooner.

CAPRICORN/THREE/NINE

Not only do you seem to have the luck of the devil you also have the most enormous cheek. You'll take risks, cut corners, even argue with the boss or insult your mother in law and somehow get away with it. However, you may not always be quite so fortunate and it wouldn't do any harm if you calmed down just a little and started toeing the line rather more often. You're much too fond of provoking aruguments; far too quick to lose you temper; and always ready to voice your opinions without a moments thought.

CAPRICORN/FOUR/ONE

Although you may never become well known for your sparkling repartee and tremendous sense of humour, it's your unflagging dedication to duty and determination to succeed that will be the subject matter of your epitaph. You're always punctual for work, never take a day off due to ill-health and more often than not are the last to down tools and go home.

CAPRICORN/FOUR/TWO

Thank goodness for your rigid discipline and icy self-control because without them, emotionally, you'd be all over the place. Unrequited love is a painful thing to suffer especially when you know it's your own fault. If only you could see the funny side of life you'd realize how silly and childish your strange, moody behaviour is. Try to make yourself more interesting and attractive, get yourself some new clothes and a different image.

CAPRICORN/FOUR/THREE

You have a quick, lively mind but an unfortunate way of voicing controversial thoughts and opinions at precisely the wrong moment. Don't be quite so blunt and brutally outspoken in future and when you do have a difficult message to deliver try wrapping it up in a few soft words to ease the blow. You could use a few private lessons in public relations as well as a few tips on the art of diplomacy.

CAPRICORN/FOUR/FOUR

Have you ever wondered why, when you are with company, people talk across you as if you weren't there? It's simply because you behave like a stuffed dummy most of the time. But in an emergency your calm, unflappable attitude helps prevent everyone else losing their heads and when you give your word nothing will persuade you to change your mind.

CAPRICORN/FOUR/FIVE

You're often guilty of hurting other peoples feelings with your biting sarcasm. Your 'me first' attitude means you can be particularly thoughtless and selfish when looking after your own interests. At work your performance is generally efficient and at home, although you're thoughtless and unimaginative, your drives and desires take precedence over everything else. You should guard against being too grabbing and demanding.

CAPRICORN/FOUR/SIX

If only you could round off a few of those hard edges and not appear quite so stern and forbidding you'd stand a much better chance of realizing your desires. A winning smile and a softer, more welcoming approach is what's needed and only you can provide either of these attributes so go to it and do something about changing your outward appearance for a new, less repelling, image.

CAPRICORN/FOUR/SEVEN

Still waters run deep and although friends and colleagues probably tend to dismiss you as nothing more than a conventional, well-meaning old fuddy-duddy that's where they could be very wrong indeed. Admittedly, on the surface you appear calm, conservative and very down to earth — in fact, quite ordinary — but behind that placid expression is a brilliant mind and deep inside that stolid exterior beats a passionate heart.

CAPRICORN/FOUR/EIGHT

There is more to life than being enormously wealthy and successful, although you probably wouldn't agree. All you ever think about is money and how to make more; status and how to rise higher; achievement and how to do better. You're mercenary, materialistic and a social climber. Charitable thoughts never enter your mind and you're only helpful when it suits you.

CAPRICORN/FOUR/NINE

Your only pleasure in life seems to be parading your book-learning and technical knowledge in front of others, hopefully to impress them. Unfortunately your efforts usually have the opposite effect of driving people away. If only you weren't so dull and unexciting you'd probably be more popular. Perhaps you should do something impulsive just to relieve the tedium and try listening for a change instead of delivering your usual lengthy diatribes.

CAPRICORN/FIVE/ONE

Your pioneering spirit could carry you far. You are certainly not afraid of hard work and regard change as both a stimulant and a challenge. In fact when things stay in the same static mould for too long you become fidgety and restless, and to counter-balance your natural inclination to be on the move, a job which involves both travel and some contact with the public would suit you down to the ground. In private a lively, stimulating partner, preferably of independent means, would suit you best.

CAPRICORN/FIVE/TWO

What you need is to come to terms with your inner turmoil as soon as possible because you're never going to feel secure if you continue to destroy everything the moment you've managed to create it. Try to stick it out in your job even though it does get boring and repetitious at times and try to keep with one partner for longer than just a few short weeks. You lack continuity and you need greater staying power and stability to create some.

CAPRICORN/FIVE/THREE

Behind that mask of respectability is a satirical, quick-witted survivor. You are talented, clever and extremely versatile. You seem able to turn your hand readily to most things and can come up with solutions to what most people would consider insuperable problems. However you'll need to keep your ego pared down to a manageable size if you don't want to become an insufferable know-it-all and you'll need to curb your restlessness if you don't want to get on everyone's nerves.

CAPRICORN/FIVE/FOUR

At work your effort is never less than one hundred per cent and your attention is always keenly focussed on the task in hand. What's more you run your home like a well-oiled piece of machinery and your financial affairs with great care. You never over-spend, act out of character or apparently seem to enjoy yourself. You often dream of breaking your conservative mould, secretly yearn to travel and desperately crave the excitement of a passionate affair.

CAPRICORN/FIVE/FIVE

What you need is a realistic goal in life and far more staying power than you've so far managed to muster. You play musical chairs with your jobs and its time you stopped being so restless and did something positive about settling down. See a job through to its conclusion more often and show some pride in what you're doing.

CAPRICORN/FIVE/SIX

Your creativity and artistic flair are not only natural gifts they're also vital safety valves. You have the perfect recipe for sanity without tears so hang on to such a precious commodity at all costs and don't feel embarassed to use it whenever you feel the need to get something off your chest or your scrambled emotions into some semblance of order.

CAPRICORN/FIVE/SEVEN

Travel has always had a great appeal for you and whether you happen to go first class, tourist or under your own steam it's immaterial just so long as you go. If you are wise you'll opt for a job which provides plenty of variety and the opportunity to move around and it would be sensible to choose a partner who shares your enthusiasm for far away places.

CAPRICORN/FIVE/EIGHT

You have a first class business brain, all the necessary qualifications and an impressive performance record in your chosen field but in the arena of personal relationships you're in desperate need of tuition. Your drives and feelings are strong and fiery but your control of them is negligible. You blow hot one moment and cold the next like an emotional yo-yo and until you reach a point of balance your private life is never going to settle.

CAPRICORN/FIVE/NINE

You are highly-strung, impulsive and totally unpredictable. Living on your nerves could, in the long term, have a dilatory effect on your health and constantly chopping and changing your mind does little to promote feelings of security. Try to practise more self-control, especially where your temper is concerned, and do whatever you can to relax and unwind at the end of the day.

CAPRICORN/SIX/ONE

You have just the right amount of drive and ambition to get you up and heading off in a constructive direction. However you tend to be easily influenced by other people and their opinions, particularly your loved ones, and although advice can be well-meaning it can also be very off-putting if you blindly act upon it without question. Don't allow personalities to stand in the way of your progress.

CAPRICORN/SIX/TWO

Your name will probably never become synonymous with success because instead of getting on with things you dither about on the sidelines wondering what move to make and whether it would indeed be advisable to make one at all. Confidence and drive are what you lack and all you seem to have in their place are unfulfilled desires and a self-effacing attitude.

CAPRICORN/SIX/THREE

What you need more than anything is security — a safe home base. Once you feel loved and wanted then you have the confidence to move mountains and the energy to achieve miracles. But without that vital backing to boost your moral and bolster your self-esteem you won't get much further than the top of the road before you go to pieces and lose heart. With constant encouragement, and of course reassurance when you make mistakes, you should eventually be able to reach quite a dizzy height in your career.

CAPRICORN/SIX/FOUR

When working behind the scenes or in a supporting role with someone else playing the lead you are, without a doubt, superb. If all you ever aspire to be is one of the Indians then no changes are called for. However, if one day you hope to become chief of the tribe, or at least one of its elders, you'll need to buck your ideas up. Don't let people walk all over you; stop being taken for granted; and remember that unless you're prepared to show your teeth occasionally no one will realize you can bite.

CAPRICORN/SIX/FIVE

Coming to terms with personal responsibilities, particularly those of a domestic or family nature, has never been an easy task for you. You find it so much easier to take than to give. Co-operation is something you need to master in order to avoid becoming labelled as mean and greedy so in future don't be too quick to take people up on offers of assistance when you don't have the slightest intention of ever returning the favour.

CAPRICORN/SIX/SIX

There have been countless occasions when you've had the chance to do all sorts of interesting and exciting things but have turned them down flat because you've wanted to put your family first. If you could go back and start again would you play things any other way?

CAPRICORN/SIX/SEVEN

You have the sort of gifts that other less fortunate souls can only dream about. You are quiet, unambitious and painfully slow at coming forward. You only feel truly at ease when totally alone, finding crowds virtually impossible to cope with and even the company of two or three close friends quite enough to handle. If only you could force yourself out of your shell you stand to gain considerably all round.

CAPRICORN/SIX/EIGHT

You are hell-bent on making it to the top in your chosen career and not even the needs and demands of your family are allowed to come between you and your goal. You leave your partner totally alone night after night, week in week out because you're far too interested in your business affairs to waste time sitting at home. What's more you are a stranger to your children, a memory to your parents and absent to all your friends.

CAPRICORN/SIX/NINE

You may profess to care about the starving millions in the Third World or the vanishing rain forests and wildlife, but when your partner is feeling off-colour or one of your children needs taking to the dentist you're usually the last person to volunteer some help. Suddenly you'll remember a pressing appointment elsewhere or come up with at least half a dozen equally good reasons why you should be excused duty. The trouble is you don't actually practise what you preach.

CAPRICORN/SEVEN/ONE

You're a well-organized, highly efficient individual. You're independent, materialistic and ambitious. You never wait around for someone to tell you what to do and you don't need help to get things done. Your life is so carefully planned out in advance that a series of goals and targets stretches ahead of you for many years into the future. However, you do know how to relax; and this is vitally important for both your physical and mental well-being.

CAPRICORN/SEVEN/TWO

Although you perform your work with care and more than a touch of pride you don't seem to get much more out of life than a little job satisfaction. Unfortunately what you don't seem to realize is that a suitable partner rarely turns up on the front doorstep outside of romantic novels. To effect a significant degree of change you're going to have to snap out of your self-imposed isolation, deal drastically with your moodiness and then launch yourself bodily into the hurly-burly of local society. You may not instantly find yourself a soulmate but a new circle of friends wouldn't go amiss for starters.

CAPRICORN/SEVEN/THREE

You are quick-witted, versatile and streets ahead of most of your contemporaries but emotionally you have the body of an adult and about as much control, or indeed understanding, of your feelings as the average adolescent. Try to come to better terms with your own sexuality and stop covering up your insecurity by running away every time a relationship threatens to get serious.

CAPRICORN/SEVEN/FOUR

Every moment of your waking life is not only accounted for but also documented, scheduled and allocated a place in your strict, unbending routine. You may believe that this is the only way to run your life but don't ever try to force orderliness on either your partner or your colleagues at work. It will only cause arguments and, in any event you probably haven't scheduled time for such contingencies.

CAPRICORN/SEVEN/FIVE

Your private affairs are furtive and clandestine because you will insist upon having several strings to your bow at any one time. Even when playing the paramour the only way to keep the music sweet is to make sure one partner doesn't find out about all the rest. It's a tangled web you weave and no mistake but it's usually only the flies who suffer any harm — seldom, if ever, the spider.

CAPRICORN/SEVEN/SIX

Where would you be without your pigeon-holes and compartments to tidy everything up into? You're one of those people who takes efficiency and organisation to the nth degree. You're inclined to be rather nervous and highly-strung and it's because of this that your compulsion for order gets exaggerated and completely out of hand at times. Do your best in future not to worry too much over trivial, unimportant details.

CAPRICORN/SEVEN/SEVEN

It's the finer things in life which are your main care and concern. You are a spiritual, enlightened being and what you need more than anything else is the freedom to think and believe exactly what you choose. So long as your mind is at liberty to soar at will beyond the confines of the human body that's all you ask – and, of course, a little privacy to indulge your thoughts.

CAPRICORN/SEVEN/EIGHT

The promise of success turns you on and the thrill of the chase holds and captivates your interest. As far as you're concerned love, romance and domesticity are necessary evils to be suffered in order to establish a modicum of personal security and a little insurance for your old age. But selection boards, annual general meetings and dining with your bankers are what life is all about.

CAPRICORN/SEVEN/NINE

You have sufficient self-control not to go flying off the handle every time a criticism is levelled or someone deliberately tries to provoke you into an argument. But you simply have to let off steam somehow and a seething letter is apparently your favourite tool. Personal grievances should be aired face to face as unemotionally as possible and the sooner you master this technique the better.

CAPRICORN/EIGHT/ONE

You rarely experience any difficulty either picking objectives or defining goals for yourself. You are also quite prepared to bide your time in order to ensure your advancement. In private your feelings never seem to be particularly hot or cold but usually balance out somewhere in between, ranging from lukewarm to gently simmering.

CAPRICORN/EIGHT/TWO

You've got a hide like a rhinocerous, a memory like an elephant and the courage of a lion. No task ever seems too big for you to handle and there's never yet been a difficulty you haven't somehow managed to find your way around. But your private life is littered with problems and obstacles like jealousy, suspicion and possessiveness, all of which are of your own making.

CAPRICORN/EIGHT/THREE

Balance is what you must strive for and it won't be an easy task for someone as outspoken as you. In private if you were a little more demonstrative your partner wouldn't have to become a mind-reader to gauge the depth and temperature of your feelings. With a greater show of affection and rather more consideration all round your personal affairs would go with more of a swing.

CAPRICORN/EIGHT/FOUR

It's quite uncanny how much you and a computer seem to have in common. You are both programmed for speed, efficiency and a phenomenal output; your memory banks are full of facts, figures and information; and you can work day and night if necessary without any apparent signs of fatigue. However, there is one vital point at which you should differ and unfortunately don't. Computers have no feelings and neither apparently have you.

CAPRICORN/EIGHT/FIVE

You may be secretly afraid of failure but you're even more terrified of total commitment in case you make an irrevocable decision which later proves to have been wrong. Unfortunately you can't hedge-hop through life forever and if you don't grasp an opportunity soon you may find there are no more golden ones left when you do finally decide to take the nettle.

CAPRICORN/EIGHT/SIX

You're well-balanced, open-minded and popular. At work you get on well with everyone because not only are you cheerful and easy-going — you're also conscientious, co-operative and efficient. At home you're the perfect companion; understanding, caring and loyal. Sexually you're rather inhibited and undemonstrative so although you're capable of experiencing great depths of emotion you find it difficult to either express or share them in a physical way.

CAPRICORN/EIGHT/SEVEN

You certainly don't shirk your duties or attempt to pass the buck even when difficulties crop up or constant repetition becomes boring. But even in the most stimulating of company you rarely appear to be having a good time. It is only on those magic occasions when you are completely alone that you really come into your own.

CAPRICORN/EIGHT/EIGHT

Set-backs never deter you, in fact they only serve to make you more determined to get on, while problems are merely minor irritations which have a certain nuisance value, nothing more. Unfortunately you not only tend to put your relationships into the same category you also deal with them in much the same offhand, unemotional manner.

CAPRICORN/EIGHT/NINE

Anyone who gets in your way, soon gets pushed out of it. You play the power game for high stakes and to ensure you always hold the winning hand you are prepared to bend the rules in your own favour or even re-write them completely should the need arise. You're a tough customer and you're like it right to the core — you don't even have a soft centre.

CAPRICORN/NINE/ONE

Fair means or foul — it's all the same to you provided you get the desired results. Not only do you have an impressive list of qualifications to help your career along, you also know every trick in the book to give it an additional boost in the right direction every now and again. You are tough, decisive and capable of great achievement provided your direct manner of speech doesn't get you into too much hot water and your impulsive nature doesn't steer you wrong.

CAPRICORN/NINE/TWO

Even though you can't bear the thought of anyone poking their nose into your private affairs, unless you can manage to straighten out all your emotional problems and hang-ups, for yourself, outside professional assistance might be necessary. You can't possibly do a good day's work when your mind is elsewhere and you can't seriously imagine half the things you suspect your partner of are really true. You are talented, creative and highly original but until you get your head together and your feelings into perspective, you can kiss goodbye to any hopes of success and fulfilment either at work or within your relationship.

CAPRICORN/NINE/THREE

You're quite an all-round firebrand because you can't bear rules, regulations or restrictions and are easily angered if someone has the audacity to take advantage of your generosity and good-nature. It doesn't take much to set you off but it does take quite some considerable time for you to settle down again after one of your explosive outbursts. In private you're also easily roused but this is no bad thing as far as either your partner or your relationship is concerned.

CAPRICORN/NINE/FOUR

You are solid, practical and down-to-earth; tough, hard-working and virtually indestructible. You're a survivor and, at the end of the day, in these uncertain times, that counts for a great deal. Not only are you well equipped to weather almost anything life can throw at you, you're also loyal, faithful and very protective towards those you care for. The family unit means a great deal to you and you'd move heaven and earth to keep yours intact.

CAPRICORN/NINE/FIVE

You may move in some rather dubious circles but at least you keep moving and somehow manage to keep one jump ahead of any problems which might be lurking in your wake. At work you sail dangerously close to the wind, while in private you blatantly poach on other people's territory. But generally speaking you're a likeable rascal with a heart of gold.

CAPRICORN/NINE/SIX

You are definitely a law unto yourself. You do things in your own inimitable way and always in your own sweet time. The only problem is that at work it's virtually impossible for a colleague to cover for you at holiday times because no one can ever fathom out what you were supposed to be doing let alone how you were doing it. At home too your loved ones never know which way to jump or quite what is expected of them because not only do you make the rules you also keep changing them every five minutes.

CAPRICORN/NINE/SEVEN

You are particularly attractive to members of the opposite sex and although faithful and loyal to your partner you're never short of suggestions to be otherwise. Life has much to offer a fascinating, talented individual like you but whether or not you decide to follow up half the opportunities which are open to you is not only another matter but also something which necessarily must be left entirely to your own discretion.

CAPRICORN/NINE/EIGHT

Unless you learn to pace yourself better and know your limits both mentally and physically, you just might go over the top one of these days without even realizing it. Admittedly you're tough, strong and almost indestructible but even stone can be worn away over the years by the steady process of erosion. By all means set your sights high, go for the top but take a few safety precautions before you set out.

CAPRICORN/NINE/NINE

You are ambitious, determined and eminently well qualified which is probably why you champ impatiently at the bit whenever cast in a subordinate role. You like to dish out the orders, not take them, and you make no secret of the fact. You're rebellious, outspoken and certainly not one to make the best of a bad job. Impulsiveness is your greatest fault and one which regularly takes you out of the frying pan into the fire.

AQUARIUS/ONE/ONE

A position of power is tailor-made for a decisive, dynamic individual like you because you're a born leader. Authority rests easily on your broad shoulders and giving orders comes as second nature. However, there's never anything tyrannical or despotic about the way you assume command. You are fair, just and popular because you would never dream of asking someone to perform a task you weren't capable of doing yourself, any more than you would ever slope off to avoid pulling your weight.

AQUARIUS/ONE/TWO

Although you would like nothing more than to reach a modestly elevated position at work you lack the necessary drive and confidence to take you there. What's more you're incapable of dealing with problems in a calm, rational manner and that's what you would be required to do if you were ever placed in authority. Power should be used wisely and with discretion, never as a lever or a tool for personal revenge.

AQUARIUS/ONE/THREE

You have the rare and wonderful gift of a truly brilliant mind; now all you need is some common sense to go with it and you could work miracles not only for yourself but for mankind too. You are versatile, original and exceptionally quick on the uptake; you have a generous nature, an enormous capacity for hard-work and the luck of the devil. Unfortunately you never know when its advisable to keep quiet, how to be tactful or what discretion means, let alone how to exercise it.

AQUARIUS/ONE/FOUR

As a partner you're loyal and faithful; as an employee you're industrious and trustworthy; but as an individual you lack that certain something which would make you stand out in a crowd. Admittedly you're calm, practical and highly respected but where's your flair, your *joie de vivre*, your spirit of adventure? You're much too cautious when it comes to weighing up opportunities, too well organized to ever do anything out of character, and too set in your ways to ever really change.

AQUARIUS/ONE/FIVE

You have a certain amount of talent, some clever, original ideas and an almost inexhaustible supply of nervous energy but you're much too restless, far too easily side-tracked and too much of a gambler to ever be taken seriously or given any great responsibility to shoulder alone. You may be the life and soul of the party but not a great leader of men.

AQUARIUS/ONE/SIX

Arguments and unpleasantness are the last things you want to get involved in because you find them not only upsetting and unnecessary but also totally unproductive. However, you're certainly not one to run away at the first sign of trouble and if something needs to be sorted out or someone needs to be put straight on a few points you won't hesitate to do so. While you could never be described as a troublemaker, there's nothing weak-willed about you.

AQUARIUS/ONE/SEVEN

You have a way of seeing right to the heart of a problem without getting blinkered or side-tracked by all the layers of muddle, confusion and opinions surrounding it. However you've never been one to volunteer for anything, preferring to keep yourself very much to yourself, so all your wisdom and experience rarely gets put to good use.

AQUARIUS/ONE/EIGHT

You don't seem to care one way or the other if people love, hate or feel totally indifferent towards you. But what does motivate you faster than anything else is your craving for power and all that goes with it. All your ideas are out of this world, your actions are larger than life and your thoughts are the biggest things going. Unfortunately once total control is yours it's debatable whether you have either the wisdom or emotional stability to wield it wisely.

AQUARIUS/ONE/NINE

Although mentally and spiritually you are both advanced and enlightened in many other areas you have much to learn and still have a long way to go. You are a born leader and a natural orator but until you've decided which way you're going, and which cause you're going to champion, it would be a good idea to lie low and keep quiet otherwise you'll only confuse everyone including yourself. The trouble is that you are too impractical and disorganized.

AQUARIUS/TWO/ONE

From a business point of view you have some pretty impressive qualifications. You are pioneering, powerful and inventive. You need neither help or encouragement to get you started nor supervision once under way. But although you're tough and decisive you have a surprisingly tender heart so where aggression or threats often fail to have any impact upon you, a good sob-story is guaranteed to provoke interest and perhaps even a change of mind.

AQUARIUS/TWO/TWO

Security, especially the emotional variety, is vitally important to your personal well-being. You expect a great deal from your partner and the majority of the time you ask more than is humanely possible to give. At work it's a different ball game; you're progressive, independent and very self-assured. To see you coping happily and efficiently with your duties it's hard to believe how difficult you can be to live with.

AQUARIUS/TWO/THREE

Your ideas are always novel and interesting but only about one in ten is ever a viable proposition because you're much too imaginative and unrealistic. The same is true not only of your notions but also of your life in general. You show tremendous flair and promise yet you lack the objectivity to see when you've gone over the top. Anyone partnering you will need to be sane and level-headed because you're not the easiest of people to either fathom or keep amused.

AQUARIUS/TWO/FOUR

You are one of those people who can't sit still for two minutes, not even to eat your breakfast or read the mail. You do everything, not only on the move, but at the double and during the course of each twenty-four hour period you get through a phenomenal amount of work of one kind or another. Slow down before you drive yourself to distraction and wear yourself away to a frazzle!

AQUARIUS/TWO/FIVE

You demand loyalty, fidelity and instant passion for which you're prepared to give absolutely no promises or guarantees in return. It is high time you realized that it's not always possible to have your bread buttered on both sides, and the sooner you break the habit the sooner your private life will reach calmer waters.

AQUARIUS/TWO/SIX

Loneliness is your greatest fear and lies at the root of all the other numerous doubts and insecurities you experience. But what you don't seem to realize is that the harder you try to escape the very thing you dread most, the more likely it will happen. You cling on to your partner with a vice like grip but instead of drawing you closer together, your emotional dependence acts like a stranglehold.

AQUARIUS/TWO/SEVEN

You find relationships difficult to handle because you're naturally shy and lacking in confidence. You must make a greater effort to overcome your self-consciousness and if you can't bring yourself to get out and about on your own then enlist the assistance and support of a close friend to help you over those awkward initial sorties. You'll soon get the hang of it and the sooner you take the plunge the quicker you'll start getting results.

AQUARIUS/TWO/EIGHT

To succeed isn't enough for an ambitious person like you. You also need to be seen to have done so by all and sundry. You want an architect-designed house, a garage full of cars and all the latest status symbols and labour-saving devices; your partner must be physically attractive, your children brilliant and your income phenomenal. However, you'd do well to check that all your skeletons are hidden away before you blossom on the social scene.

AQUARIUS/TWO/NINE

You have so many interests and hobbies outside your home that if you don't make sure you spend at least a couple of nights there a week the neighbours will begin to think you've moved out and your partner will eventually make other arrangements which no longer include you. It is not really vital for you to involve yourself in so many unpaid activities.

AQUARIUS/THREE/ONE

Curiosity may have proverbially killed the cat but it's one of your greatest assets. You like not only to get to the bottom of puzzling problems but also to find out what makes other people tick because you're lively, inquisitive and fascinated by your environment. What's more one useful by-product of all your probing and prodding is the tremendous store of knowledge you accumulate over the years on a whole variety of subjects.

AQUARIUS/THREE/TWO

Although you're neither forceful nor aggressive you certainly manage to get results. Gentle persuasion is the tool you use and it works as well in the office as it does at home. You never need to raise your voice, or indeed ask more than once, to get everyone willing to co-operate and ready to carry out your wishes. You know how to encourage, to reassure and to motivate. You are not so much a leader as a natural organizer.

AQUARIUS/THREE/THREE

You're deliberately unconventional; even your choice of clothes is a statement of your non-conformity. You take a perverse delight in being different and an even greater pleasure in being the centre of attention. You're eccentric, unorthodox and every inch the rebel. But watch out that you don't go too far over the top.

AQUARIUS/THREE/FOUR

You have a tremendous number of little idiosyncracies and foibles which set you aside in a class of your own. Try not to let your strange beliefs take over the running of your life and get yourself one 'all purpose' talisman so that in future you won't have to carry quite so many lucky charms around in your pocket for protection.

AQUARIUS/THREE/FIVE

Judging by your present lifestyle you're unlikely to experience either domestic bliss or job security because you're too much of a fly-by-night to ever settle down and really work at either. When actually in employment you refuse to work to anyone's rules and regulations and insist upon doing everything your own way, what's more you never turn up on time and invariably slope off early. And in private you rebel against everything from the commitment of marriage to honesty and fidelity within such an institution.

AQUARIUS/THREE/SIX

In all ways except one you are conservative, conventional and conform to a recognizable pattern. It's in your style of artistic expression that you stand head and shoulders above the rest. Your methods are unusual, the medium you chose to work in has many critics, but few experts, and your subject matter can at times be exceedingly bizarre.

AQUARIUS/THREE/SEVEN

Where work is concerned, you're cut out to be a researcher. Not only do you have a brilliant, analytical mind, you also have the ability to concentrate for long periods no matter how many distractions are taking place. You are undoubtedly unorthodox and unconventional but you manage to make progress. But at home, old-fashioned give and take should still be the order of the day.

AQUARIUS/THREE/EIGHT

Fair means or foul, it's all the same to you, just so long as you get what you want with the least possible delay. You're neither a pleasant person to do business with nor an ideal partner but it's doubtful whether you'll ever really alter, you'll simply invent a different set of tactics to make a change.

AQUARIUS/THREE/NINE

You are never happy unless you've got a point to prove or someone to argue with. You are full of bright ideas which you're convinced will either revolutionize industry or lighten the load of over-worked housewives. Unfortunately you seldom think them through logically or in sufficient detail to realize that your theories often won't hold water. Your temper is an uncertain commodity which needs constant monitoring.

AQUARIUS/FOUR/ONE

You're a pioneer and an adventurer. At work or at play you're a go-getter but should you discover that something or someone wasn't all they originally seemed, you will drop your enquiries immediately and leave the resultant mess for others to clear up after you. Whatever you have or manage to achieve has to be of the very best life can offer.

AQUARIUS/FOUR/TWO

Fortune certainly blessed you in terms of creativity and talent. You're inventive, original and colourfully imaginative; dexterous, artistic and quietly confident. However not all gifts are useful or indeed acceptable and as far as your moodiness is concerned the sooner you return that from whence it came the easier you'll find negotiations at work and the smoother your private life will run. Stop being such a grouch and give everyone a treat by showing the sunny side of your nature rather more often.

AQUARIUS/FOUR/THREE

If only you'd been fitted with brakes perhaps then you wouldn't run headlong into quite so many difficulties. You'll up sticks and go the minute anyone or anything threatens to interfere with the free running of your life and when restrictions bar your path you just change course and get involved in something else instead. Your attitude is 'easy come, easy go' and that's precisely what happens — you win a few and you lose a few.

AQUARIUS/FOUR/FOUR

Although change has never been something you particularly rush to embrace, it seems to feature fairly frequently in your life because alterations at work will inevitably affect the running of your private affairs. You are somewhat of a specialist in your particular field and for that reason it's necessary to go where the jobs are, not sit and wait for them to come to you. Hence all the moving around and all the upheaval that goes with it.

AQUARIUS/FOUR/FIVE

Your sight, hearing, smell, taste and touch are all finely tuned and honed to perfection but there is a sixth which is missing from your list and it has nothing to do with ESP — it's plain, no nonsense commonsense. You're totally lacking in this vital commodity so remember to add it to your shopping list.

AQUARIUS/FOUR/SIX

You may be well-educated and even better read but the milkman doesn't necessarily have to share your detailed knowledge of computers any more than your partner is forced to learn Russian with you as a second language. You must learn to live and let live rather more. It wouldn't do for everyone to be the same especially if there were many more like you around because the strain on the rest would be immeasurable.

AQUARIUS/FOUR/SEVEN

You are a pioneer, an intrepid explorer who opens up new routes for others to follow. However your expeditions into the unknown call for neither protective clothing nor expensive climbing gear because the territory you investigate exists only in the mind. You grapple with theories, ideas and concepts, you ponder the age-old riddle of man's origins; and you hope to find at least some of the answers to life's perplexing questions.

AQUARIUS/FOUR/EIGHT

Your combination of sign and numbers represents independence coupled with ambition and struggle. You're confident, decisive and tenacious. Success is what you're out for and no price is too high to pay for such a vital commodity. However, you go about achieving your desires by an unusual route, choosing to follow your own inclinations rather than the well-trodden highways. Once your mind is made up nothing will ever deflect you from your course although you might be persuaded to make a few unscheduled stops along the way.

AQUARIUS/FOUR/NINE

You are irritable, bad-tempered and irascible. Stop being such a harbinger of doom and start behaving like a little ray of sunshine instead. A cheery smile will help your working day along a treat while a few words of endearment whispered sweetly to your partner could put the sparkle back into your relationship. What should really appeal to an old scrooge like you is that none of these proposed improvements will cost you a penny — just a little thought and a bit of effort.

AQUARIUS/FIVE/ONE

You have a mind like blotting paper which makes education a relatively painless business, not to mention a determined, independent nature and a leaning towards all things mechanical and scientific. Your ideas are brilliant, your approach to problems imaginative and your potential infinite. Sexually you're an adventurer and variety is the spice you sprinkle liberally on all the dishes you choose to sample.

AQUARIUS/FIVE/TWO

Fortune tends to hand you all sorts of golden opportunities and then Fate comes along and promptly pulls the rug out from under you. Fits and starts; ups and downs; highs and lows, that's what you're in for. However, many of the pitfalls and set-backs can be avoided if you're prepared to quieten down a bit. You're much too fond of taking risks and acting like a dare-devil instead of simply getting on with your work.

AQUARIUS/FIVE/THREE

Try to get your working life into more order and routine so that you don't find yourself rushing to complete overdue orders or impossible deadlines. When your time is your own, there's no need to fill every minute of it with action-packed, non-stop socializing. Set aside at least some time each day simply to rest and unwind. You know it makes sense so make sure you do.

AQUARIUS/FIVE/FOUR

You're eccentric, unpredictable and enigmatic. At work many of your ideas are brilliant and imaginative, and even though your methods may appear cranky, you manage to achieve outstanding results time and again. You are sensual, exciting and active; however your word is your bond and once given you'll never go back on it however great the temptation to do otherwise.

AQUARIUS/FIVE/FIVE

It's virtually impossible to predict what you'll make of your life because you're made up of such a contradictory amalgum of talents and temperament. In many ways you merit the description 'genius' because you're undoubtedly capable of great things, particularly in the field of communications or the arts. However, you also behave like a lunatic at times when you turn down golden opportunities or deliberately spoil your own chances by some stupid, reckless act. You're much too restless, far too impulsive and totally irresponsible.

AQUARIUS/FIVE/SIX

You need to be stimulated, interested and fully stretched to gain any satisfaction; and it's the only way to bring out the best in you. In private, although you can be both base and vulgar in certain company, you'd be well advised to select a permanent partner with the same degree of refinement and intelligence as yourself.

AQUARIUS/FIVE/SEVEN

You have a brilliant, mercurial mind; a first-class education crowned by a whole string of qualifications and some really way-out, yet nevertheless feasible, ideas. But you spend so much time alone that you've forgotten how to conduct even a simple conversation and although your sexual drives are strong you've learned to sublimate them. You're dreamy and eccentric; rambling and confused; muddled and lazy. There's much to be achieved but only when you've got yourself organized.

AQUARIUS/FIVE/EIGHT

Success is important to you. In fact it's more than just that, it's all you ask from life — your *raison d'être*. Unfortunately you don't always play by the rules. You're hard, ruthless and determined. You cut corners, take risks and even use friends to gain a few inches of advancement. Your partners are chosen for their connections rather than their attributes and when you do marry it will almost certainly be for money, not love.

AQUARIUS/FIVE/NINE

Not only are you well qualified, efficient and prolific but you're always coming up with revolutionary ideas whereby management could cut back on resources and manpower yet still produce the same results. It's no wonder colleagues dislike you when you unwittingly put their jobs at risk. Think before you speak in future.

AQUARIUS/SIX/ONE

Although you are intelligent and of an intellectual leaning you're also particularly clever with your hands and often combine the two in your chosen career. Whatever you create bears your own distinctive hallmarks and whatever you do is sure to be original and highly unusual because there's nothing whatsoever mundane or run of the mill about someone like you.

AQUARIUS/SIX/TWO

Much of your pleasure comes from the arts either as a spectator or a participant. You are creative, talented and original and could be anything you choose from a fine artist to an exceptionally gifted musician or writer. You tend to mix with like-minded friends during your leisure time and although not actually promiscuous you do have a very free and easy attitude towards relationships.

AQUARIUS/SIX/THREE

You are jumpy, impatient and restless not to mention permissive, sensual and immoral. Your emotions are deep and turbulent yet your feelings for individuals are inconsistent and your promises totally worthless. You should concentrate more on developing your considerable gifts in order to put them to better use.

AQUARIUS/SIX/FOUR

You're hard-working yet you know when to call it a day; adventurous without being foolhardy; and cautious without being stick-in-the-mud. Occasionally you display a little impatience when progress seems slow but never enough to make you act carelessly or on impulse. Even in private you know all about give and take, sharing and co-operation. You're kind, considerate and understanding and certainly no novice when it comes to making love.

AQUARIUS/SIX/FIVE

You have rare artistic gifts and talents which border on genius and like all people blessed or cursed in this way the sanity of many of your actions is often questionable. You are odd, eccentric and aimless; totally lacking in ambition or indeed a definite course to steer. You owe it to more people than just yourself and your family to put your creativity to good use.

AQUARIUS/SIX/SIX

You care nothing for religion or politics, prefer to earn your living by your wits and conduct your relationships with as few strings attached as possible. Like a wild creature you soon grow dull and lack-lustre in captivity and on the rare occasions you remain in one place for any length of time you need to know that the cage door is ajar in case you feel the urge to run.

AQUARIUS/SIX/SEVEN

You're a law unto yourself. In fact, you're unique. You have a brilliant mind; highly original ideas and some very unorthodox beliefs. However when it comes to doing what comes naturally you're more than willing to conform and do it, although probably more often than others as you're extremely red-blooded and practically insatiable when roused.

AQUARIUS/SIX/EIGHT

Pleasures of the flesh are nothing more than that to you. Transitory moments of sensuous gratification to be enjoyed when on offer but certainly not mourned when in short supply. People are of little or no importance in your life because you need neither help nor encouragement with motivation; you're quite capable of sorting that out for yourself. You have strong individuality, an adaptable nature and a penchant for power.

AQUARIUS/SIX/NINE

People who refuse to be bound by convention, who won't toe the line or do anything in an orthodox manner set themselves apart from everyone else and often become treated like outcasts as a result. You seem to be a part-time rebel, only making a stance when the mood takes you. It's all or nothing and the sooner you make a decision the better because having a foot in both camps must be an extremely uncomfortable way to live.

AQUARIUS/SEVEN/ONE

At work you are a very specialized specialist knowing your territory inside out, but always keenly interested to find out more. In private you're spiritual and enlightened. Your moments of passion and intimacy are quite likely to be induced through meditation so take pains to find a suitably advanced partner.

AQUARIUS/SEVEN/TWO

Within a relationship you behave rather coolly towards your partner because this is the only way you can keep your moodiness and deep-seated jealousy under any semblance of control. Provided you can maintain a stiff upper lip and a relatively low profile your affairs should run like clockwork. But the moment you allow emotion to cloud your judgement that is the moment when your life will start to go haywire.

AQUARIUS/SEVEN/THREE

The danger for you lies in getting so deeply involved in all things magical and mysterious that you lose touch with reality. In other words you forget which way is up. Any investigative work you undertake, particularly when probing the inner recesses of the mind, should only be carried out under strict supervision. Do not dabble and don't be tempted to do any solo trips, always have someone with you in case of emergencies.

AQUARIUS/SEVEN/FOUR

There is a side to you which although seldom seen undoubtedly exists. Strong religious beliefs are the cornerstone upon which you build your life and despite the fact that you seldom attend formal church services your feelings are deep and sincere. You tend to play this aspect down in front of others, including your partner, but it's there in the background to sustain you.

AQUARIUS/SEVEN/FIVE

Once off on your travels you're never in any particular hurry to return, as home to you is nothing more than somewhere to hang your hat — certainly not a place to pine for while you are away. Being footloose and fancy-free you tend to be rather casual about your labours and even more so where partners are concerned. However you should try to put at least something away for your old age.

AQUARIUS/SEVEN/SIX

Try to get yourself better organized and try also to be more consistent in future. You tend to go in fits and starts; wild bursts of enthusiasm and hard work followed by periods of inertia and disinterest. You need to pace yourself better if you want to give of your best, and the introduction of a fairly flexible routine might help you gain the equilibrium you are currently short of.

AQUARIUS/SEVEN/SEVEN

You are a self-appointed psychic investigator because you're sensitive enough to pick up feelings and vibrations which more worldly people tend not to notice. You probably have unusual gifts and experiences which only serve to further fuel your interest in the unknown. You need an exceptionally level head to undertake such work and a sensible partner along for the ride is a safety precaution you shouldn't ignore.

AQUARIUS/SEVEN/EIGHT

Apart from a fine business brain you also have another valuable asset to help you along the pathway to success — your intuition. You have the ability to pick up and sense things long before they take place and with a little practice you should be able to use this gift in a positive way. Just think what an advantage this could give you over competitors. What's more it could add a new dimension to your private relationships by putting you mentally as well as physically in tune with your partner.

AQUARIUS/SEVEN/NINE

You are intelligent, intellectual and a wizard with figures, but you also attract trouble. Arguments flare up whenever you are around and unnecessary problems spring up like mushrooms in your wake. Try to be more patient and methodical in future and don't lose your temper over trifles.

AQUARIUS/EIGHT/ONE

There's nothing shy or retiring about you at all. At work you never miss an opportunity to push yourself forward any more than you ever miss a trick to gain esteem and recognition amongst members of the community in which you live. Money talks and you're hoping to amass enough to hold a great many important conversations with influential people. What's more, achieving social status is almost as vital to you as ensuring that you have financial security.

AQUARIUS/EIGHT/TWO

You're brilliant at rehearsal but when the curtain goes up and your performance has to be for real, stage fright gets the better of you time after time. Even when trying to broach a sensitive subject with your partner you seldom fare any better and usually end up apologizing for being a nuisance. It's time you mastered the art of asserting yourself; you've been an understudy for long enough!

AQUARIUS/EIGHT/THREE

You are very good at starting projects all full of enthusiasm and raring to go, but the longer a venture takes the more your interest flags so that all too often you fail to see anything through to a satisfactory conclusion. You are not tough enough with yourself when it comes to staying the course. You take the easy way out every time and this applies equally to your relationships.

AQUARIUS/EIGHT/FOUR

At work you're capable of acting in a ruthless, unscrupulous manner in order to get what you want and things aren't that much different in private. You are selfish, unemotional and for the most part detached. Anyone who partners you shouldn't expect too much from the liaison because in terms of affection and understanding you have little to offer.

AQUARIUS/EIGHT/FIVE

You are all in favour of speculating in order to accumulate but it has to be said that the majority of the risks you take are carefully calculated down to the very last penny. You are streetwise, quick witted and always open to offers. In private you're much too free to ever get trapped into marriage, although you're not averse to leading others up the garden path if it suits your plans.

AQUARIUS/EIGHT/SIX

At work you are tough, strong and determined. But at home in the bosom of your family you're a different person; gentle, caring and understanding, loving, demonstrative and generous to a fault. You're kind to children and dumb animals, always prepared to assist poor relatives and constantly lavishing gifts and attention on your partner.

AQUARIUS/EIGHT/SEVEN

You are soft, sensitive and kind although few of these qualities will be of much use to you in the cut and thrust world of modern commerce. However, in private you'll have ample scope and opportunity to show your great depth of understanding and concern, not to mention your fiery, passionate nature when aroused. And at least you'll have a happy home atmosphere to relax in after a long, taxing day on the treadmill.

AQUARIUS/EIGHT/EIGHT

You are totally ruthless and utterly without scruples. You are also cold, unemotional and unfeeling. All you care about is getting on in this world and all you ever think about is how best to achieve your ends. As a friend you're not to be trusted and as a partner you're not to be recommended. But as a parent you're surprisingly conscientious.

AQUARIUS/EIGHT/NINE

Anger is about the only emotion you ever display and then only on rare occasions when something sufficiently maddening has forced a break in your icy self-control. You're a very cold, joyless kettle of fish. Whatever it is you're frightened of experiencing, loneliness is certainly on the cards for you if you continue to shy away from all but the most essential forms of human contact.

AQUARIUS/NINE/ONE

You are tough, independent and larger than life; dangerous, determined and desperate for success. Even in private you're a force to be reckoned with because when you pledge your love to someone there's no two ways about it — it's for keeps. You're a fiery, passionate playmate and while not actually eaten up with jealousy you can certainly bite, should your partner ever step out of line.

AQUARIUS/NINE/TWO

Whatever else you do, don't give in to those anxiety attacks or even take them too seriously. It's quite natural to question the wisdom of your actions occasionally and so long as your confidence doesn't become completely undermined then no real harm will be done. Look to your partner for encouragement and reassurance and never allow problems to get out of proportion with reality.

AQUARIUS/NINE/THREE

Sometimes you can be too tough and decisive for your own good. You'll announce quite flatly and categorically that enough is enough and you'll quit a job or a relationship without further ado. However by adopting such tactics you leave no room for manoeuvre or negotiation because you've made your intentions so abundantly clear. In future try to be firm without being foolhardy.

AQUARIUS/NINE/FOUR

You are loyal, faithful and considerate; totally besotted by your partner and prepared to move heaven and earth to ensure their happiness. You also make a conscientious and fiercely protective parent and because you set great store by a good education will spare no expense where your own children's schooling is concerned. As a lover you're passionate, demonstrative and considerate; as a friend you're honest and reliable but as an enemy you are very bad news indeed.

AQUARIUS/NINE/FIVE

You have neither direction, discipline nor determination and the sooner you drum up a little of all three the sooner any further steam you decide to let off will evaporate in a good cause — namely your future prosperity. You have a good brain — use it; some brilliant ideas — cash in on them; and the elasticity of a rubber band although there's no need to stretch yourself to the limits to prove it.

AQUARIUS/NINE/SIX

You have a way with colour, a flair for design and an artistic style all of your own. You have to use your gifts just as much as you have to have air to breathe and food to sustain yourself. Don't let anyone ever stop you from doing your own thing but equally don't let it completely take over your life otherwise your career could go by the board and your relationships crumble through lack of maintenance.

AQUARIUS/NINE/SEVEN

You may understand what's going on but all you ever manage to do is confuse everyone else. Don't be so lazy in your manner of speech, try to be more articulate and collect your thoughts better before attempting to voice them. Until you can master the art of communication your career is unlikely to get more than a few inches off the ground.

AQUARIUS/NINE/EIGHT

Don't be so ruthless in your treatment of other people because the more enemies you make the more time you'll have to waste looking over your shoulder in case of attack. Keep an eye on your health too, because all work and no play eventually causes cracks to appear in even the strongest of constitutions. Do set some time aside to spend with your partner.

AQUARIUS/NINE/NINE

You are one of those 'all or nothing' people. Everything for you is either black or white with no shades of grey in between. You'll do a job whole-heartedly, enthusiastically and to the best of your ability or you won't touch it at all. With other people you take them or you leave them but you never treat anyone with indifference. You have strong convictions and fierce loyalties. You're obstinate, aggressive and very plain to understand.

PISCES/ONE/ONE

Although you are reasonably confident and usually cope with the demands of a busy job plus a home and family, there will be times when your get up and go feels as if it has gone for good. Fortunately your off-days are rare and major errors of judgement are fairly few and far between. However you will need to watch out that you don't take on more responsibility that you can comfortably handle.

PISCES/ONE/TWO

Unfortunately you are a born worrier and this can make you very trying to live with because you never seem happy unless you've got a multitude of problems to cope with. You're tense, fretful and always uptight about something or other. You should try harder to relax.

PISCES/ONE/THREE

Even though you don't like taking orders or complying with rules and regulations you do work best when part of a well-drilled team. You lack the confidence to stand completely alone not to mention the concentration and rigid discipline required under solo conditions. You're quite capable of getting yourself organized, more than happy to lend others a helping hand but rather dubious about being given too much responsibility to shoulder.

PISCES/ONE/FOUR

What others don't realize, or ever see, is the tremendous effort that goes into psyching yourself up to face each new day with courage and determination. Deep down you feel inferior and terribly insecure but the majority of the time you do a wonderful cover-up job. However, when the mask does slip, usually in private, and you temporarily lose heart it's not a pleasant sight to behold. Try to ensure that it doesn't happen too often as even the most caring of partners can only be pushed so far.

PISCES/ONE/FIVE

You need continuity and an anchor in your life and without either you're in about as much danger of ending up on the rocks as a ship cast adrift in gale force winds. You trust far too much to luck and wallow in despair when it deserts you; make all sorts of decisions and then panic because you feel pressurized; and retreat into moody silence when an impulsive action goes dreadfully wrong.

PISCES/ONE/SIX

Creative people like yourself often find the pressures and demands of everyday life exceptionally tiresome especially if they are also endowed with the excitable, nervous temperament that so often accompanies artistic talents. It has to be said that you are likely to be both moody and over-emotional and it won't be easy coping with the inevitable tension you're bound to experience.

PISCES/ONE/SEVEN

You have a colourful imagination at the best of times without allowing it to work overtime and unless you're very careful you could lose touch with reality and not even notice. Force yourself to visit friends or get out and about at least one night every week just to break the silence and make sure you get adequate rest and exercise. Health is vital and yours needs constant careful monitoring.

PISCES/ONE/EIGHT

Although you are generally confident and decisive you must admit that you don't work well under pressure and that responsibility tends to frighten you especially at times when you're feeling a bit down. Moderation should be your watchword and provided you say it to yourself each time you're tempted to overstep the mark then you shouldn't go too far wrong or suddenly find you've got out of your depth.

PISCES/ONE/NINE

You crave love and affection so desperately that it appears you'll go to any lengths to get some even if it means making a complete and utter fool of yourself into the bargain. What you can't apparently manage to do is strike up a relationship with someone of your own age group because for some unknown reason you find it virtually impossible to communicate with them. That's why you're so often seen with people several years either your senior or your junior.

PISCES/TWO/ONE

You're cultured, well-bred and refined; artistic, intelligent and imaginative; and although you may not have a hide like a rhinoceros or the cunning of a fox you still could go far. However, in private a slightly thicker skin would be a distinct advantage because you're incredibly sensitive and take everything much too much to heart.

PISCES/TWO/TWO

If there was a job advertised which called for applicants who were highly-strung, nervous and frightened of their own shadows you'd immediately be put on the short list. What's more your private life is unlikely to be a barrel of laughs when you've always got a thermometer stuck in your mouth and a permanent pained expression on your face. You should cheer up, after all it may never happen and even if it does it probably won't be as bad as you spend all your time imagining.

PISCES/TWO/THREE

You have the volatile temperament which often accompanies artistic gifts and its open to conjecture which way you'll jump in any given situation. Your main problem is that you're not very tactful, and although thin-skinned and easily hurt yourself you can never see when you're hurting others either by your attitude or choice of words. Do as you would be done by rather more often, and try to show more understanding for the feelings of others.

PISCES/TWO/FOUR

Playing safe is one thing but refusing to move a muscle for fear of the consequences is ridiculous. Not only are you over-cautious, you're also suspicious and mistrustful. At work you spend more time spying on your colleagues than you do on your actual job and in private you're so jealous and possessive that you're always checking up on your partner's movements. You're in danger of becoming paranoid.

PISCES/TWO/FIVE

For someone who worries incessantly about their health, has a bookshelf full of medical dictionaries and is always on some revolutionary diet or other you certainly are a contradiction in terms. What good will it do you living on carrot juice and bananas if you continue to smoke like a chimney and drink like a fish. Your behaviour patterns are unlikely to harm anyone but yourself but don't you think it's time you stopped being quite so hypocritical?

PISCES/TWO/SIX

In matters of the heart you lean to the romantic. You are dreamy, imaginative and artistic — certainly not decisive or well-organized at all. But you can't just sit back and hope for the best. Once you learn to be more positive and start to help yourself a little more that's when you'll begin to see some visible improvement in your general situation.

PISCES/TWO/SEVEN

You are unrealistic, impractical and muddled; lazy, confused and sensitive. You lack the drive and ambition so vital for carving a career or the emotional stability upon which to build a fulfilling relationship. What's more your health is hardly renowned for being strong and your constitution rather less than robust. However, you should still make an effort to develop greater self-confidence and to introduce a more organized lifestyle.

PISCES/TWO/EIGHT

Initiative is what you lack and unless you acquire some you will never get any of your ideas off the ground. No one is going to come along with a magic wand and get things started for you and it is high time you realized this for yourself and did something about it. Where matters of the heart are concerned, again you'll have to be prepared to give rather more freely than you normally do if you ever hope to receive anything in return.

PISCES/TWO/NINE

Although you are talented and imaginative you will probably never realize your full potential because you don't have the first idea how to promote yourself forcefully without immediately giving offence. Your tactics have much in common with the progress of a bull in a china shop. In future think things through with greater care before attempting to put any plans into action.

PISCES/THREE/ONE

Although your qualifications are impressive and you're undoubtedly capable of producing outstanding results you will need to work a great deal harder at developing some self-control and discipline if you ever hope to keep up to the mark and work at peak performance for anything more than short sharp bursts. Staying power has always been noticeably absent from your character. The potential is there and so long as your heart is in the job you're doing and your concentration improves, success is yours for the taking.

PISCES/THREE/TWO

Where relationships are concerned you make the mistake of trying to play everything much too cool when really you're getting deeply involved. You'll say things like 'see you around' when in fact you mean 'stay, don't go' or 'please yourself' instead of 'that would be wonderful'. Then when things begin to go wrong because your casual pose has been mistaken for disinterest you kick up such a fuss, declare your undying love and get laughed at for your pains.

PISCES/THREE/THREE

Despite your carefully cultivated aura of casual languidness you're surprisingly astute and far more on the ball than you'd care to let on. Very little of interest ever escapes your attention while nothing of importance ever slips through your grasp. You're intelligent, artistic and creative; quick on the uptake and particularly good with your hands.

PISCES/THREE/FOUR

The number Four has a stabilizing effect on the rather disorganized Pisces-Three character helping to put it on a more steady footing. It means that you should be able to deal with problems carefully and systematically. At work you should be a useful addition to any firm's payroll because you're hard-working, trustworthy and efficient. In private, although not exactly sexual dynamite, you can at least offer love, affection and a great deal of understanding.

PISCES/THREE/FIVE

While you may not feel the pressing need to get things done others won't thank you if you continually break their concentration or interrupt their chain of thought for no particular reason. You're also guilty of time-wasting in private, although for rather different reasons. Try not to be so casual in future, make a more consistent effort and don't lead people up the garden path. It's not only very unkind but also totally unnecessary.

PISCES/THREE/SIX

You are possibly one of the most generous, good natured people around. You'll give freely of your time and efforts if it will ultimately benefit others in any way and you're always willing to listen to people's problems without interruption or the need to pass criticism. You are sociable, gregarious and fun-loving; light-hearted, kind and warm. However, you're disorganized, inconsistent and have an attitude which is far too 'easy come, easy go' to ever get you anywhere.

PISCES/THREE/SEVEN

In matters of the heart it's not surprising that you lean to the romantic, preferring to worship from afar rather than coming to grips with passion. At work you'll take the easy way out every time as you find the necessity to earn a living both boring and restrictive. You are a square peg in a round hole.

PISCES/THREE/EIGHT

You have an abundance of talent and more than enough drive and aggression to put it to the best possible use. You may like to lounge about and be thoroughly idle during your time off but when duty calls you're hard-working, efficient and utterly determined to show outstanding results for your unstinting efforts. It's a great pity you don't show quite so much enthusiasm for your private affairs.

PISCES/THREE/NINE

If only you'd learn to look where you're going and use your brain more often you wouldn't encounter so many problems and set-backs, neither would you get involved in so many minor avoidable accidents. You go around as if you were in a trance and often fail to notice even the things taking place under your very nose. Stop day-dreaming, be more assertive and get on the ball!

PISCES/FOUR/ONE

Intuition is what will give an ambitious, success-seeker like you the edge over competitors so go ahead and don't be afraid to trust its reliability. Play your hunches because that's the only way to find out how right they are. There's no need to

272 The Wheel of Fortune

discuss the tip-off's your subconscious gives you with anyone else. Why ignore sound advice just because you receive it through extra-sensory channels?

PISCES/FOUR/TWO

At work you should experience relatively few problems either selecting a suitable career or seeing that it progresses in the right direction because you're practical, efficient and astute. It is during your leisure hours that you are likely to run into difficulties. Don't get involved with people who you somehow sense to be wrong for you, let your feelings be your guide in emotive situations and try not to let your colourful imagination blow doubts and suspicions out of all proportion.

PISCES/FOUR/THREE

There's rather more to someone like you than meets the eye because, like an iceberg, a good two-thirds of you is hidden beneath the surface away from public gaze. Your everyday image is one of convention and respectability. You are efficient at work, prompt at paying bills and, from all appearances, reasonably prosperous. However the true brilliance of your mind is rarely glimpsed because you prefer to play it down as much as possible. Deep down you are clever, versatile and shrewd; intelligent, original and far-sighted.

PISCES/FOUR/FOUR

You are practical and down-to-earth in your attitude towards people and problems. What's more, domesticity suits you and home is undoubtedly where you can be seen at your best. Your other frequency is of a higher, spiritual nature because your thoughts are never solely confined to worldly, material affairs. Predictive dreams often reveal to you glimpses of what's yet to come, while your intuition can be invaluable in times of decision.

PISCES/FOUR/FIVE

You thrive on stimulation, mental or physical and once your curiosity has been roused you'll know no peace until you've followed up whatever happens to be bugging you. Travel particularly appeals because it offers the opportunity to gain first hand experience of different cultures and lifestyles. Your sexual drives are strong and although you try hard to be faithful there could well be occasions when your normal constraint is pushed beyond its limits.

PISCES/FOUR/SIX

Don't discuss anyone else's private business but your own, remember that when something is told to you in confidence that's how it should be kept and try to be more tactful and discreet in future. Special talents should be treasured, not paraded as party tricks or shamelessly abused if you don't want them to backfire on you.

PISCES/FOUR/SEVEN

To look at you no one would ever guess what you get up to in your spare time and that's just how you like it. First appearances say you're conservative, respectable and not the slightest bit out of the ordinary. However, in the privacy of your own home, and in the company of your carefully chosen friends, the occult, the supernatural and the paranormal are all areas you're passionately interested in. Fortunately you're too sensible to ever lose complete control but nevertheless care should be exercised at all times when delving into the unknown.

PISCES/FOUR/EIGHT

The trouble with you is that you start to doubt your own sanity when the same rather disturbing dream keeps recurring night after night or when something deep within you almost forces you to reject a certain course of action. What you are actually experiencing is premonition even though you believe such incidents to be the early stages of madness. You always have to have logical reasons for the events that take place in your life and sometimes they are not always possible to produce.

PISCES/FOUR/NINE

It's time you came down off that high horse of yours, stopped being so haughty and superior, and learned to muck in just like everyone else. You have never heard of give and take, haven't the faintest idea what co-operation is all about and don't even know how to keep your opinions to yourself. There's no time like the present to find out.

PISCES/FIVE/ONE

There are just two things which stand between you and the success you're always day-dreaming about. The first is the fact that you are basically lazy and the second is your refusal to come to terms with reality. You've got a colourful imagination and a penchant for playing make-believe. But unless you knuckle down and apply yourself soon you'll have nothing tangible to show for yourself when all your peers have beautiful homes and enviable incomes.

PISCES/FIVE/TWO

You are untidy and totally disorganized. You never seem to know whether you're coming or going and have the happy knack of infecting others with the same malaise. What's more, you are weak-willed and easily-led. Your moods change as often as the prevailing weather conditions and your partners with almost the same speed and frequency.

PISCES/FIVE/THREE

When it comes to conjuring up wonderful visions of a brilliant future no one can possibly equal, let alone imitate, your undeniable skill with words. You're so persuasive that you could sell clothes pegs to a gypsy. Whether or not your flattery is sincere or the opinions you voice are strictly honest makes no difference; people want to believe you simply because you are a spinner of dreams.

PISCES/FIVE/FOUR

The number Four gives you just a shade more commonsense than most other Pisces-Fives, but not enough to make you see reason where members of the opposite sex are concerned. You can understand the need to concentrate and apply yourself at work, even financially you can appreciate the disastrous consequences of over-spending and living beyond your means but you can see no harm whatsoever in arranging as many clandestine rendezvous as there are days in the week with a couple of weekend matinées thrown in for good measure.

PISCES/FIVE/FIVE

You are restless, lustful and impatient. You're always trying to swim in two directions at once while, at the same time, burning the candle at both ends. Try to get yourself into some semblance of a routine, and don't be so quick to throw in the towel when the going gets tough, particularly at work. The sooner you grasp the fact that there is more to life than gratuitous sex the sooner you'll cross that thin dividing line which separates adults from adolescents.

PISCES/FIVE/SIX

Not only is your act coming apart at the seams but its also quite likely to be a source of distraction to anyone and everyone you come into contact with. Basically you're a time-waster who can't resist trying to get other people involved in hair-brained schemes. Your opening lines are well delivered and extremely convincing. What's more your tremendous charm and considerable stage presence goes a long way to ensnaring the more sceptical members of your audience.

PISCES/FIVE/SEVEN

The call of the open road is one you've never been able to resist and whether you travel first class or economy it makes no odds just so long as the fields and pastures you visit are new and the people you encounter on the way are genuine and authentic. Fakes and posers are not what you're looking for, that's why you prefer to stay away from tourist haunts and get as far off the beaten track as possible.

PISCES/FIVE/EIGHT

You'll boldly go where only a fool would follow and then look surprised when you inevitably come unstuck. Be more realistic; check and double check all your calculations with the greatest of care and don't shout quite so loudly about what you're hoping to achieve. In future wait until you have some tangible proof of your success before you begin to crow.

PISCES/FIVE/NINE

It's a great pity you are not more organized and decisive because you have a perfectly sound brain just crying out for a good workout to prevent it from malfunctioning completely. What you need is self-discipline, staying-power and a goal to aim at which is neither too easy nor too difficult for you to achieve.

PISCES/SIX/ONE

You are rather inclined to model yourself on someone you admire and when, because you're not that person, you find you can't achieve the same outstanding results you quickly lose heart and become despondent. You should make every effort to work within your own boundaries and the only way you'll be able to do that is to know yourself better and to identify your own strong points and weaknesses.

PISCES/SIX/TWO

You'll allow personal likes and dislikes to colour your judgement, and other people's personalities to stand in your way. Stop thinking with your heart all the time, clear your head and get things into better perspective. Don't treat your partner like a pet which must be kept on a leash and don't treat your colleagues to temper tantrums followed by moody silences.

PISCES/SIX/THREE

Everything seems to come very easily to you and for that reason you don't value benefits nearly enough. You're so versatile and talented that there are few things you can't turn your mind or your hands to. What's more, you pick up new skills with apparent ease and have the infuriating habit of outshining everyone. Where people are concerned you're rather inclined to take them for granted and seldom remember to treat friends or lovers with the respect and consideration they deserve.

PISCES/SIX/FOUR

Not only are you well organized, efficient and systematic you're also neat, practical and domesticated. These are all commendable attributes but unfortunately you just can't leave it there. Once you are running like well-oiled clockwork, you then have to start on everyone else. You're a compulsive tidier and unless you stop it you're going to drive everyone to distraction.

PISCES/SIX/FIVE

The minute something new or interesting appears on the scene you'll drop whatever it is you're doing and rush off to investigate. At work you barely have time to settle into one job before you're writing off letters of application to other companies who appear to have more to offer. Your personal relationships bear a striking resemblance to a game of musical chairs although in your version the music hasn't always stopped when you decide to make a move!

PISCES/SIX/SIX

You are far too fragile and easily hurt to be able to survive for long without getting damaged. You need someone strong to lean on and to shield you from the stark realities of modern life. You are sensitive and unworldly; creative and artistic; romantic and dreamy. You take everything at face value and everyone at their word which is not only unwise it can also be dangerous. Stand on your own two feet and learn to cope just like everyone else.

PISCES/SIX/SEVEN

You are receptive to the moods of others, open to many influences and often confused when two sources of information overlap but fail to tally on certain points. By all means be guided by your sub-conscious but don't make the mistake of allowing it to take the place of common sense or use it as a crutch. You must learn to be accountable for your own actions and you must try to make progress even though you're not particularly ambitious or dynamic.

PISCES/SIX/EIGHT

You tend to experience extremes of emotion, often in the space of a few short hours — one moment wallowing in the depths of despair only to rise phoenix-like from your anguish and soar to a point of ecstacy. You never know whether you're coming or going so it's highly unlikely that your partner will ever be able to fathom you out.

PISCES/SIX/NINE

The way you go about showing your love and friendship leaves much to be desired because you go too far in the opposite direction. You kill people with kindness, smother them with affection and go so far out of your way to please that the situation becomes embarrassing. There are two things you need to learn — tolerance and moderation.

PISCES/SEVEN/ONE

Thanks to the influence of the number One you stand a better chance than most other Pisces-Sevens of achieving success in this life. However, nothing will guarantee this unless you're prepared to put in many long, weary hours of hard work and to show unswerving dedication to duty. Fortunately you do have an enquiring mind, and an open one at that, not to mention a fair amount of drive and energy.

PISCES/SEVEN/TWO

When left to your own devices you lack the will or the discipline to ever get anything done. You're attracted to all the wrong things and even though, deep down, you probably realize the folly of your ways, you either can't or won't do anything to stop yourself. Emotionally you're not very stable and would be well advised not to experiment with either people or stimulants which could do you harm.

PISCES/SEVEN/THREE

In terms of business your ideas are original and the thinking behind them sound, however you lack the initiative to capitalize on them. In private you're charming, entertaining and witty but terrified of forming lasting associations because of the inevitable responsibility such liaisons bring with them. Once the conversation turns to marriage you're off like a shot and it will take a pretty hefty rope to tie you down for any length of time.

PISCES/SEVEN/FOUR

Your plans seldom if ever get past the drawing-board stage as they're either unrealistic or far too expensive to fund. What progress you do make is generally at a snail's pace and even then full of mistakes and errors which could so easily have been avoided. It's high time you stopped being so vague.

PISCES/SEVEN/FIVE

There's no two ways about it, you're an escapist. There's nothing realistic or down to earth about you at all. Life for you is one long fantasy which you're going to live out come hell or high water. You are over-imaginative, weak-willed and easily seduced. You're always on the look out for new experiences and should think twice before experimenting with new sensations.

PISCES/SEVEN/SIX

Your combination of sign and numbers produces not only people who are creatively talented but also some highly imaginative and intuitive individuals. Therefore it's hardly surprising that you have a very definite leaning to the arts and that you are capable of producing some outstanding results. What's more you have more than just one string to your bow. Perhaps your greatest single problem is knowing in which direction to specialize for the best.

PISCES/SEVEN/SEVEN

You are as vulnerable as a snail without a shell or a piece of ice during a heatwave. Try as best you can to protect yourself from the more obvious pitfalls of life such as running into debt or getting involved with the wrong kind of people and remember that if in any doubt, it's best to do nothing than something you might live to regret.

PISCES/SEVEN/EIGHT

You have a reasonably good nose for business but unfortunately you have no scruples and for that reason alone many of your methods and tactics are dubious to say the least. Try not to cut corners in your haste to make that first million and avoid dealing with sharks and conmen at all costs as you're very often judged by the company you keep.

PISCES/SEVEN/NINE

You're a very soulful, spiritual individual. Your thoughts are nearly always on higher things and you're not really properly equipped to deal with the inevitable demands and limitations of an earthbound existence. What's more you wouldn't feel happy in a job which was too stressful or competitive so when choosing a career you should opt for something creative and relatively easy-going. In private, although you need a partner who can hold the purse strings, you also need one who's prepared to hold your hand when life gets you down.

PISCES/EIGHT/ONE

You need to stand or fall by your own decisions and abilities, not be carried along or held back by other people. In private, although this is never usually practical advice, you'd do well to remain single for as long as possible as relationships only cause you unnecessary complications, due entirely to your changeable and insecure emotional state.

PISCES/EIGHT/TWO

Life never seems to be much fun for you because even at the best of times feelings of insecurity eat away at you like a worm in an apple. You are fretful, tense and devoid of humour. If only you could relax a little and learn to laugh at yourself not only would you feel better inside you would also be more attractive to other people. Take a deep breath, put on a smile and with your best foot forward take life as it comes for a change.

PISCES/EIGHT/THREE

You are one of those lucky individuals who Fate saw fit to bless with brains and talent. However sensitivity must have been missing from the list because you seldom seem to care about anyone other than yourself and rarely display such feelings as kindness, understanding or compassion. All in all you're a very cold fish and an even cooler customer.

PISCES/EIGHT/FOUR

You appear to have few ordinary feelings let alone finer ones and about the only values you understand are of the material variety. You are cautious, mercenary and at times downright mean and penny-pinching with yourself as well as others. You're also incredibly superstitious which is an odd trait to find in such a down-to-earth person like you.

PISCES/EIGHT/FIVE

Your deep-seated restlessness usually manages to ruin your career chances somewhere along the line because you find it difficult either to concentrate or settle to anything for any length of time. Your rampant sensuality is practically guaranteed to land you in trouble, sooner rather than later. Deep down you feel muddled and insecure but your actions only serve to confuse you even further and instead of life being simpler it grows progressively more difficult.

PISCES/EIGHT/SIX

You have a vivid imagination, creative flair and a positive genius for arranging things to their best effect but where you generally fall flat is in situations where you need to be not only hyper-confident but also quick-thinking and decisive. You wilt under pressure and don't give your best performance when put on a spot. You need plenty of time to collect your thoughts and open-ended completion dates for all your work.

PISCES/EIGHT/SEVEN

You seem unable or unwilling to keep your emotions on anything vaguely resembling an even keel and spend far more time on your own than is really necessary or indeed healthy. You are prone to fantacizing, and have an extremely colourful imagination with the end result being a distorted picture of reality. It's very sensible to work frustrations out of your system but not if it means directing them at the nearest person who happens to be handy.

PISCES/EIGHT/EIGHT

You do at times run the very real risk of biting off far more than you can comfortably chew let alone swallow, and it would be a sensible idea if in future you voluntarily came down a peg or two and cut your cloth in a style more in keeping with your means. What's more your massive ego could do with some trimming back before someone else tries to take the wind out of your sails. You should aim to show rather more consideration all round.

PISCES/EIGHT/NINE

Your obsession with personal hygiene is beginning to get out of hand and if you're not careful people might start to think there's something rather odd about you. They could even be right because you don't find it easy to relate to others without getting involved in unnecessary arguments and even when conversations don't disintegrate you still have the happy knack of always getting hold of the wrong end of the stick.

PISCES/NINE/ONE

You need to remain as optimistic as possible even when annoying problems and set-backs upset all your schedules. Never lose sight of your objective for even a second because once you allow yourself to become side-tracked the whole picture could change drastically. Where relationships are concerned try to select a partner who comes from a similar background and don't ever mistake infatuation for the real thing.

PISCES/NINE/TWO

You have never found it easy to strike up a relationship and find it even more difficult to nurse one along for any appreciable length of time. Possibly you could be accused of trying too hard to please and almost certainly the fault lies somewhere with you for most of the time. What's more you're in danger of seeking solace from a bottle and although this may temporarily dull the pain it's not the long term solution to your dilemma.

PISCES/NINE/THREE

Anything novel or slightly out of the ordinary acts as a stimulus to your creative imagination. You love to take ideas one step further, explore different variations albeit on old themes and have it in your power to be one of the architects of a new tomorrow. You look at things in a different light to everyone else and can often provide simple solutions to problems which have been baffling others for a considerable time. However, when it comes to putting your own affairs into order that's another matter entirely. All too often you'll hear opportunity knocking at your door and pretend you are not at home.

PISCES/NINE/FOUR

You're very much like a worker-bee, because not only do you know where you stand in the pecking order of things, you also know precisely what's expected of you. You're practical, down-to-earth and extremely well-organized. You never waste time on anything frivolous or unnecessary. However you do shy away from personal involvements for fear of getting stung, resist change in any shape or form for fear of losing your bearings, and won't even dare sample the nectar you help produce for fear of becoming addicted.

PISCES/NINE/FIVE

The Five influence on a Pisces-Nine combination is a recipe for disaster because it highlights and blows out of all reasonable proportion the sexual problems that already exist. You are impulsive, irrational and quite prepared to try just about anything once — twice if you enjoyed it the first time. Anything goes where you're concerned!

PISCES/NINE/SIX

You have much to commend you to members of the opposite sex, unfortunately you're attracted to all the wrong ones. Don't go for the big-timers because they'll walk all over you, and leave the misfits and lame dogs to those professionally equipped to deal with their problems because they'll only drag you down. Go for one of your own kind for a change.

PISCES/NINE/SEVEN

Not only are you easily-led, emotionally confused and generally rather muddled, you're also lacking in direction, commonsense and initiative. It is a great pity because you have a brain capable of grasping theories and concepts which would leave others open-mouthed in bewilderment. With determination on your part and a loving partner to provide encouragement and understanding, there's nothing you shouldn't be able to overcome given sufficient time and patience.

PISCES/NINE/EIGHT

Fate has a nasty way of intervening in your affairs at all the wrong moments which is one of the penalties of being influenced by the number of reversals

— Eight. For this reason you'd be well advised not to go counting your chickens until they have hatched, and not to broadcast your success too far and wide for fear of what might happen. Try to be more understanding and when you can sense an argument brewing it might be a good idea if you went out for a long walk and didn't wait around for the firework display to get under way.

PISCES/NINE/NINE

What you must realize is that there are some aspects of life from which it is not possible to escape. Don't you think it's time you faced up to reality, responsibility and commitment in an adult manner. Very often, when you have the courage to stand up to adversity, you find that it's never quite so menacing in the flesh than when blown out of all proportion by your imagination.

CHAPTER SIX

Your Year Ahead

By combining birth sign, date of birth number and initial letter number, we have hopefully provided a 'thumb nail sketch' of you as an individual, whether good, bad or indifferent. The final stage is to apply that basic knowledge to your year ahead.

It is important to understand that the year we are looking at is not a calendar year but a personal year. Your personal year runs from birthday to birthday.

The normal rules of numerology apply — reducing compound numbers to a single number. Let us imagine that you reached the age of 56 on your last birthday. Your personal year will run from that birthday to the next and, by reduction, we can see that the number which governs the year is 2.

$$56 = 5 + 6 = 11 = 1 + 1 = 2$$

Bearing in mind the assessments given in previous chapters, turn now to the section covering your personal year number to see what's in store. However, even armed with all this information *you* still remain in ultimate control of the personal events in your year ahead. Remember, forewarned is forearmed!

PERSONAL YEAR ONE

A personal year One marks the beginning of a whole new cycle of destiny and is therefore particularly powerful, fateful and auspicious. It is a time to consider wiping the slate clean if you don't like the story so far, by perhaps starting afresh or attempting to find new solutions to perennial old problems. However, in order for a new regime to be brought to power it will be necessary to lay careful plans, which will mean identifying areas where adjustments are called for, and maybe even giving up bad habits which you've drifted into during the course of the last nine-year cycle.

No one ever suggested that a personal year One was going to be easy but there's no other time like it for making a supreme effort and giving life a good old shake-up and spring-clean. If you are lacking in confidence, conditions look favourable for acquiring some now and if you usually find it hard to be decisive you shouldn't experience too much difficulty under this vibration. So assert yourself, push yourself forward and whatever it is you're after go for it without further delay.

For anyone considering a change of job this is a favourable time to put out feelers and do something positive about it. Off with the old and on with the new is an appropriate maxim for a year like this, and as all the omens are favourable all that is required of you is to make the effort and act. For those not wishing to make any drastic changes in their working life, but nevertheless with one or two grumbles and grievances to air, you mustn't suffer in silence any longer. Speak up, don't be afraid to stand up for yourself — after all if you don't complain when things are wrong how will anyone else get to know of your dissatisfaction? However, do remember there's no need to get carried away, just be firm not ferocious. This is a year for tremendous development and progress if you concentrate on one thing at a time and don't look to anyone else for help and encouragement.

It is also particularly good for all those involved in creative work of any kind as well as engineers, designers, inventors and explorers if there are any still around to be included.

Finances should be beneficially highlighted during the course of this twelve month period and although improvements are on the cards they're unlikely to be rapid or earth-shattering. One other point where money is concerned: any outstanding obstacles should be removed now and overdue debts should be settled so as to put everything in order for the new cycle. The buying and selling of cars and various items of machinery as well as personal effects, is very much in the spotlight and a move of home is more likely during this year than at any other time. So if you have been thinking of moving house, but haven't done anything positive about it, there's no time like a personal year One for setting the ball rolling and opting for a change of scenery.

Relationships need to be carefully examined at this time, especially those which are limping along or defying all efforts to revive them. A clean break is probably the best solution here although admittedly any action of this sort is always rather drastic because it's so final so have just one last go at the kiss of life before reaching your decision.

Those of you who are blissfully happy or have little to complain about still shouldn't be feeling too smug and complacent. Familiarity can eventually breed contempt and in order to avoid such a contingency try not to be quite so predictable and dream up a few surprises for each other just to make sure that the magic's still there and stays there.

No year, however well aspected, is without its pitfalls and drawbacks, and a personal year One is certainly no exception. In between bouts of tremendous energy and productivity the temptation to rest on your laurels and do nothing further will always be there. But unless you make a concerted all-out effort, you will miss opportunities which may not repeat themselves, so don't give in to laziness however much you feel a break is in order.

What is more, you certainly can't afford to be stubborn over certain issues any more than you can afford to hesitate when snap decisions are called for. On the home front watch out for your tendency to become bossy and selfish, and at work insubordination is a real danger. Learn to take orders without resentment, although if you feel you are being unjustly treated, that's another matter and you must say something about it before matters degenerate even further.

KEYWORDS
Positive: new beginnings, movement, adjustments, energy
Negative: stubbornness, laziness, selfishness, bossiness

PERSONAL YEAR TWO

Personal year Twos are nearly always rather uneventful but this doesn't for one moment mean they have to be dull. However as night follows day, two follows one which is usually a very difficult and exhausting act to continue and all that most people want to do under this vibration is to relax and get their breath back.

This is also a period which those with religious leanings should put to good use, because spiritual development is well aspected and anything which might possibly bring greater enlightenment or personal comfort shouldn't be dismissed out of hand, but explored to the full with a view to elevating your thoughts onto higher planes of existence. But for the more mundane and down-to-earth although you may not literally 'see the light' you will almost certainly have the opportunity to get your thoughts in order and instigate some sort of routine. While things are relatively quiet and peaceful, it's not a bad idea to take a long, hard look at yourself in order to better assess your character strengths and weaknesses. This is by no means a futile operation designed purely and simply to fill in time, but one which, at some later date, you'll be very glad you bothered to carry out.

As with all other aspects of life during a personal year Two you can't look for a great deal of improvement or action on the career front so patience will most definitely be part of standing orders. No major changes or unexpected promotions look likely to take place and the emphasis during this period is on team work and co-operation. Group projects take the spotlight and you'll need all the tact and diplomacy you can muster to come up with good results when having to fit in with other people. Give and take is something you'll have to learn about fast if you don't already know the rules because balance, agreement and harmony are all vitally important when responsibilities are shared out between several people who may not necessarily even like each other in the first instance.

Careers which are particularly favoured under the year Two vibration are the diplomatic service, politics, teaching and sales as well as clerks in all fields and agents handling anything from club catalogues to property deals. These people can expect the odd lucky break to occur but still nothing in the way of a major breakthrough.

Where home and personal finances are concerned, don't expect anything very much to happen on these two fronts. By all means mull over future plans and indulge in as much wishful thinking as you like but there should be nothing in the way of material advances made during this twelve month period and little of note about the house except perhaps the odd spot of decorating or cosmetic touching-up. Turn your attention to the garden because that seems about the most profitable area to focus your energies on as fresh salad vegetables are always in demand.

In private any changes which take place will certainly not be for the better, but problems are only likely to occur if you're stupid enough to provoke incidents and cause emotional scenes. We all experience moments of insecurity but the trouble is that under this vibration you could quite possibly make the mistake of letting your doubts show. Don't let your anxieties get out of proportion as sanity and a sense of balance will definitely be needed to see your relationship through this year unscarred. More self-control is definitely called for and it would be a good idea to keep any inflammatory opinions to yourself for fear of the havoc they could wreak if voiced at an inopportune moment. Keep a low profile, spend more time around the home and become a better listener. This won't guarantee your safety but it should go a long way to helping to keep trouble at bay. There's also a little brain teaser for you — what is the difference between actions and reactions? Once you've discovered the answer year Two may have ended but you'll be that much wiser for knowing.

With regard to things to watch out for during a personal year Two the list is short but the repercussions could be far-reaching if you fail to heed the warnings. Don't get too over-emotional or moody as this will probably cause more problems than are solved and if anything is told to you in confidence, see that it *remains* confidential information. You may find it difficult to keep secrets but during a year Two it could cost you your relationship for starters if you fail to do so.

KEYWORDS
Positive: co-operation, peace, balance, tranquillity, breathing-space
Negative: moodiness, indiscretion, over-emotional, careless talk

PERSONAL YEAR THREE

The influence of a personal year Three is on the mind and the intellect in particular. During such a period you should be on top form mentally because this is a peak year for really stretching yourself and running your brain in top gear, perhaps even occasionally in overdrive. If you have talent develop it further in order to reach your full potential and even if you don't feel particularly creative yourself, you could broaden your horizons considerably by visiting galleries, exhibitions and concert halls to gain a greater understanding and appreciation of the arts. You won't go too far wrong either if you join the local library and read a book occasionally as an alternative to watching television. This is a time not only to stop, look around you and listen to what's being said but also to learn, study and amass as much knowledge and experience as possible.

On the career front although a personal year Three has never been noted for bringing major changes certain advantages are likely to fall into your lap which should not be ignored. This is a period for gaining technical and specialist skills so that even though you're narrowing the field all the time you're becoming more of an expert in your own small area of operation. Any opportunities to go on seminars organized by your employers should be snapped up the minute you're offered a place and even a temporary attachment to a different department could be enormously educative. In addition, if your local authority runs evening classes in your particular subject and by attending each week you stand to gain further useful qualifications which you don't already have, make sure you enrol and stay the course even if it does mean that your social life suffers as a consequence. Travel perhaps in the form of visits overseas to clients or suppliers is also a distinct possibility under this vibration.

Journalists, writers and artists should all find Fate treats them well during such a creative year as this promises to be. Musicians and entertainers, in fact anyone who earns their living through personal expression are also likely to enjoy the same preferential treatment.

As far as home life is concerned a Three year is unlikely to go down in family history as the year you took leave of your senses and ploughed up the garden or even decided to sub-let part of the house to students, but you could well decided to instal a computer system not only to help with the domestic accounts, but also as a means of storing facts and information. This would also be as good a time as any to stock up the bookshelves with reference books or even a new set of encyclopedias. Culture is the name of the game now so you're quite likely to take up writing poetry, experimenting with water colours or strumming a guitar. However, the main item of expenditure is almost sure to be a special holiday as this is also a time for unrestrained movement, the further afield the better so that you can experience other lifestyles firsthand and by so doing build up your awareness of what is taking place outside your immediate environment.

A personal year Three has very little direct bearing on relationships although indirectly it's influence can be felt quite distinctly. During such a period, opportunities will present themselves to gain a deeper understanding of your partner and with it, hopefully, greater respect. The slant is definitely one of hearts, flowers and romance so if you feel like penning the odd sonnet or composing a love song, go ahead, it will probably turn out better than you would imagine.

Sentimental journeys could also be on the agenda and there's nothing like a trip down memory lane to either rekindle passion or re-awaken interest but watch out you don't re-open old wounds in the process.

There are both positive and negative sides to most things and with a personal year Three you need to watch out for the following undesirable traits. Don't allow cynicism to make you over-critical and sarcastic; pessimism will get you nowhere and being boastful will lose you many friends. Try not to let your growing list of accomplishments go to your head because even though you may be quite an expert by the end of this year there's no need to shout about it.

KEYWORDS
Positive: talent, potential, knowledge, skills, the arts, travel
Negative: big-headedness, cynicism, pessimism, boastfulness

PERSONAL YEAR FOUR

If you are looking for excitement then you're going to be sadly disappointed during a personal year Four, because there's nothing of that nature on the agenda. The theme is very much one of hard work and attention to detail interspersed with welcome periods of rest and relaxation. After the changes experienced during year One, the soul-searching traditionally associated with a year Two and the quest for knowledge during year Three, now comes the time to put everything in order and yourself into some sort of a routine. Don't worry that under the influence of this vibration it will be an uphill climb all the way, because there will be ample opportunities for enjoyment thrown in for good measure.

Health matters always come under close scrutiny in this particular twelve month period. Not because things are going wrong but in order to prevent them from doing so. Mental and physical well-being should both be considered and this would be as good a time as any to have a complete check-up by your GP just to make sure that you're firing on all cylinders. It would also be wise to take a careful look at your lifestyle and habits, and ask yourself whether you are taking adequate exercise, assess how much you smoke and drink, and whether you unwind sufficiently at the end of one week before plunging headlong into the next. Make sure your batteries are fully charged and that you look after yourself properly because no one else is likely to bother on your behalf.

There's unlikely to be much happening in terms of advancement or pay increases just now and if you're thinking of changing jobs it would be unwise to do so at present as the likelihood of such a move turning out successfully seems pretty remote. It would be better to leave such ideas for later in the nine-year cycle and concentrate instead on building yourself a better future where you are now. Try to learn something positive from any errors of judgement you have made in the past, take more pride in the responsibility already entrusted in you and don't allow gloom and despondency to get you down. You're likely to be experiencing a patch of the doldrums where your career is concerned and once a fresh wind fills your sails your usual optimism and confidence should both return with it.

The only people likely to experience a slight upturn in their business affairs during a year Four term of office are workers who fall in the following categories:- farmers, accountants, builders, executives, engineers and chemists. However, even these well-aspected individuals shouldn't look for miracles if they don't want to see their hopes raised for nothing.

Around the home there are bound to be plenty of chores to be done or outstanding work to be finished. None of these tasks is likely to be either stimulating or particularly rewarding; however they need to be attended to and that is what a year Four is all about — tidying up loose ends. As with work, this is not a good time to be considering moving house but any plans for building an extension, modernization or generally improving your property should meet with success if set in motion now. You have the foundations and it's quite permissible to take them a stage further so long as you don't try to move everything from one place to another, which would be inviting trouble.

Your bank balance could also be causing you concern during this period so don't take on any new household commitments which would only serve to put a further strain on your rather slim resources.

For unmarried couples now is the time to start planning your future with a vengeance. Thrift, economy and saving schemes are all highlighted and although you may be in a hurry to put your relationship on a permanent footing, don't tie the knot under this influence as this is a year for preparation only. Those of you who are already established and have been together for some time shouldn't take any risks at the moment particularly financial ones as money worries always put extra strain on relationships and often cause rows and disagreements. Your best advice is to tread water and do nothing irresponsible or impulsive which could in any way rock the boat even slightly. Keep a low profile and hopefully no insuperable problems should arise.

From a negative point of view, a year Four can make people very conscious of their duties and at the same time resentful of the burdens they have to bear. Try not to make any silly moves on the spur of the moment, especially when responsibilities are weighing you down as such actions usually only make things worse and cause a whole lot more problems to add to your load.

KEYWORDS
Positive: hard word, relaxation, organization, calm, thrift, health
Negative: irresponsible, impulsive, over-laden, hard done-by

PERSONAL YEAR FIVE

You are half-way through the cycle when you've reached the personal year Five point. You've probably already gathered that Five is a number with strong sexual overtones but although exciting private encounters are quite possible under this vibration, they are by no means the order of the day and there's going to be much more going on throughout this twelve month period than mere dalliances with attractive members of the opposite gender.

The emphasis for a year such as this falls on subtle change rather than the drastic all-round variety associated with the beginning and end of a nine-year span. You are likely to be feeling rather restless having come this far but fortunately travel, intellectual development and spiritual growth are all on the menu, so this bears all the hallmarks of being an interesting period of experience.

At work just about anything barring a change of employer seems likely. What is more, for every conscious decision you make there will almost certainly be an equal number sprung on you at very short notice. Voluntary and involuntary, that's what this period is all about. You must not allow yourself to get too bogged down with the tedious, mundane tasks which you could so easily delegate to someone else. Tackle any outstanding problems with as much ingenuity as you can muster, then break the routine a little and do something about keeping abreast with new ideas. Visit trade exhibitions, find out what competitors are up to and keep abreast of the latest advances in technology by reading everything you can lay your hands on on the subject and asking the opinions of those qualified to have them. Don't allow the march of progress to pass you by otherwise you could later find yourself as redundant as outdated methods and machines. Even if you can't get one jump ahead of everyone else, keeping in step is the next best thing but whatever you do don't lag behind because it's the strays and stragglers who are always the most vulnerable members of any group or society.

Those careers particularly well aspected during a personal year Five include all those involved in the world of communications and public relations as well as authors, writers, journalists, linguists and anyone in any way connected with travel, from bus drivers to air hostesses, astronauts to lorry drivers, plus all those in between who move about a great deal to earn their livings. All these people can expect a few surprise lucky breaks during the year ahead and if not actual promotion then perhaps a few extra pennies in their pay packets each week as an added incentive.

Physical movement on the home front is not all that likely under the influence of a year Five with the exception of changes from big city or suburban dwelling to the great out-doors and a more countrified atmosphere. If you've been wanting to get away from the crowds and noise not to mention pressures and traffic this is an excellent vibration under which to effect the transition but if you only feel like moving from one side of town to the other you'd do better to wait a couple more years till nearer the end of the cycle. Those of you not wishing to do anything of this nature won't go far wrong if you continue to get some savings behind you although if some items of furniture have grown shabby and need replacing the odd carefully selected piece probably wouldn't break the bank and would give the whole room a major face-lift.

Now's also the time to review the motoring situation. A change of car seems quite likely as does some major repair work which will then hopefully guarantee you a few more miles of relatively trouble-free travel.

For the footloose and fancy-free this can be a year to remember. If variety is what you're after, then you're in for a treat especially when travelling away from home, as an exciting holiday romance could be just what you're looking for and quite an experience too. Those of you in established relationships should seek new ways of enjoying yourselves together, as a partnership which is allowed to go stale could easily run into trouble. Don't be afraid to break with routine or get involved in new joint interests. Monotony must be avoided at all costs, besides which, new experiences broaden the mind.

Unfortunately those of you who don't feel like making an effort and are getting restless and bored with the present arrangements could easily be tempted to break their vow and go off the rails as infidelity and extra-marital affairs are both distinct possibilities during a year Five. This can be a testing time for even the strongest of personal relationships and how well you fare depends entirely on your frame of mind and the amount of self-control you decide to exercise.

Every year has its list of do's and don'ts and the things you should avoid doing under a Five vibration sound like the warnings issued by most caring parents to their rapidly maturing offspring. Be careful with your money because it's hard to come by but very easy to get parted from; avoid doing anything to excess which includes eating, smoking and drinking and be selective in the company you keep especially in your choice of partners.

KEYWORDS
Positive: money-conscious, progressive, minor changes, travel, variety
Negative: infidelity, promiscuity, over-indulgent

PERSONAL YEAR SIX

Six is a number traditionally associated with love, beauty and harmony on the one hand, and domesticity on the other so it's hardly surprising that during a personal year Six the emphasis falls heavily on family ties, the home and, to a lesser degree, artistic expression.

This is a year which shouldn't be allowed to slip by unnoticed because it's a time to put into action plans which have been on the drawing-board for some considerable time. Careful preparation is essential to the success of any ventures undertaken now and spectacular results, especially with creative endeavours, are not beyond the bounds of possibility. New ideas are also likely to take shape in your mind although it may not be appropriate to take them much further than the embryo stage at this juncture in the cycle.

Those of you who are budding composers and poets or who show flair with a brush or raw clay can expect not only to make tremendous progress but also to see your style alter as it matures. Learn to appreciate the subtlety of shape and form; use colour sparingly but with flair; and don't be afraid to experiment with new methods and mediums as this is all part and parcel of your artistic development.

Family businesses are in the spotlight during a year Six but you don't necessarily have to be the proprietor of one to reap some of the benefits, as employees of such concerns are likely to feel the effect of their firms' prosperity and, indeed, possible expansion at this time. Those of you who are self-employed may consider taking one of your own offspring into partnership as the year goes by and although personalities can sometimes clash in an agreement of this nature, when inaugurated under such a favourable influence any misunderstandings should be quick to die down — after all, Six is a number of peace and balance.

Anyone not included in either of the categories already mentioned needn't think they've been forgotten. There are benefits for you as well and this could be an auspicious year in more ways than one. The review of pay structures is likely to produce some unexpected but nevertheless beneficial results and any schemes to modernize and update your place of work should go a long way to easing pressures and lightening your load. Don't expect to be offered a seat on the Board at this time but don't be tempted to look any gift horses in the mouth even if what is being offered seems rather paltry as this may be only the first of a series of opportunities designed to improve your lot, not merely a one-off which on the face of it seems a bit insulting.

Anyone involved in caring occupations where a service is performed for the good of others, hospital and welfare workers in particular, medics and vets not to mention ordained and lay-members of the Church, marriage guidance counsellors, and last but not least the grossly underrated housewife; these people should all benefit directly or indirectly during a personal year Six although not necessarily in financial terms. So don't go expecting huge bonuses or cash settlements of outstanding wage disputes as you're likely to be disappointed.

Where bricks and mortar are concerned, a personal year Six is a time for putting down roots so if you've only been in temporary or rented accommodation up until now it's about time you considered investing in a home of your own and looked into the possibility of taking out a mortgage to enable you to do so. Property owners and secure tenants are unlikely to be feeling restless or wanting to make a move but they could well be considering an extension to existing buildings, structural changes such as a loft conversion or just a face-lift with new colour schemes and soft furnishings. Now is the time to make yourself as comfortable as possible and if it means dipping into your savings then so be it. There's nothing guaranteed to give a person the blues quicker than gloomy surroundings so if there's a danger of your decor causing depression do something about ringing the changes without delay.

Relationships of all kinds are well aspected during a personal year Six especially those of a personal nature. Single people could meet their life partner, young couples are likely to be getting engaged and making plans for marriage, while young marrieds could well be looking seriously at the possibilities of parenthood. Responsibility is the keyword here and it's the family unit which is in focus. This is a time for communication, commitment and long-term plans, not a year for light-hearted flirtation or recklessness. Those of you with elderly relatives could be called upon to show extra sympathy and understanding at some point during this twelve month period as the rough always has to be taken with the smooth in any relationship, which is after all what caring is all about.

There are one or two points to watch out for during the rulership of the number Six: Don't be over-protective of your loved ones, this applies particularly to mothers with growing children. Know when to let go as all offspring have to fly the nest eventually. Try not to be too bossy and dominant, don't force your views and opinions on others and never make people feel completely dependent on you for their existence. Encourage them to stand on their own two feet whenever possible, but make sure you are there to offer a back-up service in times of difficulty and indecision.

KEYWORDS
Positive: love, beauty, harmony, family ties, domesticity, creative expression
Negative: bossy, domineering, opinionated, forceful, over-protective

PERSONAL YEAR SEVEN

A personal year Seven is not an easy period during which to accomplish anything tangible or concrete. Seven is traditionally the number of magic and mystery so the emphasis here is more on thoughts and ideas than material leaps and bounds. This is a year for getting your brain working efficiently, your concepts into order and seeking the answers to all manner of deep questions.

Whether you like it or not, circumstances are likely to conspire and force you to take a long, hard look at yourself. Time spent on your own is vital for your inner growth and you should make a greater effort to read, catch up on neglected studies and gain a deeper knowledge and understanding of life and what it's all about. Personal wisdom is what you should strive to attain and whether you reach your goal through meditation or personal experience is immaterial, just so long as you get there in the end. You'll find yourself trying to unravel perplexing riddles, wrestling with truths, going back over the past but all the time you'll be making progress towards personal enlightenment as you consolidate and adjust everything you not only discover but also already know.

Careers are likely to prosper particularly if promotion hangs on good examination results, as all attempts at further education should meet with success under this vibration. What is more you could find yourself involved in the training of new recruits so a little revision wouldn't go amiss to ensure your instructions coincide with those in the book. Financially you don't stand to gain a great deal from assuming a temporary teaching role, but there will be benefits of a more subtle nature which you may not fully appreciate until well into a year Eight or even Nine. The trend where any changes are concerned seems to be in a positive direction although you won't be given much warning when they do take place nor opportunity to do anything much except go along with them. It is likely to be a case of 'you will' rather than 'would you like to?'

Highlighted jobs and occupations under the rule of a personal year Seven include students of any shape, size or form, archaeologists, astrologers, philosophers and anyone connected either directly or indirectly with research and library work. You would all be advised to study hard, pay greater attention to detail than normally necessary because you might either miss something interesting or you could spoil your future chances over a silly, avoidable mistake, if you don't bother to heed this warning.

As far as the home and any other property is concerned what you need to do is get your priorities right. This means don't go spending vast sums of money installing costly kitchen equipment when the roof is leaking and more urgently in need of repair, or if your car is in any doubt of passing its MOT you would be rather foolish to pay out to have it resprayed before you know where you stand. Be sensible, decide what is urgent and what is not and attend to the more pressing matters first before embarking on anything of a cosmetic nature. Above all else, make sure you know how far your bank manager is prepared to let you go, before making any moves at all — vital or otherwise.

Relationships and health will both need careful and indeed constant monitoring during the Seven influence, not because problems are guaranteed, but simply to prevent them from arising. Any changes experienced on either count are likely to be so subtle as to arouse no immediate interest or suspicion, and it is precisely for this reason that vigilance at all times is particularly advocated. If you expect the unexpected then you shouldn't go too far wrong.

Within your marriage or relationship try not to let personal problems get out of proportion. Strive to make yours a union of minds as well as bodies because getting onto a similar, if not exactly the same, wavelength could work wonders for your togetherness, not to mention the physical side of things.

What you must be on your guard against is that well-known temptation the seven-year itch. You'd hardly be human if you didn't grow a little bored with things when they stay the same for so long, but provided you only experience the irritation and don't ever decide to scratch then all should be well. After all, infidelities of the mind don't actually count as such so long as you don't talk in your sleep.

There are many pitfalls and draw-backs to a personal year Seven, the worst of which is a fear of failure and loneliness which comes upon most of us, to a certain degree, under this influence. Try not to be unreasonable when dealing with others or too hasty when handling financial decisions. Above all don't turn down any opportunities to be trained in new skills or disciplines because an unwillingness to learn will see many doors closing in your face over the course of this particular year.

KEYWORDS
Positive: self-analysis, inner growth, study, meditation, analysis, priorities
Negative: over-hasty, stubborn, unwilling to learn, fearful, sexually restless

PERSONAL YEAR EIGHT

The number Eight has a strong, powerful influence and during a personal year ruled by it almost anything is possible. However, you would do well to remember, particularly when tempted to push your luck, that this is traditionally the number of great reversals so, if you grow careless, spectacular failure is just as likely to be the result as resounding success. However, whatever the outcome, this is most certainly not a year to be wasted.

After the years of gradual preparation and development you should by now have learned not only how to stand on your own two feet but also the true meaning and value of freedom. During this year you must demonstrate that you can conduct your life in a responsible manner by means of the self-control and confidence which you have built up and somehow prove that you can handle money matters wisely and with the utmost respect. The approach to the peak of this cycle is well under way and having come this far, hopefully with flying colours, there is no going back now, as the pace quickens and the atmosphere becomes charged with a feeling of expectancy.

At work, this is a year to make your presence felt and to push for greater authority and power. You must learn to delegate wisely when your workload gets beyond manageable proportions, although heavy reliance on other people just in order to get by is never advisable, nor standard business practice. With hard work, good organization and sound judgement you should be able to channel your energy in a constructive direction either at one specific goal or a whole series of smaller targets to be reached, rather like stepping-stones fording a river. Those of you working for big companies should make every effort to get yourself noticed during the next twelve months with a view to promotion or a change of duties as the cycle draws to a close, while those working for smaller firms should do everything they can to make themselves indispensable. The self-employed could find this a particularly challenging year as there are big orders to be landed if you set your sights marginally higher and even bigger money to be made if you are ambitious enough to make a flat-out effort and really go for it.

The number Eight always smiles on business and finance because it's influence is such a material one, and the occupations particularly favoured by this vibration are bankers, brokers and financiers as well as executives, lawyers and all those engaged in supervisory or administrative roles. This is a year for big financial killings provided you remember to wear suitable protective clothing.

Any of you with properties to sell at this time should hold out for a good price as you are bound to find the right buyer eventually but if you are dealing in items of antiquity an expert valuation might be a good idea as it's so easy to be sold a fake or swindled if you're not well up on such matters.

By and large, repairs and decoration are usually high on the list of priorities during a personal year Eight because having once put your house well and truly in order it is all ready to go on the market in tip-top condition during a year Nine when many of you feel the need for a move of home. Even if you're frugal by nature, try not to scrimp on materials or labour, as a job worth doing should be done well first time round thereby avoiding the occurrence of all sorts of irritating problems at a later date.

Relationships don't hold much of your attention, when the number Eight is in office and those that do feature usually only do so because they've run into trouble. If you don't know what to do for the best where your private affairs are concerned it would be best to do nothing at this moment in time as the situation can always be reviewed later when circumstances might be more favourable. Avoid rows and arguments at all costs, especially over money, but if you feel like splashing out on a few surprise treats these might help the course of true love to run just a little more smoothly during a potentially bumpy and hazardous period.

Generally speaking this can be a rewarding twelve months if you don't get too tough and demanding. Remember your manners, don't go riding rough-shod over all and sundry and try not to stoop to low, underhand measures to get your own way. Be firm without getting aggressive and never treat anyone in a manner you would find offensive yourself if the roles just happened to be reversed.

KEYWORDS
Positive: power, authority, ambition, finances, goals, progress
Negative: aggressive, mercenary, ruthless, rude, underhand

PERSONAL YEAR NINE

A personal year Nine marks the end of a cycle of experience which should end on the crest of a wave. Very often the first and last years of a sequence have much in common and changes put into effect during a year Nine have a way of not showing up until well into the next year. This sort of thing frequently occurs during such transition periods when the old cycle tends to overlay and run into the new for the first few months at least.

Full cyclic maturity should now be yours. The unexpected should no longer be able to take you by surprise, tolerance and understanding should by now be second nature and ideals should be things you automatically live up to as a matter of course. A year Nine is a period of opportunity when you should be setting your sights on the future and making long-term plans. Travel for pleasure rather than business is also a distinct possibility and even if you don't set foot very far afield, new faces and new places are all part and parcel of this lively vibration. Friendships struck up now should stand the test of time particularly if you already have shared interests or acquaintances.

A change of job certainly appears on the bill at this point in the proceedings as this is a time for tidying up loose ends or leaving situations which have failed to live up to their initial promise. However, don't be in too much of a rush to effect changes because it is never a wise idea to burn your boats before you have a definite promise of alternative employment. You may be called upon to be patient for just a while longer but there's nothing to stop you brushing up your knowledge and qualifications in the meantime. Keep abreast of current affairs as something taking place in the world outside could well have a knock-on effect on the course of your destiny at some later date.

The humanitarian influence of number Nine has a more beneficial effect on some jobs than others and those it particularly favours are as follows — public service workers, teachers, lecturers and doctors as well as statesmen, diplomats and politicians. These groups of workers all have one thing in common in that they perform their duties for or on behalf of others to a greater or lesser degree.

As with jobs, changes on the home front are quite likely to come under serious consideration. This is a year for endings and if you feel you've been in one place quite long enough now would be an appropriate juncture to do something about that rut you've become stuck in. However, don't make any impulsive, spur of the moment moves as a decision as important as this shouldn't be entered into lightly and needs careful handling if it is to go smoothly and without a hitch.

Unfortunately a personal year Nine could also sound the death knell for any relationships which have gone past their sell-by dates. Do your best not to let past injustices colour your judgement or in any way influence your thinking, after all bygones should be regarded as such, but there may be some old scores which need to be settled and it would be a good idea to do so now in order to move forward into the future and a new cycle, unencumbered by outstanding debts of honour. However there are some relationships which you may feel still have something to offer, and in such cases you would be ill-advised to give up half-way even if you feel progress is slow and very one-sided. Sometimes its not easy to pin-point and identify your own faults but if you adopt a policy of do as you would be done by when relating to your partner maybe problems will iron themselves out and you'll eventually get yourselves back onto a more even keel.

Family responsibilities and demands could weigh particularly heavily on your shoulders as this cycle draws to a close and you may find yourself feeling that there's never any time to call your own. Don't despair, the problems will pass and the way things turn out you'll be glad you decided to offer your help and support from the start.

There is no room for petty-mindedness anywhere during a personal year Nine. Neither should you be uncharitable, intolerant or impulsive. Keep your temper under firm control and learn how to enter into a discussion without losing it. Hot-heads seldom get anywhere but so long as you keep your cool, control and mastery of the situation should always rest with you.

KEYWORDS
Positive: endings, tying-up loose ends, changes afoot, look to the future
Negative: impatient, impulsive, quick-tempered, intolerant, uncharitable.

CHAPTER SEVEN

How To Use Your Wheel of Fortune

The Wheel of Fortune is made up of three discs in reducing size order. You will find it attached to the cover of this book. There is no need to remove it from the book — the discs revolve easily and The Wheel of Fortune can be used conveniently at any time to predict influences and prospects.

THE AGE DISC

The small numbers show actual ages, the large numbers are the year numbers. Find your age in one of the disc segments and refer to the large numeral in the same segment. This number will influence the year from the date you achieved that age. For example if you are 47, the number 2 would have influenced your year starting on your 47th birthday.

THE MIDDLE DISC

The initial number is found by using the initial letter of your first name. Find this in one of the segments of the middle disc and refer to the number in the same segment. For example: your first name is Anne, then your initial number would be 1.

THE BIRTH DISC

This is the smallest disc. Using your date of birth number (see page 25) this disc will provide the third component for analysis using the Wheel of Fortune.

WHAT THE NUMBERS MEAN

Once you have determined the three influencing numbers, revolve the discs so the segments in which they appear all line up. These will reveal all the influences for your particular age year. If two or three numbers are the same (for example 233 or 333) the following trends apply:

ONES — A year to express yourself forcefully, but heed the feelings of others.

TWOS — In this year rely upon your intuition and first impressions for success.

THREES — Don't let social activities distract you this year from important tasks. Take advantage of creative abilities.

FOURS — You risk biting off more than your can chew this year. Plan how to use your skills more carefully.

FIVES — You run the risk of an emotional confrontation this year. Avoid being too over-confident.

SIXES — A period when you must use your logic and reason to make decisions. You could be easily carried away by over-enthusiasm for an idea or project.

SEVENS — You will learn vital lessons this year from both good and bad experiences.

EIGHTS — Efficiency and organization are the year's watchwords, but make sure too much self-control doesn't damage emotional relationships.

NINES — The chances for disappointment are strong during this year. Be more realistic. Set any goals you have within reason.

ALL EVEN NUMBERS — A year of general harmony and happy home life.

ALL ODD NUMBERS — A year in which to make progress both at home and work.

MORE ODD THAN EVEN NUMBERS — A risk of rows and arguments developing during the year. Don't go looking for trouble.

MORE EVEN THAN ODD NUMBERS — You need to give more than take this year and if in doubt about a decision, do nothing.

SPECIAL NUMBER COMBINATIONS

These combinations are extra influences which only occur occasionally and should be given special regard. There is no particular order of numbers so a combination of 159 can appear as 195, 519, 591, 915 and so on, on your Wheel of Fortune.

123 — A time when you could cause confusion and chaos — get organized and lay plans with care.

147 — The time is right for action not words. If you use your hands for work, opportunities arise for great benefits.

157 — A year in which you need to learn as much as you can. Don't let emotions interfere with your intellectual progress.

159 — You will need to draw on all your resources of patience: be persistent and determined if you want to get ahead.

248 — A good year for finances but relationships might suffer.

258 — Boost your self-esteem but temper it by achieving balance in all things.

357 — A year to truly discover yourself and lay major plans for the future.

369 — A year of growth for inspiration, creativity and relationships. Don't waste time during this period.

456 — Don't let minor set-backs hold you back from what you want to do. Don't lose sight of your major goals.

789 — A good time for health and wealth. You will have boundless energy and a full engagements diary.

STAR SIGNS

Your own star sign will either boost or counter the number influences during your year. Use the astrological keywords and compare them to the year influences.

ARIES — energy, enterprise, self-assertion
TAURUS — patience, practicality, realism
GEMINI — expansive, versatile, enquiring
CANCER — resourceful, receptive, reserved
LEO — flambuoyant, dramatic, larger than life
VIRGO — logical, critical, precise
LIBRA — charming, diplomatic, balanced
SCORPIO — subtle, secretive, purposeful
SAGITTARIUS — adventurous, spontaneous, free and easy
CAPRICORN — calculating, methodical, responsible
AQUARIUS — unorthodox, unpredictable, imaginative
PISCES — sensitive, emotional, unrealistic

Of further interest . . .

The Book of
LOVE NUMBERS

Find your ideal lover with this amazing exposé
of the secret love numbers of your life.

David and Julia Line

The Book of Love Numbers
Use your love number to find your perfect partner

David and Julia Line

Now at last the special and secret numbers that rule your love-life are here revealed.

As individual as fingerprints they highlight the most intimate aspects of your nature to enable *you* to:

● identify the partner of your dreams
● choose between potential suitors
● discover if your lover is your ideal

David and Julia Line here expose the true, full and fascinating facts — at one time the most carefully guarded secret of the ancients — so that *you* can discover, and use, your secret love number to find romance, satisfaction and lasting happiness.

HOW TO
COMPUTE
YOUR
DESTINY
THE SECRET OF ASTRO-NUMBERS

Are you a doer or a thinker? Why isn't your life more exciting?
How can you get on better with your friends?
Compute your destiny and find out!

PAUL AND VALETA RICE

How to Compute Your Destiny
The secret of Astro-Numbers

Paul and Valeta Rice

Here at last is a simple guide to astro-numerology which will help you plan your life — if you can count on your fingers you can use this book. After a few minutes you can use the vibrations of the numbers to see yourself and your associates in a new light.

With this fascinating and easy-to-use book you will become aware of your failings and be able to plan how to better yourself. You are also shown how to calculate what lies in the months and years ahead and smooth your pathway through life.

Knowledge of the numbers will confirm much that you already suspected and reveal things you merely imagined to be true!

Magic For Lovers

Kathleen McCormack

Most people 'read the stars' but here Kathleen McCormack, a noted astrologer and psychic, has gone one step further. In this easy-to-read, exciting and fun-filled volume she has gathered together tried and tested methods of divination to help YOU to:

- find your ideal mate in the stars
- interpret the romantic messages of your dreams
- make a talisman to protect your lover

Is she an unpredictable Gemini? Is he an idealistic Virgo? Love and marriage are too important to be left to chance. *Check your choice with the stars.*

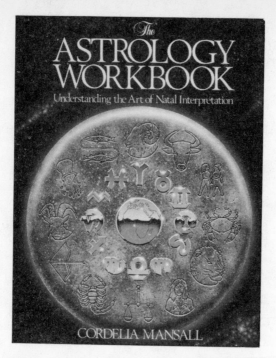

The Astrology Workbook

Understanding the art of natal interpretation

Cordelia Mansall

For anyone who wishes to learn the ground rules of modern astrology, this book provides the ideal starting point.

A tutor with the Faculty of Astrological Studies since 1977, Cordelia Mansall has used her experience of teaching astrology to beginners to produce a manual that takes a fresh and original approach to the problem of understanding astrological concepts and techniques.

In a clear and accessible style, THE ASTROLOGY WORKBOOK explains the first principles of astrology and gives full instructions on how to construct, analyse and interpret a birth chart. It also considers:

- the growth and development of astrology
- the symbolism of the zodiac
- the houses and their meanings
- the significance of the planets
- how to interpret aspects and harmonies

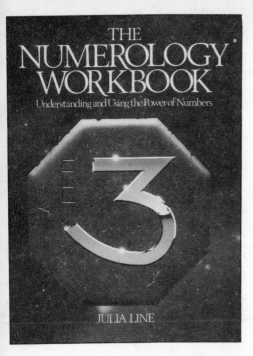

The Numerology Workbook

Understanding and using the power of numbers

Julia Line

Through numerological analysis we can not only discover what we are best qualified to do, and how to fulfil our destiny, but we can also recognize our limitations. Once we have discovered our personal numbers we can, with practice and understanding, use them to solve the enigmas of our existence.

Julia Line takes a comprehensive look at the many systems of numerology, with special emphasis on the Pythagorean, Golden Dawn and Cheiro methods, explaining what numerology is all about and what it ultimately sets out to achieve.

Through first hand experience, experimentation and personal involvement, students will be able to use this occult science in a way which suits both their needs and their personality. Among the many fascinating topics covered are:

- numbers and your name
- the significance of the date of birth
- numerology and the alphabet
- the numbers of the planets and the zodiac
- numerology and the tarot

Napoleon's Book of Fate

Ancient Egyptian Fortune-Telling for today

H. Kirchenhoffer
Revised and edited by Bonnie Parker

In 1801 a member of Napoleon's famous expedition to Egypt discovered in a royal tomb near Thebes, under a mummy's armpit, a long roll of papyrus covered in beautifully painted hieroglyphics — hieroglyphics said to relate to the Oracles themselves. Intrigued, Napoleon ordered immediate translation; the result was said to change his life, for he never made a decision without consulting it.

NAPOLEON'S BOOK OF FATE is a straightforward and absorbing form of divination. From a list of 32 questions, you choose the one most closely resembling your own dilemma. Then you allow your subconscious to focus on an answer, offered by one of the 32 Oracles, by a simple process of almost literally plucking numbers out of the air — there are a possible 1024 alternatives, all in one small book!

The original work was purported to have been dictated by Hermes Trismegistus, the Thrice Great of philosophers, priests and kings. Such was his genius that the answers given bear as much relevance today as they must have done thousands of years ago. With this English version, we can all now benefit from the BOOK OF FATE and regulate our future according to the counsels of the Oracles.